Hannah Arendt's Ambiguous Storytelling

Also available from Bloomsbury:

The Bloomsbury Companion to Arendt
edited by Peter Gratton and Yasemin Sari
Ethics and Time in the Philosophy of History: A Cross-Cultural Approach
edited by Natan Elgabsi and Bennett Gilbert
Action and Appearance: Ethics and the Politics of Writing in Hannah Arendt
edited by Anna Yeatman, Charles Barbour, Phillip Hansen, and Magdalena Zolkos
Philosophy of History: Twenty-First-Century Perspectives
edited by Jouni-Matti Kuukkanen

Hannah Arendt's Ambiguous Storytelling

Temporality, Judgment, and the Philosophy of History

Marcin Moskalewicz

BLOOMSBURY ACADEMIC
LONDON • NEW YORK • OXFORD • NEW DELHI • SYDNEY

BLOOMSBURY ACADEMIC
Bloomsbury Publishing Plc, 50 Bedford Square, London, WC1B 3DP, UK
Bloomsbury Publishing Inc, 1359 Broadway, 12th Floor, New York, NY 10018, USA
Bloomsbury Publishing Ireland, 29 Earlsfort Terrace, Dublin 2, D02 AY28, Ireland

BLOOMSBURY, BLOOMSBURY ACADEMIC and the Diana logo
are trademarks of Bloomsbury Publishing Plc

First published in Great Britain 2024
This paperback edition published 2026

Copyright © Marcin Moskalewicz, 2024

Marcin Moskalewicz has asserted his right under the Copyright,
Designs and Patents Act, 1988, to be identified as Authors of this work.

For legal purposes the Acknowledgments on pp. x–xi constitute
an extension of this copyright page.

Cover image © Christian (Keilo) / Getty Images

All rights reserved. No part of this publication may be: i) reproduced or transmitted in any form, electronic or mechanical, including photocopying, recording or by means of any information storage or retrieval system without prior permission in writing from the publishers; or ii) used or reproduced in any way for the training, development or operation of artificial intelligence (AI) technologies, including generative AI technologies. The rights holders expressly reserve this publication from the text and data mining exception as per Article 4(3) of the Digital Single Market Directive (EU) 2019/790.

Bloomsbury Publishing Inc does not have any control over, or responsibility for, any third-party websites referred to or in this book. All internet addresses given in this book were correct at the time of going to press. The author and publisher regret any inconvenience caused if addresses have changed or sites have ceased to exist, but can accept no responsibility for any such changes.

A catalogue record for this book is available from the British Library.

A catalogue record for this book is available from the Library of Congress

ISBN: HB: 978-1-3502-9587-2
PB: 978-1-3502-9591-9
ePDF: 978-1-3502-9588-9
eBook: 978-1-3502-9589-6

Typeset by Integra Software Services Pvt. Ltd.

For product safety related questions contact productsafety@bloomsbury.com.

To find out more about our authors and books visit www.bloomsbury.com
and sign up for our newsletters.

Translated by Ben Koschalka and Marcin Moskalewicz.
This translation has been funded by the Foundation for Polish Science.

To Kasia and Tosia

Contents

Acknowledgments	x
List of Abbreviations	xii
Introduction: Aporiae of Meaning	1
1 *The Origins of Totalitarianism*—477 Pages Wrong	13
2 Bare Life and the End of History	31
3 Thinking History through Time	39
4 The Science of History as Ideology	51
5 Performative Self	69
6 The Temporal Conflicts of the Mind	85
7 The Contingency and Decline of History	97
8 The Beauty of the Past	107
9 Redemption of Contingency	135
10 Pieces of the Past	159
Conclusion: In Praise of Inconsistency	179
Notes	184
Bibliography	241
Index	255

Acknowledgments

My first idea to write this book came in 2003 during Martin Jay's seminar "Aesthetics and Politics" at the University of California at Berkeley, where we closely read Arendt's "Lectures on Kant's Political Philosophy." Crucially, some of the issues having to do with Arendt's aestheticization of politics and history struck me as unresolved, despite many scholarly publications on the theme. At that time, I certainly merely hoped to write my book on Arendt but obviously did not consciously design or even imagine publishing one in Polish in 2013 and then in English, with Bloomsbury, in 2024. After all, I was just a graduate student who suddenly realized that there is more to Arendt than he initially believed. But did I really hope to write this book in 2003? And would I have now recalled the hope if I had not written it? I doubt it.

This retrospective impression associating a tangible end with a hypothetical beginning lies at the core of storytelling, but Arendt's take on it is far from unequivocal. On the one hand, as Arendt rightly argues, particular and contingent events from the past appear as events and show their historical meaning only when looked at from the perspective of their unintended consequences—an equally contingent present. At that moment, they somewhat lose their haphazard reality and appear in the guise of necessity. Simultaneously, however, the very same events should contain their full meaning regardless of whatever happened in their respective future. A historical appreciation of their particularity beyond the chain of previous and subsequent affairs should open up the gap in the continuity of time and redeem the false sense of the inevitability of historical happenings. This is the basic aporia of Arendt's philosophy of history, which is the point of departure for this work.

My 2013 book published in Polish with the Nicolaus Copernicus University Press was titled *Totalitaryzm, Narracja, Tożsamość. Filozofia historii Hannah Arendt* (Totalitarianism, Narration, Identity. Hannah Arendt's Philosophy of History). Although largely based on the same research, the current book is substantially different from the Polish edition, shorter in length but expanded in content, with an entirely new arrangement of chapters and paragraphs.

I would like to express my gratitude to my teachers and guides in the field of philosophy of history, Frank Ankersmit and Wojciech Wrzosek. Frank Ankersmit taught me how deeply the narrative goes, and how to think aesthetically about the past. From Wojciech Wrzosek I have learned to think historically about the present, and that time itself is a historical phenomenon.

I am also deeply grateful to the academic colleagues with whom I have discussed the various contents of this book: Oliver Bruns, Maciej Bugajewski, Daniel Ciunajcis, Annelies Degryse, Ewa Domańska, Thomas Fuchs, Antonia Grunenberg, Marek Hetmański, Martin Jay, Axel Körner, Reinbert Krol, Hans-Peter Krüger, Waldemar Łazuga, Rudolf A. Makkreel, Allan Megill, Waltraud Meints-Stender, Agata Mergler, Magdalena Moskalewicz, Piotr Nowak, Herman Paul, Rolf Petri, Andrzej Przyłębski, Andrzej Szahaj, Maria Solarska, Wiktor Werner, Dirk Jan Wolffram, Stuart Woolf, Marijke Wubbolts, Kathleen Vandeputte, Eva de Valk, and Arjan Zuiderhoek.

Finally, I would like to thank the institutions that supported this work: the Adam Mickiewicz University in Poznan, Poland; the University of Groningen, the Netherlands; the Marie Curie Fellowships Program; The State Committee for Scientific Research at the Polish Ministry of Science and Higher Education, the Maria Curie-Skłodowska University in Lublin; and the Foundation for Polish Science, who financed the translation of large parts of the Polish edition into English. I completed the book in Heidelberg in 2022 while supported by the Alexander von Humboldt Foundation. I would like to thank Ben Koschalka for his work on the translation and Anastazja Szuła for helping me with the index. I also enjoyed working with Tim Churcher who assisted me in giving the book its final polish as well as with the Bloomsbury editors, Lucy Harper, Suzie Nash, and Alexander Bell.

Abbreviations

Works by Arendt

BPF	Between Past and Future
CR	Crises of the Republic
EU	Essays in Understanding
HAP	Hannah Arendt Papers, Library of Congress
HC	The Human Condition
LKPP	Lectures on Kant's Political Philosophy
LOM I	The Life of the Mind, Vol. 1
LOM II	The Life of the Mind, Vol. 2
MDT	Men in Dark Times
OR	On Revolution
OT	The Origins of Totalitarianism
RV	Rahel Varnhagen

Work by Kant

CPJ	Critique of the Power of Judgment

Introduction: Aporiae of Meaning

Intrinsic Contradictions

For Karl Marx, labor was necessary and defined the characteristics of man. However, it was ultimately to be abolished by the revolution. Commenting in *The Human Condition* on Marx's apparently contradictory attitude toward labor, Hannah Arendt wrote:

> Such fundamental and flagrant contradictions rarely occur in second-rate writers; in the work of great authors, they lead into the very center of their work.[1]

Arendt was not a second-rate writer, and there is no shortage of scholars who place her at the level of Marx. And this is not surprising as there is an analogous, fundamental, and flagrant contradiction that leads to the very center of her work. It is the contradiction between meaning in itself, which is intrinsic to political action, and retrospectively imposed historical meaning. Recognizing this contradiction, in turn, leads to the core argument of this book.

Numerous scholars have drawn attention to several unresolved tensions in Arendt's thinking. Most often recognized is the tension between philosophy and politics. Jennifer Ring interpreted it as resulting from the German and the Jewish elements of Arendt's thought.[2] From the point of view of political philosophy, the fundamental tension concerns deliberative and performative politics. In Seyla Benhabib's and Jürgen Habermas's reading, Arendt was a "reluctant modernist" who perceived politics as the striving for a consensus.[3] In Dana Villa's more postmodern interpretation, Arendt was a proponent of agonistic politics accentuating differences at the expense of identity and in Bonnie Honig's reading, an agonistic feminist.[4] For Norma Moruzzi, the key inconsistency concerned the relationship between social identity and political agency.[5] Philosophically speaking, meanwhile, the crucial discrepancies correspond to early and late Arendt and concern *vita activa* and *vita contemplativa*. These were noted by, among others, Richard Bernstein and Leah Bradshaw, who described Arendt's later work as a "dramatic turn" in her thinking.[6]

Not excluding the tensions mentioned above, this book argues that the fundamental aporia of Arendt's thought concerns two types of meaning: meaning in itself and historical meaning. This is reflected by two incommensurable functions, which Arendt attributes to historiography. The first is redemption from contingency—weaving a particular sense of action into a greater whole, grasping it in the form of a story. The second function is redemption from the image of necessity and the continuity of history—unstitching the thick fabric of a story and recovering the original, particular meaning of every act.

When it comes to Arendt's historiography, the above two functions correspond to the tension between her stories in the plural and a larger story (or meta-narrative) that organizes them into a whole. On the one hand, as the example of *The Origins of Totalitarianism* will show, Arendt proposes an understanding of the past through seemingly unrelated fragments or scraps of history and provides a convincing methodological justification for this approach. On the other hand, however, especially in *The Human Condition*, she creates a meta-narrative structure, into which she squeezes the entire history of Western civilization, which appears as a single and coherent History of decline (and thus "History" with a capital H).

In the essay *Tradition and the Modern Age*, Arendt describes Søren Kierkegaard, Karl Marx, and Friedrich Nietzsche as nineteenth-century philosophical forerunners of a later break in tradition associated with twentieth-century totalitarianisms.[7] She presents their philosophical systems as a series of failed reversals against tradition. Kierkegaard's transition from doubt to faith actually introduced an element of doubt into the concept of faith. Marx's turn away from theory to practice eventually brought the theory of historical laws into practice. Lastly, Nietzsche's abandonment of the transcendental in favor of the sensible exposed their co-dependence. This, Arendt argues, demonstrates the trouble with rejecting tradition entirely.

Arendt insisted that Kierkegaard's, Marx's, and Nietzsche's reversals continued a long tradition initiated by the original Platonic reversal from the world of phenomena. This original reversal established a dichotomy that would haunt generations of thinkers like a philosophical curse from then on. Ironically, Arendt's own rebellion against traditional academic means of comprehending the past followed the same pattern and was likely to be tangled up in the dichotomous logic. The scientific historiography, turned on its head by Arendt's fragmentary historical method, returned with redoubled vigor as a speculative philosophy of history.

Arendt's work is full of internal contradictions that are not only concerned with its particular stages but are intrinsic to the work itself. The founding contradiction between the two types of meaning must be more than a mere oversight. Like Marx's, it is a contradiction that, as it were, organizes Arendt's multidisciplinary work from within and sustains it in a tense state of balance as it exposes one of the fundamental and irremovable aspects of the human condition.

Recollecting the Fragments

This book is an act of interpretative violence performed on Arendt's extraordinary intellectual oeuvre. Every act of violence, Arendt would say, is **justified** by its practical goal. In the present case, the goal is understanding. It aims at rationalizing Arendt's fragmentary, anti-systematic, and sometimes even purposefully chaotic work. Arendt's comment from the end of *Thinking* that any conclusive summary of her argument would stand in flagrant contradiction to what she was trying to say equally well applies to her reflections on historical narratives and the aesthetics of history.[8] This raises the question of how a direction can be found in this disorder.

The key to finding this direction is the philosophy of history—the theory of historical process (ontology), the methodology of historical research (epistemology), and historiography (historical representation). Both ontology and epistemology materialize, so to speak, in historical representation. What makes an excellent historical narrative? What is its political function? Should one judge the past when telling stories about it? Despite being fragmentary, Arendt's work approached from the perspective of the philosophy of history provides powerful conceptual tools and insights to address these issues, particularly the problem of the narrative representation of the past and its political function. The philosophy of history is thus the key that both opens the box of recollections and is found inside the box. This general interpretative strategy goes strictly against the grain of Arendt's methodological premises, and this is why speaking about interpretative violence is justified.

Arendt's renowned work *The Origins of Totalitarianism*, from 1951, constitutes the axis around which the other philosophical and theoretical topics discussed in this book revolve. These mostly concern time, storytelling, historical judgment, and the overriding issue of what makes a good and politically sound historical narrative. In the final reckoning, *The Origins of Totalitarianism* is a bitter diagnosis of Arendt's contemporary times, but it is also the most perceptive example of the successful implementation of her unique historical method, referred to throughout this work as **fragmented historiography**.

Arendt sees totalitarianism as the most significant phenomenon of late modernity. It is an extraordinary and unprecedented event, which (as every genuinely historical phenomenon) shatters the past expectations of historical actors. As such, it is simultaneously the most demanding of explanations and yet the most inexplicable. This character of unprecedentedness makes it paradigmatic for any political event. At the same time, Arendt's theory of totalitarianism remains of interest to such an extent that it influences the interpretation of her conception of historical judgment and historical representation.[9]

Several interpretative problems that are both directly and indirectly related to totalitarianism were to stay with Arendt until the end of her life. Indeed, it is no exaggeration to claim that this book played a decisive role in her entire intellectual career and that the issues raised in *The Origins of Totalitarianism* directly led to her mature thought.[10] The books written in the late 1950s—*The Human Condition*, *Between Past and Future*, and *On Revolution*—were in a sense unintended consequences of a major research project funded by the Guggenheim Foundation and titled *Totalitarian Elements in Marxism*, and were thus closely related to the issues present in the study of totalitarianism.[11] Finally, Arendt's last, unfinished work, *The Life of the Mind*, also contains numerous topics that indirectly refer to some interpretative problems stemming from her intellectual confrontation with Western totalitarianism.

When it comes to Arendt's other papers that are referred to in this book—essays, lectures, letters, and notes, both published and archived—inevitably, many are marginalized and some are excluded. The principle applied for the selection and exclusion of papers outside of the corpus of Arendt's major works is their relevance to her narrative theory and conception of historical judgment. This book also puts aside the more historical context of events and crises in the United States that Arendt often took as a point of departure for her thinking and analyses. These include the Cold War, desegregation, the Vietnam War, and the civil rights movement. Contrary to her own self-characterization, Arendt was a **philosopher**, and philosophers don't need biographies. As in Derrida's paraphrasing of Heidegger's alleged description of Aristotle's life—she was born, she thought, she died. And the rest is pure anecdote. Or rather, the rest would have to be another story.

In light of the last point raised above, this book is not an exercise in intellectual history. It only aims to inject a sense of order into the remnants of the wind of Arendt's thoughts on storytelling and judgment—a task that she would herself be against. After all, it was the poignant force of the blow rather than its consequences that gave them their power. In her essay on Walter Benjamin, Arendt recalls the figure of the collector, who "gathers his fragments and scraps from the debris of the past."[12] Since the past is already broken, the collector is not a destroyer—he saves the precious objects from oblivion, even if these are mere quotations. It is not unlike Arendt's fragmented oeuvre, a result of lifelong collection—not continuous, somewhat shattered, and possibly ambiguous.

The reconstruction of Arendt's ontology, epistemology, and practice of history requires a recollection of what was never a coherent whole. However, even if the passages interpreted below are selective and self-serving, this book follows the hermeneutic assumption of the unity of meaning necessary to build up a story. This assumption is necessary even if the message finally extracted would explicitly contradict the existence of such a coherent and complete oeuvre. More precisely, the presupposed coherence embraces the three levels of reflections mentioned above: historical ontology, appearing as the analysis of the human condition; historical epistemology, taking the form of reflections on storytelling and judgment of the past, and the concrete practice of history writing, the point of departure and arrival of this book—*The Origins of Totalitarianism*.

The Underlying Temporal Structure

The organizational theme of this book is temporality. It might seem that this is mostly due to its author's philosophical interest, but it was Arendt's reflections on temporality that shaped this interest in the first place. Firstly, and as argued further on, the central concept of the whole of Arendt's oeuvre is the concept of a **gap in time**. Secondly, both Arendt's hierarchical arrangement of the categories of the *vita activa* and her distinction between the faculties of the mind have temporal foundations. Thirdly, this is a book on the philosophy of history, and the shortest definition of history, in the well-known words of Marc Bloch, is **man in time**. The thread of temporality shall thus slowly emerge as linking Arendt's ontology of history with her theory of judgment and fragmented historical writing.

While *The Origins of Totalitarianism* constitutes the major exemplification of Arendt's fragmented historiography, one has to extract the more theoretical considerations from her two most philosophical works—*The Human Condition* and *The Life of the Mind*. Most importantly, Arendt's meticulous and powerful conceptual distinctions, which shall be taken advantage of in the reconstruction of her critical philosophy of history, are found in these latter books.

The Human Condition cemented Arendt's position in the American academic community and is commonly recognized as her most important work in political philosophy. Its subject is active life—*vita activa*—the Latin equivalent of Aristotle's *bios politikos*. Challenging its traditional Greek and Christian understanding, Arendt presents a phenomenology of practice divided into labor, work, and action. These categories supposedly correspond to the primary conditions of earthly human life, namely: life in the sense of a biological process; worldliness—a superstructure of life in the form of the material world; plurality—the fact of irreducible human diversity among equal beings. The whole structure is grounded in human finitude, specifically natality and mortality. Here, these categories shall be further interpreted from the perspective of Arendt's non-orthodox speculative philosophy of history and not the philosophy of politics, as is usually the case. They will be presented as ahistorical forms of action that predefine the possibilities for a historical process as a whole—the principal task of various speculative philosophies of history.[13]

As far as Arendt's philosophy per se is concerned, one of the primary theses put forward in this book, the consequences of which for the narrative understanding of the past shall be elaborated upon later, is that the typification of *vita activa* has temporal foundations. Not only is the whole structure grounded in human finitude, but the notions of labor, work, and action stem from three distinct conceptions of time. Moreover, this hidden temporal grounding discloses a hitherto rarely noticed correspondence between the forms of action and the types of mental activities. This explains the importance of *The Life of the Mind*—Arendt's late exercise in phenomenology.[14] Despite the favorable reception that it received upon publication in the late 1970s,[15] it is much less known than *The Human Condition*, if only judged by the considerably smaller number of academic publications that address it. Nevertheless, its significance in the context of Arendt's entire output is indisputable. This is not just because *The Life of the Mind* is chronologically the last and thus contains Arendt's most mature thoughts. In the present context, the analyses concerning the temporal dimension of the mind's activities fill the gap left by her reflections on the temporalities of practical life.[16]

As far as the critical problem of a historical judgment of the past is concerned, it is unfortunate that the third and the last volume of this work, devoted to the faculty of judgment, was never written. Scholars of Arendt agree that the posthumously published *Lectures on Kant's Political Philosophy* serve as its substitute and are currently the primary source of information on her ideas on the power of judgment.[17] The chief challenge here is to separate Arendt's views from those of Immanuel Kant and his *Third Critique*. In the following reflections, the passages on judgment that are threaded through many of Arendt's other texts, especially *The Life of the Mind*, provide a context for this venture. This task, however, requires one to look past the letter of these readings and delve deeply, and quite paradoxically, into the Kantian aesthetics. The latter occupies a unique position in this book's argument on the beauty of the past. What justifies this move is Arendt's idea taken from the *Lectures* and defended below (mostly in Chapter 8 on Kant)—that of the spectator's superior position in the infinite interpretation process.[18]

The three activities of the mind are thinking, willing, and judging. They are autonomous with regard to each other and to the world, in the sense that willing is the "cause" of willing, thinking is the "cause" of thinking, and judging is the "cause" of judging.[19] All are invisible and involve intentional withdrawal from the immediate world of sensory experience.[20] Furthermore, all are not directly conditioned—people can judge as they see fit, want the impossible, and think about the unknowable. The word "life" in the context of the mind does not denote life in the biological sense, but the reflective capacity to transcend the given.

This book argues and expands on the claim that the underlying principle distinguishing these activities is temporality: judgment refers to the past, willing concerns the future, and thinking inhabits the lasting and extended present. Moreover, in the context of the philosophy of history, the analysis of the mind's activities constitutes the temporal backbone of historical cognition. There is an underlying thread of temporality that links Arendt's fragmented historical writing, every narrative about the past, and every autobiographical story. This thread also ties together the ten chapters of this book. Temporality, therefore, slowly emerges as its central theme. A chief argument, delivered and defended in Chapters 2 to 7, speaks of three corresponding levels of practical and theoretical activities and their hierarchical order. This order is ultimately based on three different time concepts—circular, linear, and hermeneutic (see Table 1 at the end of Chapter 7).[21] Labor and logical reasoning are embedded in circular time, work and cognitive activities in linear time, while action and thinking stem from a finite, hermeneutic temporality. Based on this hierarchy, Arendt's grand narrative of Western history presented in *The Human Condition* may appear as a history of decline. It is a decline that involves a gradual transition from proper, finite temporality, via linear and infinite clock time, to the indifferent, circular change.

Overview of the Chapters

Chapter 1, entitled "*The Origins of Totalitarianism*—477 Pages Wrong," examines Arendt's key and methodologically groundbreaking historical book. It presents the debates and controversies that accompanied its publication in academic circles. The first two volumes of the book devoted to anti-Semitism and imperialism are discussed in greater detail to give the reader unfamiliar with this work (but accustomed to conventional and standardized historical writing) a sense of its idiosyncratic content. The discussion then moves to unravel some hidden normative explanations of Arendt's narrative. The chapter closes with a discussion on the essence of totalitarianism—terror, which is governed by speculative philosophies of history. The tension between Arendt's fragmented narrative and her conceptual model of totalitarianism is shown as the first manifestation of the fundamental aporia.

Chapter 2, entitled "Bare Life and the End of History," shows that the concurrence of totalitarianism with the consumer society is not accidental as both phenomena stem from the historical victory of the indifferent, circular temporality of labor. Both are also decisive for the crisis of modernity and the break in the continuity of Western history. Therefore, this chapter looks in greater depth at Arendt's category of labor and her concept of the break in tradition. It shows how Arendt's entire oeuvre revolves around the notion of a gap in time and why time is at the forefront of her philosophical and historical concerns.

Chapter 3, entitled "Thinking History through Time," explores the very concept of the philosophy of history. Crucially, it argues, following Dray, Popper, Ankersmit, and White, among others, that the speculative or metaphysical dimension of history is indispensable for any thinking and writing about the past—a claim often, though unjustly, considered to be postmodern. Further on, it analyses the activity of thinking as transcending the cognitive capacities and focused on meaning. The chapter ends with the analysis of the temporal structure of all mental faculties—thinking, willing, and judging—in the contexts of the phenomenology of time. This analysis is significant for two complementary meta-historical reasons. Firstly, temporality is a prerequisite for an ontologically conceived history—it is "common to both history in the singular and stories in the plural," as Koselleck put it. Secondly, it is a prerequisite for knowing the past.[22] In the latter sense, temporality preconditions the task of reclaiming the past after the postmodern break in historical continuity (the gap in time), which for Arendt is the proper task of historiography today.

Chapter 4, entitled "The Science of History as Ideology," explores Arendt's category of work and its essential affinity with science and ideology. Taking advantage of Hempel's and Topolski's models, it analyzes the structural similarities between totalitarian ideologies and the positivist ideals of explanation. Furthermore, via Popper and Koselleck, it addresses the problem of the fabrication of truth in science and history. Attention is also paid to the relationship between mass culture and the logical thinking characteristic of totalitarianism. These discussions constitute the background for the chapter's arrival point, which is examining Arendt's critique of social scientific methods in historiography, alongside her debates on the function of historical writing. The chapter thus presents Arendt's fragmentary method as a means to overcome traditional, "utilitarian" ideals of historical explanation through aesthetic representation.

Chapter 5, entitled "Performative Self," focuses on Arendt's view of political action and its source in the activity of willing, and the consequences of that view for establishing historical meaning. Contextualizing Arendt's ideas with those of Heidegger, the chapter elaborates on the idea of action as an unpredictable communicative interaction serving the purpose of identity disclosure. Arendt's concept of an absolute beginning (a notion that underpins the possibility of breaks in historical and temporal continuity) is reconstructed via her inspirations, St. Augustine, Duns Scotus, and Kant. The chapter then constructs an argument—which is further developed in Chapter 8—on Arendt's profound aestheticization of action. Following Julia Kristeva, Martin Jay, and Richard Wolin, the analysis purposefully moves beyond Arendt's scholarship toward Kant, whose idea of genius (a source of fine arts) becomes an ultimate paradigm of political action. Adolf Portmann's and Hans-Georg Gadamer's characterization of self-presentation (*Selbstdarstellung*) enables a further elaboration of action as a performative and aesthetic being. Finally, the chapter presents the aforementioned, and rarely noticed, structural interdependence of action and thinking—both of which occupy the top of Arendt's hierarchy of human activities.

Chapter 6, entitled "Temporal Conflicts of the Mind," concentrates on the internal conflicts between the acts of thinking, willing, and judging, which stem from the clash of different dimensions of time. It introduces the notion of authentic, unpredictable future, which will prove relevant for Arendt's politics of historiography. Crucially, the chapter presents judgment as the mental faculty for dealing with the past. It also explores the age-old antagonism between the actor and the spectator, demonstrating why only the latter is capable of discerning the meaning of events. The reciprocal dependence of action and thinking is finally shown as based on finite hermeneutic temporality and the metaphysical (and not historical) sense of the gap in time.

Chapter 7, entitled "The Contingency and Decline of History," shifts focus to Arendt's view of the political nature of the historical process as the web of contingencies, conceived against her constant adversary, the speculative philosophy of history—the "philosophy of politics" in her nomenclature. It moves on to discuss the consequences of history's political nature—its unpredictability, purposelessness, and irreversibility. The chapter ends by presenting Arendt's grand narrative of decline from *The Human Condition* as standing in contradiction to her metahistorical reflections. In conclusion, this decline is presented as based on the hierarchy of three different concepts of time—circular, linear, and hermeneutic.

Chapter 8, entitled "The Beauty of the Past," concentrates on extracting the role of reflective judgment for historical understanding. The argument returns to Kant's *Critique of Judgment*, whose meticulous distinctions contextualized with Arendt's scattered remarks constitute a substitute for the nonexistent third volume of *The Life of the Mind* devoted to judgment. An emphasis is placed on the role of imagination in historical judgment and the function of *sensus communis*, which is reinterpreted as being paradigmatic of a historical sense—a sense for judging the past. The chapter also examines the Kantian hierarchy of genius and taste, transforming it into a hierarchy of past actors and present historians—the beautiful past and the aesthetic expertise capable of its appreciation. The notion of purposiveness without a purpose (characteristic of beautiful objects in the Kantian aesthetics) appears as particularly suited to illustrate Arendt's concerns regarding the nature of historical representation devoid of the scientistic baggage. As a result, the whole of the past is presented as the work of the Kantian genius, awaiting a historian capable of appreciating its beauty. The chapter concludes by highlighting the issue of the unwanted teleological implications of judging the past in the wrong way.

Chapter 9, entitled "Redemption of Contingency," is entirely devoted to narrative as a medium of historical cognition. The primary thesis, going against many existing interpretations, is that Arendt's ideas on storytelling anticipate the narrative anti-realism of Louis O. Mink and Hayden White. In briefest terms, although life and a story have much in common, ultimately, life is not a story. Narrative already operates on a personal level as a means to achieve the retrospective continuity of self over time. Its fictionalized causality and purposiveness provide redemption from the contingencies of the self. This function, however, becomes problematic when it comes to historiography. The discussion of the conflicting functions of the historical narrative—redemption from the contingencies of the past and liberation from the past as necessary for present existence—proves how Arendt, contrary to the mainstream view, ultimately maintains the anti-realistic stance. A fundamental theoretical problem is how the contingency of the past can be redeemed without an implicit projection of any future scenarios. In many of her essays on storytelling that are discussed later, Arendt repeatedly confronts the aporia of the historical and political meaning of events without providing an unequivocal answer. The chapter closes by presenting Arendt's masterpiece, *The Origins of Totalitarianism*, through the prism of Kantian aesthetic reflective judgment. It is a story that is purposive without a purpose, the continuity between its different elements is superimposed by historical spectators.

Chapter 10, entitled "Pieces of the Past," begins again with *The Origins of Totalitarianism*, now fully regarded as a historical work written in the literary trope of irony (as defined in Hayden White's model). The idea of reenactment of the past—showing how it really was—is presented as not viable, as asserted further by contextualizing Arendt with Robin Collingwood and Walter Benjamin. Overall, the argument has somewhat constructivist implications insofar as it presents storytelling as a performative political action and defends the autonomy of the present with regard to the past. Finally, the chapter examines the question of narrative identity. It follows the example of Odysseus, who wanders in search of himself, both knowing and yet not fully realizing who he really is. His story, which for Arendt is paradigmatic for history, further exemplifies the fundamental aporia and the principal motivation behind historical writing—reconciliation with the past. The aporia is never definitively overcome, pointing to a permanent, temporal gap between history and politics within a subject.

As stated initially, this is as much a book on Hannah Arendt as it is a book on the philosophy of history, where the latter appears as the key to recollecting Arendt's ideas. The philosophy of history is required in order to unpack and understand Arendt's idiosyncratic and transdisciplinary oeuvre. Most of Arendt's intellectual struggles are a response to totalitarianism as both a system of governance and an extreme form of storytelling. The trouble is that narrative continuity superimposed upon the past, and necessary for the unification of the self may easily turn into retrospective prophecy in which the past serves as a promise of the future. In Arendt's view, this is the predicament of the science of history, which as a result, produces an erroneous image of time. The proper response to totalitarianism lies in the radical manner of historical writing—the fragmented historiography grounded in the new, aesthetic philosophy of history. The past may be a pile of debris, as Arendt would say, yet it might still be approached in a completely novel fashion—as a performative aesthetic object.

At the same time, haunted by the dichotomous logic attributed by Arendt to Plato and the philosophers Arendt's rebellion against academic historical writing ultimately produces another speculative, even if negative, philosophy of history. The incongruity of these two approaches constitutes a shaky and ambiguous foundation of Arendt's theory of history, which is the main subject of this book.

1

The Origins of Totalitarianism—
477 Pages Wrong

The book as a whole is not really scholarly despite the wealth of footnote references and a large bibliography.
Klaus Knorr, World Politics 1952

The only work of real genius to have appeared this decade.
Al Alvarez, The Listener 1957

An Amateur Historian: The Reception of *The Origins of Totalitarianism* in Professional Circles

First published in the United States in 1951, *The Origins of Totalitarianism* remains Hannah Arendt's most widely read contribution to the field of history. The work on the text began at the end of the war, if not earlier, precisely as many of the events under discussion were only coming to light. The book is dedicated to Heinrich Blücher, Arendt's second husband, who actively contributed to its completion.[1] *The Origins of Totalitarianism* appeared highly controversial, especially in the circles of professional historians. The book was greeted with both devastating criticism and zealous praise. As was often the case with Arendt, there were few moderate or balanced judgments.

The Origins of Totalitarianism consists of three volumes—each of them almost a book in its own right—that provide answers to two fundamental questions. Firstly, what is totalitarianism—an unprecedented and historically novel form of government? Secondly, how did it emerge and become viable? The second question directs Arendt toward examining the influence and ramifications of previous events. Crucially, however, Arendt's temporalities are not held together by any classical causal relation. *The Origins of Totalitarianism* is not a standard historical work. The first two historical volumes are more of a collage of sometimes loosely related fragments and metaphysical insights mixed with short biographies, anecdotes, and personal observations.

This fragmented nature is not a professional shortcoming. When the book was first published, some of the reviews were practically idolatrous. Dwight MacDonald cited Arendt's work as the greatest achievement of social thought since Karl Marx.[2] Al Alvarez in *The Listener* declared the book to be "the only work of real genius to have appeared this decade."[3] An endorsement by Hans A. Reinhold in *Commonweal* went so far as to assert that Arendt's "deductions are so pregnant with thought and fact that only an equal of hers could dare condense the book."[4] Arthur Darack in *The Cincinnati Enquirer* described the book as "a massive searching and altogether stunning performance in which the most intimate mastery of European history is combined with a probing, brooding intelligence."[5] Josef Maier in *Aufbau* (published in New York in German) spoke of "great ingenuity" and "unusual acumen and passionate humanity" of Arendt's analysis.[6] Having read the manuscript, sociologist David Riesman, the author of *The Lonely Crowd* and a personal friend of Arendt, declared in correspondence that he was "overwhelmed" by her vision, which "touches genius."[7] The book was likewise privately praised by Carl J. Friedrich, a leading post-war authority on totalitarianism.[8] Lastly, the influential *Times Literary Supplement* declared: "There are books which are in themselves historical phenomena, and mark some important phase or turning-point in human thinking."[9]

There was, however, another side to the coin as numerous divergent and critical reviews appeared. For the sake of clarity, let us divide these opinions into three basic groups as reproaching Arendt's work for (1) its **exaggerated coherence and logic** (a criticism that was largely directed at the theoretical model of totalitarianism presented in its third part); (2) its supposed **interpretive incoherency** between the methodology adopted in the first two parts (respectively devoted to anti-Semitism and imperialism), and the aforementioned third section—this line of criticism was largely attributed to the fact that Arendt "to put it mildly, is no historian,"[10] as the respected historian of ideas Georg Lichtheim asserted; and (3) its overly **emotional attitude** toward the subject matter, combined with unprofessional moralizing. Let us scrutinize these generalizations one by one and uncover the basis upon which they each rest.

The first most striking and controversial element of Arendt's work was the thesis that Soviet and Nazi totalitarianisms were structurally identical and supposedly based on analogous power structures and worldviews. Arendt's definition of the term "totalitarianism" also differed from its common usage.

It was too narrow to be applicable for comparative research. Moreover, many scholars disapproved of Arendt's selective choice of historical sources and excessive focus on Nazism at Stalinism's expense.[11]

Raymond Aron laid out a plain critique of the excessive coherence and logic of Arendt's theory. Aron, who himself authored *The Opium of the Intellectuals*, a work critical of sympathies for Marxism within Western academia, underlined that in trying to capture the essence of totalitarianism, Arendt was necessarily driven to exclude or marginalize facts that did not fit with her model.[12] A similar accusation concerned Arendt's thesis on the supposedly unprecedented nature of totalitarianism. Aron claimed that Arendt simply ignored relevant details that would have challenged her argument.[13]

Robert Burrowes leveled similar charges, accusing Arendt of reductionism and producing an "essentially fantastic construct." Arendt's overly coherent work supposedly ignored the diversity of historical facts and thereby reduced a multi-dimensional power structure to the concentration camps. The criticism was primarily focused on the third part of the book entitled *Totalitarianism* and sought to discredit Arendt's professional competence. Burrowes wrote that Arendt "does not confront reality with the tentativeness and skepticism of the scientist." As a result, her theory of totalitarianism is "brilliantly wrong." Its "chief virtue—its logicality—is also its chief vice."[14]

While entirely unconventional, the first two parts of *The Origins* dealt with questions that seemingly demanded professional historical reflection. Thus, the reception of *The Origins of Totalitarianisms* was least unfavorable among academic historians, who accused Arendt of scientific inadequacy and a lack of professionalism. Most of them did not recognize Arendt's innovative historical method. All they had noticed was chaos. This is hardly surprising given that the book challenged some core ideals prevailing in the social and historical sciences at the time and still prevalent today.

In *The American Historical Review*, Charles H. van Duzer wrote that Arendt's work is "in part brilliant and suggestive […] as a whole conveys an impression of miscarriage."[15] In *The American Economic Review*, Werner Baer stated that "the unsatisfactory methods used by the author make the book of little value as a contribution to the taxonomy of comparative political and economic systems."[16] Another reviewer concluded: "The book is 477 pages wrong."[17]

Reactions focusing on the methodological idiosyncrasies of *The Origins of Totalitarianisms* also followed its release in the United Kingdom. James Parker captured this overriding sentiment saying that it "is not a historical study" because "historical material is not presented in a way to give a clear picture of the sequence of events." Parker argued that Arendt, enthralled with existential philosophy, demonstrated a "lack of concern with the past and future [that] involves the substitution of subjective patterns for an attempt at an objective estimate of facts."[18]

These critical remarks were principally directed at the book's apparent incoherence—"an ever-shifting eclecticism," as Thomas Cook put it in *Political Science Quarterly*. Cook rightly observed that in Arendt's historical narrative, "the pattern, the trend, the relation of cause and consequence, are not always clear."[19] Van Duzer further expressed his disapproval in terms of a "disregard for the concept of historical continuity."[20] Historian and author of comparative analyses of totalitarianisms of the 1930s, Hans Kohn, stated that Arendt provided "no clear and convincing pattern of the origins of totalitarianism in anti-Semitism and imperialism."[21] The reviewers argued that Arendt should have developed a definitive scheme explaining the origins of totalitarianism—an aim actually contradictory to her methodological aspirations. This is because in point of fact the reviewers were right—the coherence of the book is elusive.

Let us glimpse some of these troubles by looking at the book's continuously misleading title. Initially, Arendt planned to call her work *The Elements of Shame: Anti-Semitism—Imperialism—Racism* or *The Three Pillars of Hell: Anti-Semitism—Imperialism—Racism*.[22] Both titles pointed to "elements" or "pillars," and not to origins, insofar as the work did not intend to provide a genealogical investigation into historical causes. The editor of the Houghton & Mifflin publishing house, Paul Brooks, ultimately rejected the manuscript since, in his words, it contained "material for several books."[23] In 1949, two years before publications, Arendt's work was referenced simply as *A History of Totalitarianism*. Half a year later, Robert Giroux, an editor of the Harcourt publishing house (which finally accepted the manuscript), rejected Arendt's title proposal, *The Twin Myths of Destruction*, and suggested the title *The Burden of Our Times*. It was in September 1950 that the name *The Origins of Totalitarianism* appeared in correspondence with the publishers.[24] However, Arendt's intentions were better mirrored by the British edition's title—*The Burden of Our Time*,[25] and even more, thanks to the usage of the concept of an element by the 1955 German publication—*Elemente und Ursprünge Totaler Herrschaft* ("Elements and Origins of Total Rule").[26]

The latter, amended edition was acclaimed throughout Germany. *Gewerkschaftliche Monatshefte* wrote that "none of the many attempts to interpret totalitarianism comes close to Hannah Arendt's great study."[27] Julie Pohlmann in *Welt der Arbeit* called it "an extraordinary work of history" and an "incorruptible striving for clear, naked truth."[28] Richard Reich in *Neue Zürcher Zeitung* praised Arendt's "brilliant political-sociological interpretation"[29] and Wolfgang Berkefeld in Hamburg's *Sonntagsblatt* her "unusual clarity."[30] Meanwhile, Wolfgang Höpker in *Die Welt* described Arendt as "smart and almost frighteningly clever"[31] and later in *Christ und Welt* hailed the book as an X-ray picture of totalitarianism—"an analysis penetrating to the very core."[32] Finally, Robert Haerdter in *Literatur* wrote, "This immense work has provided us with an instrument of self-knowledge that is both indispensable and irreplaceable."[33]

As far as the book's apparent incoherence is concerned, the irony is that the critical remarks targeted at its discontinuous narrative and methodological eclecticism were entirely justified. One cannot help but agree with Klaus Knorr, who wrote:

> The book as a whole is not really scholarly despite the wealth of footnote references and a large bibliography. Again and again, the author makes the most surprising statements without giving us her own reasoning, or that of anyone else, upon which such statements are based.

There is no exaggeration in saying that *The Origins of Totalitarianism* is not a scientific work but "a large essay or series of essays in the tradition of the littérateur."[34] Isaiah Berlin supposedly regarded the book as "sheer metaphysical free-association."[35] The paradox is that both intuitions were correct. It is only the negative conclusions drawn from them that were far-fetched.

Raymond Aron was in a limited company in remarking positively on the work's unscientific character, concluding that an overly coherent attempt to capture the essence of totalitarianism would clash with the methods applied in the historical portion of the work. Aaron appreciated the variety of methods and modalities of elucidation employed in the text. What he especially welcomed was the avoidance of social and economic determinism and a departure from the pragmatic interpretations of totalitarian terror ("pragmatic" meaning rational with respect to its goals).

Particularly vital in this range of responses was the voice of Eric Voegelin—an American political philosopher born in Germany, an immigrant with a life trajectory not unlike Arendt. Voegelin was the only reviewer to receive a reply from Arendt, in which she explained the heuristic assumptions underlying her research. Voegelin accused Arendt of endowing "historical causality with an aura of fatality" and putting the "gradual revelation of the essence of totalitarianism"[36] as the central thread of the book. Just like the historians mentioned above, he criticized the lack of a defined research methodology.[37] The overall picture emerging from the reviews is thus ambiguous and inconsistent. David Riesman considered the book to be "extraordinarily penetrating" and "densely imaginative." Similarly to Voegelin, he critically noted that Arendt sometimes "assumes historical rationality and inevitability" in the development of historical events[38]—an opinion that seems entirely inaccurate.

The third and final category of criticism accused Arendt of superfluous and unprofessional moralizing. Only very few scholars saw this apparent moralizing in a positive light. Among them was Philip Rieff, who argued that Arendt is "moralizing history as the burden of our time," without succumbing to the "pseudo-objectivity which masks itself as the moral achievement of modern social science."[39] In his preface to the first German edition, Karl Jaspers wrote that the book aims to "contribute to a moral-political way of thinking" and "provides insight through which philosophical thinking becomes a judgment of political reality."[40] And speaking of the same edition, German philosopher, Max Bense, said in a 1956 radio broadcast:

> Hannah Arendt has opened the door to a modern historical research in which political tendencies and philosophical attitudes can never be completely suppressed and in which scientific objectivity is not the same as disinterested curiosity. Her confident way of writing history is simultaneously a topical kind of historical criticism.[41]

Stephen Whitfield put things slightly more provocatively in saying that "given a choice, Arendt would rather have been original than right." Aron added that Arendt often "affects a tone of haughty superiority."[42] While correctly observing that she did not shy away from moral judgments, Riesman misread Arendt's negative evaluation of the nineteenth-century bourgeoisie as a suggestion that it deserved its decline. Arendt's verdicts, however, did not result from confusing scientific analysis and moral judgment. It was a purposeful strategy originating in her belief in political entanglement and the judgmental activism of historical storytelling.

Incommensurable Layers of Anti-Semitism

The contradictory reactions of the reviewers often reflected their perplexed impressions of *The Origins of Totalitarianism*'s overwhelming contents, as though representing the book's inner contradictions. The sheer volume of facts, the mass of surprising interpretations, unexpected twists, and the apparent inconsistencies in reasoning must all have been confusing. Most of the observations were accurate regarding the details but at the same time missing the broader context. This section will tackle the idiosyncratic contents of the first volume of Arendt's historical *opus magnum*. Since the book eludes any simple generalizations and classifications, this summary must remain superficial and is intended merely as an overview for readers who are unfamiliar with Arendt's work.

Having read the first volume entitled "Anti-Semitism," one seeking to find out what anti-Semitism is will likely be disappointed. This extensive volume is not only lacking in structure and does not give any cohesive description of the problem, but it gives the impression that anti-Semitism as such has never existed. Certain leitmotifs that connect various historical anti-Semitisms, such as mechanisms of marginalizing the Other, do not form any cohesive whole.[43]

Arendt provides a hint of an explanation in the introduction to the 1967 (third) edition of *The Origins of Totalitarianism*, when she states that her objective was to destroy the illusion of continuity between various historically incommensurable forms of anti-Semitism.[44] In Arendt's fragmented, historicist view, not only Jewish but also Christian and secular historians succumbed to the "optical illusion" of the eternal persecution of Jews.[45] The idea of pure or ahistorical anti-Semitism, Arendt suggested, also partly results from the Holocaust, for it led to the retrospective projection of continuity upon the fragmented past, a projection performed by the perpetrators and the victims alike.[46] Consequently, developing this line of thinking in historical narratives reproduces the perpetrators' perspective used to justify genocide.[47] In reality, the ancient Roman aversion toward Jews was different from the religious-based hatred from the Middle Ages, and the diverse forms of nineteenth-century anti-Semitism that Arendt analyzed in-depth were quite unlike its imperialistic and totalitarian forms.

Anti-Semitism, Arendt maintained, is neither uniform, nor one-dimensional, nor ahistorical. By contrast, it is a diverse, multifaceted, and frequently fleeting phenomenon. Its various forms are mutually incommensurable. In addition, it **was not** a cause of the Holocaust—the only effect of the nineteenth-century anti-Semitisms was Zionism and not Nazism.[48] Taken as a cause of genocide, anti-Semitism outrages common sense, Arendt claimed, as if being on the other side of the spectrum to Daniel Goldhagen's much later controversial thesis regarding the "eliminationist" German hatred of Jews.[49]

A careful reader will count several, divergent types of anti-Semitism in the book: two early forms in Prussia (the conservative anti-Semitism of aristocrats and the radical anti-Semitism of intellectuals and liberals); a later short-lived anti-

Semitism of German parties with supranational aspirations; Austro-Hungarian anti-state anti-Semitism stemming from national liberation movements; French leftist economic anti-Semitism resulting from the strong position of bankers; French postwar nationalist anti-Semitism; French irrational anti-Semitism of Louis-Ferdinand Céline; clerical anti-Semitism; military anti-Semitism; anti-Semitism of the mob; anti-Semitism of Jewish communities torn between operating outside of society as pariahs and participating within it as parvenus.

Not only are the different types of anti-Semitism incommensurable, the overlapping layers of its various manifestations also do not cumulate in the manner of archaeological strata. Arendt intends to show how at first, at the turn of the twentieth century, anti-Semitism seemed to be a relic, and then how it suddenly reappeared in a totally novel and unprecedented form. It was the hatred of anti-social elements directed against a satiated and orderly society and now allegedly transferred onto its symbol—the assimilated Jewish intelligentsia.

Some parts of *Anti-Semitism* bear the hallmark of an indirect, structural explanation mixed with a history of ideas. At times, Arendt delves into social psychology and focuses on depicting a specific space of social experience underlying possible reactions toward Jews within it. For example, she focuses at length on how the concept of the chosen people operated in the secularized world and how the idea of an innate personality drifted across religious, national, and economic discourses before its ultimate transformation into hereditary Jewishness free of any religious bonds, convictions, social positions, or behaviors. Another modus of a more normative narrative explanation is based upon the mostly tacit distinction between the social and the political, expounded by Arendt much later in *The Human Condition*. In *Anti-Semitism*, Arendt presents a story of Jewish emancipation and assimilation as a conceptual trap, in which more equal opportunities paradoxically become a Jewish privilege. The failure of emancipation stemmed from the fact that Jews became synonymous with the bourgeoisie while remaining the others within society. This gave birth to a new kind of social anti-Semitism that was simultaneously attracted toward the Jews and discriminating against them. Only in a world in which the social dominates over the political, Arendt claimed, was such a double-orientation possible. Jewishness was transformed into a quasi-magical quality, which could be viewed through the figure of an exceptional Jew, but it could also become an innate vice that is impossible to escape. All in all, whilst this new constellation of anti-Semitisms paved the way for its later twentieth-century European forms, it did not directly cause them.

Throughout *The Origins of Totalitarianism*, the reader also encounters several micro-stories that interrupt the narrative flow and function as case studies designed to illustrate some of the phenomena in question. They resemble a much later genre of microhistory as developed in the 1970s by Carlo Ginzburg and other Italian historians; the exception is that in Arendt's case, these stories are more fragmented, for example, a brief section on the Rothschild family illuminates the origins of the anti-Semitic idea of the global government. Meanwhile, a short interlude on the former British prime minister, Benjamin Disraeli, shows how the idea of Jewishness stripped of its messianic transcendent girdle became reduced to the mere fact of birth and, as such, even more inalienable. Furthermore, Disraeli's puzzling belief in conspiracy theories exemplifies the nineteenth-century views on the secret societies governing the world. Something of an arrival point in this fragmentary narrative is the Dreyfus Affair, which in Arendt's words was "a kind of dress rehearsal for the performance of our own time."[50] The metaphor of dress rehearsal alludes to indirect links between the anti-Semitism of that age and totalitarianism. Arendt is concerned with showing how an essentially innocuous spark could set the political world alight and reveal structures buried within it—a knot of various types of anti-Semitism that was invisible just a moment before. The goal is to show the hidden potential and yet unrealized possibilities contained in overlapping and accumulated layers of heterogeneous forms of hatred.

Inconsistencies of Imperialism

The section on imperialism is similarly fragmentary, albeit considerably more theoretical. It makes an argument corresponding to the thesis on the incommensurability and historical unprecedentedness of various types of anti-Semitism. Arendt presents different kinds of imperialism—overseas, continental, pan-Slavic, and pan-Germanic—in a historicist manner and also as being incommensurable and unprecedented. Comparably to various examples of anti-Semitism, there is a discontinuity between these cases of imperialism and their totalitarian form.

Arendt defines pre-totalitarian imperialism as an essentially purposeless expansion of the ruling bourgeoisie—an expansion for its own sake. Her narrative aims to do justice to the historical contingency and "absent-mindedness" that led to the development of the British Empire.[51] Here lies another similarity with anti-Semitism—the disparity of causes and effects. Nevertheless, this part contains more elements of structural explanation than the fragmented story of different forms of anti-Semitism. For example, Arendt claims that the affinity of overaccumulation of capital with the mob is "a force that had always lain in the basic structure of bourgeois society."[52] Among the essential factors demonstrating the unprecedentedness of imperialist expansion is its connection to capitalism. The classical view of Joseph Schumpeter defines imperialism as an irrational and purposeless inclination toward war. It is somewhat of an expansion for expansion's sake that historically precedes capitalism, which is essentially pacifist despite its possible alliance with imperialism.[53] By contrast, Arendt maintains that capitalism is a prerequisite of imperialism. The expansion of power requires the expansion of capital. The expansion of "superfluous" capital also depends on "superfluous" people—the social outcasts who are the products of capitalism.

In this respect, Arendt's non-Marxist analyses complement some Marxist explanatory models. Arendt's arguments concerning the alliance of capital with the mob in overseas imperialism and the role played by thinking in terms of race in this process are non-Marxist.[54] Similarly non-Marxist is her explanation of the German and Russian continental imperialisms, which emphasizes the role of nationalistic and "tribal" factors and the specific mentality of the declassed mob. On the other hand, the abovementioned thesis regarding the relationship between imperialist expansion and the superfluous capital (which implies the historical unprecedentedness of this expansion) is fundamentally Marxist and, in Arendt's case, influenced by Rosa Luxemburg's *The Accumulation of Capital*. According to this theory, capitalism requires a non-capitalist Other. Unlike for Marx, expropriation and accumulation are permanent. Is Arendt then a Marxist, a non-Marxist, both or neither? Does the fragmentation of her historical narrative go beyond its form and style toward theoretical, explanatory premises, where one can also discern inconsistencies and even contradictions?

Whitfield pointed to the conflict between the explanation of Stalinism through pan-Slavism (which is indifferent to economics) and Marxist economic categories. And Klaus Knorr quite correctly stated that Arendt "manages to be a strict Marxist and a strict non-Marxist."[55] Among the inconsistencies concerning Marxist theoretical premises is Arendt's use of the concept of class. Lenore O'Boyle, who considered Arendt a Marxist, argued that the construction of the class structure in the book is "shaken." Arendt's application of the concept of class, which O'Boyle believed is her fundamental research tool, is thus "incoherent."[56]

In an equally idiosyncratic fashion, Arendt narrates the story of one of imperialism's fundamental elements—racism. It is a story full of ruptures, dissimilarities, and discontinuities that expose the methodological limits of the classical history of ideas. Imperialist racism proper, Arendt claims, is heterogeneous and different from its historical forerunner, race-thinking, which also adopts diverse forms, being different in aristocratic France, Germany, and England. As with anti-Semitism, the point is that pure racism, whose history might be "endowed by some 'immanent logic'" simply does not exist.[57] Arendt emphasizes the fundamental discontinuity between the various types of race-thinking and actual, imperialist racism. Analogously to the argument on the nineteenth-century forms of anti-Semitism, race-thinking would have vanished if not for the unexpected colonial invasion of Africa that radicalized the racist views instead of dissolving them.

Furthermore, several passages from the book fit into what one would today call the history of mentalities. Arendt presents several ideological doctrines from various historical epochs that became components or **crystallized** into later speculative philosophies of racial and class struggle. The ideas of eighteenth-century French Germanism espoused by Count Henri de Boulainvilliers are examples of proto-naturalistic thinking in terms of race and class; Arthur de Gobineau's theory of the inequality of races presents the idea of history as a natural science governed by a single law; there is also polygenism, Darwinism, and other evolutionary doctrines, along with the curious fortunes of *The Protocols of the Elders of Zion*. The mentalities discussed by Arendt include the mass inclination to see the world in terms of historical necessity, the deification of coincidence in Russian thought, the tribal belief in the existence of a chosen nation and the divine origin of chosen groups, and the idea of an innate personality (although not in the Jewish sense this time). Arendt also introduces a new type of anti-Semitism, the leitmotif of which is jealousy toward the supranational organization of Jews. As in the previous volume, she underlines the discontinuity between this thinking and its later political application.

The resulting complexity, heterogeneity, and highly fragmented character of the second volume of *The Origins of Totalitarianism* is unlike any professional historical narrative. As in the first volume, the reader is treated to brief, partly biographical stories, this time on Lord Cromer, Cecil Rhodes, and Lawrence of Arabia. Lawrence exemplifies the fascination with the lack of responsibility and thinking about oneself as a functionary of an impersonal historical process. Cromer represents a type of philosophy of bureaucracy. Rhodes epitomizes bureaucratic, proto-totalitarian lawlessness, the belief in the infinite nature of the process of expansion, and the role of secret societies. Meanwhile, the short story about the gold rush in Africa portrays the insanity of a search for the absolute value of material wealth. In these matters, Arendt's "primary concern," as one of the reviewers rightly noticed, is "psychological" and focused on motivations and feelings that made totalitarianism possible.[58] However, this is only partly true. Smoothly and effortlessly moving between social, economic, philosophical, and other levels of explanation, Arendt indeed explores human psychology, but what she aims to grasp are those ways of Western thinking that made the later belief in an alliance between a man and the hidden forces of history possible. Thus, despite the changing circumstances, what links these micro-stories together are the overlapping mentalities of their protagonists.

Tacit Explanations

The fragments of the past of totalitarianism, its origins, various types of anti-Semitism, racism, and imperialism **do not cause totalitarianism in any logical way**. Indeed, they are its constituent parts but not in the sense of continuities building up. They are only "dissonances, discontinuities, and contradictions."[59] The elements comprise a particular historical space of experience for political actors who undertake autonomous decisions within it. Arendt speaks about elements and not causes, but that does not mean that she totally disregards historical continuity and development or that she merely juxtaposes incongruent fragments and detached facts.

Despite the absence of strict causal connections, the book includes explicit structural explanations as well as implicit narrative explanations at various levels of generality that are necessarily required in any narrative form. It also takes advantage of more expressive explanatory forms that presuppose specific general laws. Regarding anti-Semitism, for example, Arendt shows how a relatively marginal issue of modern European history suddenly stood at the forefront of events. Thus, continuity is maintained if only because it is ultimately the Jews that are the constant object of various accumulating forms of hatred. Particularly important, however, are the arguments based on psychological explanation. These include the relationship between bourgeois mentality and otherness, which, according to the model, find the latter entertaining due to its alleged abnormality. This model serves Arendt's argument on how Jewishness, synonymous with otherness, might have become attractive and repulsive at the same time.

Another psychological model comes from Alexis de Tocqueville's *The Old Regime and the Revolution*. According to Tocqueville, wealth devoid of power creates a greater hatred than wealth combined with power. Even if the latter is exploitative, powerless wealth appears useless. Arendt calls this idea a "general rule." This rule is more specific than, for example, the rule according to which "every power arouses hatred."[60] Arendt then uses the model to explain anti-Semitism and dispute "the scapegoat theory," according to which the Nazis' choice of victim was entirely arbitrary. The abovementioned micro-stories exemplifying thinking about the world in terms of historical necessity also constitute micro explanatory models.

Arendt's narrative also contains elements of explanatory normative political philosophy, which prove essential for her argumentation. For example, she presents political structures conditioning totalitarianism, such as the nation-state (of which she is highly critical as potentially leading to the deification of the nation)[61], the continental multi-party system (of which she is again highly critical for its potential toleration of the independence of the ruling party from the state), and state bureaucracy. The section on imperialism that begins with a chapter on the political emancipation of the bourgeoisie includes an exhaustive analysis and devastating critique of Thomas Hobbes's philosophy of power. Arendt claims that Hobbes establishes a bourgeois community based on care for one's private interests, which excludes the idea of humanity. As a result, he becomes the founder of later racial doctrines. In this context, Arendt unravels the hidden temporal premise of the key ideas of the liberal worldview: the infinite accumulation of capital and the related idea of infinite progress—the false image of infinite temporality. This critique reads as if directly stemmed from Heidegger's existential analysis of finitude from his *Being and Time* (1927).

Hidden Essentialism: Purposelessness of Totalitarian Terror

Arendt's account of totalitarianism is controversial. The provenance of the concept of totalitarianism is fascist. It initially had positive connotations, particularly in the rhetoric of Benito Mussolini and Giovanni Gentile.[62] In American journalism, Walter Lippman used and popularized the term starting from the 1930s. A decade later, due to numerous research studies by German immigrants, such as Franz Neumann and Friedrich von Hayek, it became part of the American intellectual discourse.[63] Immigrating to the United States in 1941 and entering New York's intellectual circles, Arendt came across the nascent term, but she creatively changed its meaning.

Apart from the claims on its historical unprecedentedness and structural correspondence of the Soviet and Nazi regimes, what distinguishes Arendt's heterodox theory is her narrow understanding of the concept of totalitarianism and its limited applicability.[64] Fascist Italy or communist Poland in the worst period of Stalinism, and even Nazi Germany and Soviet Russia for most of their history were not totalitarian.[65] This is because in Arendt's model, fully fledged totalitarianism is a movement geared toward the radical transformation of reality, yet lacking any final objective and fundamentally without an end—"a chaotic, non-utilitarian, maniacally dynamic movement of destruction."[66] Despite designs on global domination, which Arendt claims are essential for maintaining the coherence of a totalitarian world view, the movement's only goal is the total domination taking place in work and extermination camps. This domination exceeds a mere objectification of humans into a means to an end (such as a source of an unpaid workforce or material for manufacturing industrial products) and its core is the elimination of unpredictability.

The heterodoxy of Arendt's theory is easiest to comprehend by showing it against the classic, influential, and somewhat common-sense model of Carl Friedrich and Zbigniew Brzezinski from their 1956 book *Totalitarian Dictatorship and Autocracy*. Like Arendt, Friedrich preferred not to speak of the causes of totalitarianism but rather of its general conditioning factors, such as the development of scientific technology, the predilection to dogmatism that is characteristic of Christianity, and mass democracy. Friedrich also appreciated Arendt's theory for sharing his belief in the historical uniqueness and contingent nature of totalitarianism.[67] Nevertheless, from the point of view of Arendt's theory, Friedrich and Brzezinski's six basic and necessary conditions for a totalitarian rule (monopoly of state communications, monopoly of state weapons, subordination of armed forces to the party, a centrally directed economy, police terror as the method of governance, and a monopolistic state ideology) are simply insufficient.[68]

Comparably with Friedrich and Brzezinski's model, a totalitarian system is ruled by a single, hierarchically organized party. This party, however, not only assumes control over the state but stands above it. The party leader is not a classical dictator but a replaceable functionary of the masses, reliant on broad social support. Despite the seeming transparency of the hierarchy, the totalitarian movement is, in Arendt's view, "shapeless." It contains parallel structures of power, police, army, state, and party administrative institutions, whose competencies are unclear—offices and positions might be duplicated and multiplied, the center of power remains elusive. The shapelessness adds to the lack of understanding of the current hierarchy and of responsibility. Unlike in a classical dictatorship, the secret police not only organize purges but are also targeted by them. All citizens, including the system functionaries, co-constitute the system and are under constant suspicion. The totalitarian economy is also centrally directed, notably though, in a way that does not bring economic benefits. Arendt refers to this fact as economic anti-utilitarianism, the quintessence of which is the concentration camp, in which productiveness is subordinated to the aim of total domination. As in Friedrich and Brzezinski's model, the method of rule in the entire system is terror put into motion by a monopolistic ideology. In this respect, however, unlike in the first two parts of *The Origins of Totalitarianism*, Arendt's account becomes, most surprisingly, quite essentialistic.

This essentialism was already visible when Arendt spoke about the structural identity of Nazism and Soviet Communism as well as the concentration camp as a central institution of the system—a thesis likely influenced by Blücher.[69] It becomes most conspicuous when she tries to grasp the alleged spiritual core—*l'esprit général* of totalitarianism. In this respect, Arendt returns to the eighteenth-century classification of the forms of government by Montesquieu—republic, monarchy, and tyranny. The reason is that Montesquieu imagined these forms as temporarily dynamic and propelled by their principles of motion—virtue in a republic, honor in a monarchy, and fear in a tyranny. The principle of motion, Arendt claims, allows the structure of governments to be conceived not as ahistorical but encompassing "history and the historical process."[70] Montesquieu also theorized about the nature of different forms of government—the rule of the people in a republic, the lawful rule of an individual in a monarchy, and the unlawful rule of an individual in a tyranny—which is another essentializing idea that Arendt borrows from him speaking of terror as the essence of totalitarianism.[71] The spiritual basis is also Montesquieu's concept supposedly uniting the nature of government with its principle of motion. Arendt interchangeably uses various terms to describe this spiritual basis: "existential experience," "fundamental experience," "fundament," "common ground," and "origin," but they all point to an imagined hidden and essential core that supposedly permeates the entirety of the reality pertaining to a given form of government.[72] In a republic, this ground is the love of equality, in a monarchy, it is the love of distinction. Montesquieu does not describe it in reference to tyranny, but Arendt posits that it is the impotence of isolated individuals. Following these somewhat obsolete categories, Arendt defines totalitarianism as a system whose nature or essence is terror, whose principle of motion is ideology, and whose basic existential experience is the omnipresent sense of loneliness and superfluousness. Before totalitarianisms, this superfluousness had never been fully revealed—it remained "hidden."[73]

What is most surprising is the rigid and almost stiff nature of this characterization built upon the scaffold of Montesquieu's old-fashioned eighteenth-century language. While Arendt refuses to speak about the history of Nazi Germany or Soviet Russia in essentializing terms, when it comes to describing their totalitarian systems, she succumbs to the essentializing language of *l'esprit general*. This language, paradoxically, belongs to the same arsenal as Thomas Mann's belief in the almost ahistorical German *Innerlichkeit*—the "essence of Germanness," whose evil potential had also remained hidden—with which she so vehemently parted.[74]

According to many commentators, Arendt failed to convincingly answer the question of the historical uniqueness of Russia and Germany and its role in totalitarianisms. For example, Rieff argued that Arendt failed in explaining why the same anti-Semitic ideas as those found in Germany did not lead to totalitarianisms in other Western European countries.[75] A mirror image of the same argument was the reason for why the lack of strong anti-Semitism in Russia led to the emergence of totalitarianism there. Meanwhile, the mass society, a significant element of totalitarian rule in Arendt's theory (albeit, as Whitfield stresses, insufficient to explain its emergence), existed in Italy and France, where no totalitarian governments formed.[76] One could say the same about other elements of totalitarianism. Most of them were a part of the political culture of non-totalitarian European countries. Was it an explanatory failure or a purposive strategy aimed at showing that the whole of Europe was potentially totalitarian?

Such charges, Margaret Canovan emphasizes, could only make sense if Arendt had talked about the causes and not the elements of totalitarianism.[77] An attempt to explain Soviet and Nazi totalitarianisms by appealing to Russia or Germany's historical uniqueness were more pernicious in Arendt's view than confusing totalitarianism with tyranny or dictatorship. This is because such an explanation disregards totalitarianism's most terrifying menace—its pan-European potentiality.[78] The idea of a so-called German *Sonderweg* was fundamentally incorrect for it showed alleged precedents for the unprecedented. It is accepted that certain vital elements of the modern world constitute essential totalitarian conditions and Arendt's arguments are in many respects parallel to those of the Frankfurt School, or more recently, Zygmunt Bauman.[79] Totalitarianism belongs to modernity, yet it proves to be historically exceptional. Its uniqueness is possible only in specifically modern conditions. Despite numerous modern continuities, a fundamental discontinuity occurs between various totalitarian elements and their crystallization into the solid, actual phenomenon of totalitarian rule. Concerning the fact of crystallization, there is no German or Russian problem. Explaining totalitarianism solely through some preceding phenomena, for instance, Prussian militarism or Tsarist terror, effectively trivializes the issue. For Arendt, there had never been a German problem. There was only a problem of Europe—the supranational problem of fascism.[80] And this is why in Arendt's model, despite their completely different historical, cultural, and ideological circumstances, the Nazi and Soviet totalitarianisms were structurally identical and shared a common essence.

This essence was terror—the term to which Arendt ascribes a totally new meaning. In her view, all other concepts are inadequate for capturing the unprecedented. The qualitative difference between totalitarian terror and all previous forms of state violence is its non-utilitarian and perpetual character.[81] In a dictatorship, the *raison d'être* of terror is the elimination of political opponents—a goal which is possible to achieve. Even revolutionary terror that devours its own children is not permanent. Totalitarian revolution, on the other hand, is perpetual. Paradoxically, the terror strengthens along with the consolidation of regimes and the physical elimination of the opposition. Its victims become increasingly random. In Germany, for example, these are no longer solely Jews, but also the Roma, sexual minorities, and people with mental illnesses. There are plans to eliminate individuals with heart disease. Such purposelessness applies to both Soviet Russia and Nazi Germany, and in both variants of totalitarianism, the victims are ultimately innocent. Their guilt results not from their actions but from who they are. Simultaneously, as everybody is potentially guilty, the difference between perpetrators and victims vanishes, including the leader's closest circles. Everyone can become a victim, and almost everyone can become a perpetrator, an unwitting and irresponsible executor of orders, unaware of the significance of his deeds.[82] Totalitarianism thus blurs the very division between the rulers and the ruled, between the perpetrators and their victims.

The permanent movement of terror is also unprecedented because it is governed by allegedly absolute laws of a higher order—the laws of (historicized) nature or (naturalized) history, which in the end are the same. These laws are not arbitrarily introduced but eternal and immutable. As in speculative philosophies of history, they demarcate the meaning of the whole of history. Furthermore, unlike traditional laws deriving from the authority of tradition or nature, they are the laws of the movement. They determine the true and just character of the changes that take place in nature and history. They do not limit human actions but propel them through terror, which "functions as the executor of Natural History."[83] Being the essence of the system, terror, an "instrument of acceleration," is designed to ensure a faster realization of what would have happened anyway.[84] The essence of totalitarianism is thus governed by a speculative philosophy of history, but Arendt's description of it is also largely speculative. Looking at the historiography of the Holocaust through the prism of Isaiah Berlin's distinction between the two types of thinkers, the hedgehogs and the foxes, Michael Marrus put Arendt's approach among the hedgehogs—those presenting a single and coherent grand vision (and not the foxes, whose understanding is more scattered and diffused).[85] It is as if the tension between Arendt's fragmented historical narrative and her strict conceptual model of totalitarianism was the first manifestation of the fundamental aporia of her oeuvre—the aporia of the meaning in itself and the meaning of the whole.

2

Bare Life and the End of History

Ghastly marionettes with human faces, which all behave like the dog in Pavlov's experiments, which all react with perfect reliability even when going to their own death.

Hannah Arendt, *The Origins of Totalitarianism*

The Circularity of Life

The ghastly marionettes with human faces from the quote above are the inmates of both the gulags and the Nazi concentration camps—the central institutions of totalitarian power. In Arendt's historical presentation, the figure of the camp works as a magnifying glass aimed at totalitarian aspirations. It reveals the full extent of the blurring of the difference between perpetrators and victims, as well as the anti-utilitarianism of terror and the elementary experience of superfluousness. The camps are a testing ground of the limits of what is possible and attainable—an experiential field of total domination. Ideally, their boundaries should expand sufficiently to embrace the entire totalitarian world.[1]

Arendt argues that the results of this experiment with human nature radically transform humanity into a set of physical, chemical, and biological reactions, as revealed by the fundamental experience of superfluousness and loneliness of its subjects.[2] The final level of total domination is killing human individuality and spontaneity. One is reduced to the sum of organic reactions to external stimuli. What is left is life in the purely biological sense.

This reductive reasoning from *The Origins of Totalitarianism* can be rendered through the conceptual framework of Arendt's later work, *The Human Condition*. The difference between classical tyranny and totalitarianism corresponds to that which is found between *homo faber* and *animal laborans*. The fundamental experience of *homo faber*, the producer, is isolation. In the conditions of tyranny, politically isolated figures still form relations with others although these are formed exclusively through the exchange of goods on the market.[3] In cases of totalitarianism, these figures become lonely and lose both the external world and themselves.[4] In agreement with the premises of phenomenology underlining the intentional character of consciousness, Arendt notes that "self and world, capacity for thought and experience are lost at the same time."[5] They become physiological laboring animals, deprived of others, reality, and themselves. The only practical activity left is metabolism with nature, and the only theoretical activity available is the logical processes of the brain.

Exploring the analogy further, the category of labor associated with *animal laborans* facilitates the comprehension of the existential experience of totalitarianism. The circular nature of labor—both the labor of one's body and one's brain—exemplifies the purposelessness of totalitarian power. The temporality underlying late modern consumer society and the temporality of totalitarianism appear identical and ultimately circular.

In Arendt's phenomenology of practice, labor is one of the three categories of the *vita activa*, alongside work and action, which will be gradually introduced in the next chapters with their corresponding theoretical counterparts. Labor is the first and fundamental human activity, stemming from life in a biological sense or *zoe*, as opposed to life in a biographical sense or *bios*.[6] Arendt uses Marx's definition—labor is a "metabolism with nature," its goal being to remain alive.[7] It operates at a species level where nature is immortal, and memory and history are negligible.[8] Furthermore, Arendt contends, following John Locke, labor is physical, and as such, it belongs to the domain of *oikia*, to privacy.[9]

As a means whose sole purpose is to keep oneself alive, Arendt's labor is fundamentally purposeless. This might not seem obvious. After all, the reproduction of life is the ultimate goal of labor, even if it is not durable. Therefore, one must add, labor's goal is given, whereas in fabrication, it is imposed by the producer.[10] Labor is subjected to the necessity of nature. Its circular character corresponds to the circular character of nature.[11] In labor, there is no past that is different from the future. Labor and consumption are two aspects of the same process. The outcome of labor serves to sustain life and is meant for consumption, which, in turn, produces the strength for labor. The surplus of life and consumption follow each other like day and night.[12] The toil of labor and joy at being alive, exhaustion and rest, effort and regeneration, are all closely and inextricably connected.[13] There is a continuous movement in which one produces in order to consume and consumes in order to produce. The products of labor are thus the least durable of all human products. Although they last for a while, their disappearance is inherent in their being, as they are meant to be consumed.

Notably, in Arendt's view, the concept of labor not only denotes activities directly aimed at sustaining life, such as eating, excretion, sleep, and reproduction of the species, but also many other activities, such as washing the dishes, shopping, or entertainment.[14] As long as it solely serves the bureaucratic process (as long as its products disappear consumed by the circulating bureaucratic machine), the intellectual work of a bureaucrat also belongs to labor.[15] Therefore, its circular character extends further than the fact that one eats to work and works to eat. If one buys a suit or a car that one needs for work, which one does to earn money and pay off a loan, one remains a laboring animal.[16]

Such life-sustaining consumption is different from use, and consumer goods are not use objects.[17] This distinction also corresponds to the distinction between *animal laborans* and *homo faber*. Destruction, which immanently belongs to consumption, is incidental to use. In Arendt's view, therefore, the difference between consumption and use is principally temporal. When labor products are durable enough to become part of the world, the worldlessness of *animal laborans* transforms into the worldliness of *homo faber*.[18]

Furthermore, and crucially, the circular nature of labor does not exclude growth. The distinction between unproductive and productive labor employed by Adam Smith and Karl Marx only seemingly mirrors the difference between Arendt's labor and fabrication.[19] Labor is indeed unproductive insofar as it only produces life. And yet, despite not leaving a permanent product behind, it can produce a surplus-value, which serves the reproduction of labor, and thus its further increase. Hence, even the surplus-value does not alter the immanent repetitiveness, the circular character of the whole process.[20]

This has significant historical and existential implications. Modernity accelerates the circularity of life well beyond the necessity of nature into the social sphere, which leads to what Arendt deems the unnatural growth of the natural—a historically unprecedented accumulation of wealth and self-multiplying capital.[21] As a result, previously restrained circularity transforms into a progressive process.[22] The ultimate effect of the entire process is the emergence of a new biological subject of a socialized humankind that Arendt terms "a society of jobholders."[23]

Arendt's speculative critique of the temporal structure of modernity is aimed at showing that in a utopian society of absolute consumption (which no longer requires labor), consumption becomes labor. Putting the toil of creating products onto machines does not abolish necessity but only conceals it. Consumption itself becomes a necessity. The rhythmic labor of machines resembles the circular movement of nature. A capitalist market appears as a form of life where money circulates analogically to the planets orbiting the earth.[24]

Circular labor has a theoretical equivalent that, analogously, occupies the lowest rung in Arendt's hierarchy of human activities. It is logical reasoning. Arendt touches upon this issue in *The Human Condition*, whereas in *On Revolution* she asserts that the truths of reason are rooted in the brain's physicality.[25] The brain as a part of the body is subject to the laws of natural necessity that manifest themselves as principles of deductive reasoning. Intelligence—the biologically given power of an organ measurable analogously to physical strength—also corresponds to labor.[26] Since brain power, as muscle power, can successfully be replaced by a machine—a computer, whose calculation powers exceed ours—the position of these capacities in the entire hierarchy is the lowest.[27]

Circular temporality is the hidden link between labor and totalitarianism. Metaphorically at least, a replaceable and interchangeable jobholder is analogous to the superfluousness of a concentration camp inmate. There is an obvious difference between the two, but the point is that totalitarianism radicalizes the already present elements of Western consumer society. The totalitarian movement is purposeless like labor. Its goal is total domination, and not, as in cases of tyranny, peace and the elimination of enemies. Totalitarianism excludes everything spontaneous and unpredictable, and ultimately strips one of oneself. Without others, without experience, understanding, and action, the self appears as nothing more than bare life, the logic of the brain, a generic identity of all. Both totalitarianism and consumptionism represent a victory of physiology over politics.

A Gap in Time: A New Perspective on the Past

The late modern victory of *animal laborans* represents no less than a negative end of history.[28] This end coincides with totalitarianism, which, as it were, brings it to a conclusion. Totalitarianism marks the culmination of the crisis of the modern age and the transition to the modern world. As Arendt puts it, "totalitarian domination as an established fact ... has broken the continuity of Occidental history."[29] And break in continuity is a fundamental premise of Arendt's philosophy of history.

In the final pages of *Thinking*, Arendt describes the broken "thread of tradition" as the "basic assumption" of her investigation. She points to the fragmentary nature of her reflections in *Thinking*, but one may well apply these words to her entire oeuvre.[30] The break in continuity is a key concept that develops throughout most of Arendt's works. She makes it clear that it is this break that enables the process of exposing or dismantling traditional metaphysics and philosophy. More broadly, it enables the dismantling of the whole of tradition—the past that is no longer given. It is not so much the past that is lost but rather its continuity and consistency—"what you then are left with is still the past, but **a fragmented past**, which has lost its certainty of evaluation."[31]

Arendt does not consider this process of dismantling destructive:

> [I]t only draws conclusions from a loss which is a fact and as such no longer a part of the "history of ideas" but of our political history, the history of our world.[32]

Although the loss is irrevocable, Arendt presents it as an opportunity. The demise of metaphysics has twofold benefits in her view. Firstly, it allows us "to look on the past with new eyes, unburdened and unguided by any traditions ... without being bound by any prescriptions as to how to deal with these treasures."[33] Secondly, it abolishes the traditional distinction between professional philosophers and non-specialists.[34] When it comes to the philosophy of history, the first benefit is crucial.[35] One can now look at the past in a way unencumbered and unmediated by any previous explanatory templates. It is a unique opportunity for new, post-scientific historiography that can utilize the resources of the past in a free and unfettered way. Arendt uses René Char's aphorism to express this idea: "our heritage was left to us by no testament."[36]

In consequence of the crisis, the scientific approach to the past ceases to be convincing. The break in tradition becomes a point of departure for a new conception of historical writing emphatically expressed in *The Origins of Totalitarianism*. This non-classical conception is **fragmented historiography**.[37] As David Luban rightly noted, the break in tradition is an epistemic condition, to which Arendt responds with the radical fragmentation of reality.[38] The new task entails reclamation of the past in fragments that expose and dismantle historical metaphysics, with all its traditional categories of understanding.[39] For Arendt, dismantling metaphysics is both a destruction and a rescue from forgetfulness. The fundamental problem that permeates Arendt's oeuvre, a direct consequence of the break in tradition, is the formation of a proper relationship with the past.

Thinking hermeneutically and assuming the coherence of meaning of Arendt's diverse and multifaceted work, one faces the troublesome impossibility of grasping it as a whole. Arendt's output is dispersed—it is scattered, as it were, through several discourses. It is compiled from fragments that have to be recollected. It lacks both an overarching, leading concept and a clearly defined core of meaning. It does not fit into any specific academic discipline, such as history or political science, research paradigm, or subject matter. It is precisely for this reason, however, that the concept of the break and the consequential loss of the past, which together result in the crisis of late modernity, are central categories that establish a common denominator for Arendt's diverse and transdisciplinary reflections. This is paradoxical since after the break, no concept should occupy a privileged and central place.

As a consequence of this rupture, the gap between past and future appears—the gap in the continuity of time. The concept of the gap has two incongruent meanings in Arendt. Firstly, there is an ahistorical (ontological) gap belonging to the activity of thinking. It does not originate in late modernity, but "seems to be coeval [co-temporal, as *aevum* means time] with the existence of man on earth."[40] Secondly, there is a historical (ontic) gap, related mostly to the victory of *animal laborans* and the totalitarianisms. With the late modern break in tradition, the ahistorical gap becomes broadly actualized—it becomes a political fact for all.

In the introduction to the collection of essays tellingly entitled *Between Past and Future*, Arendt writes:

> For very long times in our history, actually [for] thousands of years … this gap was bridged over by what, since the Romans, we have called tradition. That this tradition has worn thinner and thinner as the modern age progressed is a secret to nobody. When the thread of tradition finally broke, the gap between past and future ceased to be a condition peculiar only to the activity of thought and restricted as an experience to those few who made thinking their primary business. It became a tangible reality and perplexity for all; that is, it became a fact of political relevance.[41]

In other words, the temporal locus of thinking becomes the temporal locus for acting.[42] Everyone finds oneself in the standing now. It is a literally postmodern situation in which "the past has ceased to throw its light upon the future," and thus "the mind of man wanders in obscurity."[43] To extend Arendt's metaphor, the homelessness of pure thinking becomes the homelessness of the acting man.

Arendt renders her concept of tradition through the metaphors of thread or chain—it represents historical continuity that has been lost. However, it is worth noting that the gap in the historical sense (concerning politics and not thinking) is not only the domain of late modernity. In one of her final manuscripts, at the end of *Willing*, when commenting on the founding ancient legends of the West, Arendt presents a view that there is always a revolutionary hiatus between the no-longer and the not-yet—between the liberation and the establishment of freedom. This hiatus demonstrates that "time continuum is an illusion." Arendt calls it an "abyss of freedom."[44] But above all, Arendt's historical works—*The Origins of Totalitarianism* and *On Revolution* in particular—indubitably show that there are gaps in historical time, which are especially visible in the periods of transition or during revolution, and are based on and conditioned by the ahistorical gap.[45]

Despite these previous historical discontinuities, the latest break in tradition retains a central unprecedentedness—both in terms of its scope and its extremity. Arendt presents modernity as a future-oriented epoch, one that puts the faculty of willing onto a pedestal. As in Koselleck's later influential model of the temporal structure of modernity, the extent to which expectations are determined by historical experiences diminishes, and the gap between the space of experience and the horizon of expectations grows.[46] For Arendt, though, ultimately the expectations become fully detached. The demise of modernity marked by the victory of *animal laborans* and totalitarianisms breaks temporal continuity for all.

Arendt saw a fundamental danger in disregarding historical discontinuities.[47] She argued that they had been traditionally interwoven *post-factum* with a cognitively constructed continuity, which she deemed fictional. Her historiographical response to the latest break in time was supposed to be different, as *The Origins of totalitarianism* prove. The latest crisis had far-reaching epistemological consequences. This led directly to the negation of traditional, metaphysical historical writing—"fictional stories" or "ideology" in Arendt's nomenclature—stemming from an outdated substantive image of history. Like a political actor, the historian was freed from the wisdom of the past.

In Arendt's story, the crisis culminates the history of decline. The end resembles the Nietzschean death of God for it destroys any stable system of reference and initiates a process of overcoming, except that no affirmation carried out by the Übermensch follows. Instead, the new fragmented historical writing brings a critical appraisal of the past and creates a new space of political experience. This new Arendtian perspective on the past leads to a form of liberation that—unlike those proposed by Nietzsche and Heidegger—is not supposed to be metaphysical but genuinely and performatively political.

3

Thinking History through Time

The activity of thinking can be understood as a fight against time itself.
Hannah Arendt, *Thinking*

Speculative Historiography

Arendt's project of historical writing was aimed at saving the past in fragments, and it was essentially meant to minimize the traditional speculative entanglement of historiography. Arendt openly and consistently criticized any substantive speculative systems looking for patterns of historical development with the intention of explaining the past and predicting the future.[1]

Despite her aversion to speculative systems, Arendt was a philosopher interested in the nature of historical process, and had, as Richard King put it, "a powerfully sensitive historical consciousness."[2] In the words of Annette Vowinckel:

> Arendt does not think **about** history, she thinks history ... The outcome is not a new philosophy of history but **philosophized history**.[3]

Surely, Arendt did not construct any historiosophical theodicy (to use Martin Jay's expression) and showed how substantive images of history may lead to genocide. Nevertheless, she reflected on the historical process as a whole. Her thinking resembled Adorno's negative philosophy of history in saying that there is no historical developmental scheme that proper speculative systems proper posit.[4] Should one regard such a transformed philosophy of history—in fact, a negation of traditional positive speculative systems—as a philosophy of history at all?

Eminent historical theorists argued that speculativeness is inextricable from historical science. Frank Ankersmit wrote that "there is no intrinsic difference between speculative systems and history proper; they are used in different ways. Speculative systems are used as master-narratives to which other narratives should conform."[5] Hayden White essentially expressed the same idea even more succinctly: "every philosophy of history contains within it the elements of a proper history, just as every proper history contains within it the elements of a full-blown philosophy of history."[6] Every historian is thus a philosopher of history in a speculative sense. And every philosopher of history is also always, at least in part, a historian. All historians function in what Jerzy Topolski metaphorically called ontological spaces that precede their choice of research methodologies leading to historical narratives.[7] Wojciech Wrzosek, in turn, spoke of "microhistoriosophies"—a philosophy of history in a nutshell, so to speak, consisting of historians' unarticulated premises concerning their understanding of the very nature of the historical process and also preceding their scientific endeavor.[8] In short, the speculative philosophy of history cannot be entirely abandoned.

Arendt rejects the notion of history as a whole, its purpose and its mechanism. She regards history as a sphere of coincidence, a more-less random assembly of stories in the plural. However, Arendt maintains that things are a certain way for a reason, and in this limited sense, speaks of history as a whole. Utilizing the concept of speculative philosophy is thus justified only insofar as Arendt's theory applies to the whole of history that is labeled as being impossible to define. Applying William Dray's classification of speculative philosophies of history, Arendt's view of the historical process would follow the chaotic pattern.[9] With this view, history is mostly a game of chance. There is no purpose to it nor is there a mechanism that propels it. Nevertheless, the negative response that the chaotic philosophy of history evokes with regard to the whole of the process is sufficient to call it speculative (as opposed to critical or analytical).[10] Karl Popper was of a similar mind, asserting that the historicist way of thinking acknowledges it as certain that either "the world is ruled by superior powers" or that it is "a mere wheel of chance."[11] Arendt's insight concerning the impossibility of systematization of history speculatively leads to its very core.[12]

The goal of understanding Arendt's original conception of historical writing as materialized in her most important historical book, *The Origins of Totalitarianism*, therefore requires attention to both its methodological justification (her critical philosophy of history) and to her vision of historical process as a whole (her speculative philosophy of history).[13] The methodological justification emerges from Arendt's reflections on storytelling that, admittedly, refer to daily life practice, and only secondarily to professional historiography.

The speculative issues are, in turn, openly considered under the auspices of political theory. In this interpretative endeavor, historical writing is both the point of departure and the point of arrival, while the philosophy of history in both the critical and speculative sense marks the path of understanding.

The Human Condition as the Metaphysics of History

Hans Jonas remarked that the best label associating Arendt with this area of fundamental questions is philosophical anthropology.[14] As Passerin D'Entrèves put it, Arendt "provides the framework of a phenomenological anthropology," which differs from the "theory of human nature."[15] This comes across as surprising, given Arendt's harsh critique of Western philosophical tradition as being focused upon man. Arendt would certainly not have called herself a philosophical anthropologist, if only by being Heidegger's student.[16] However, there is a more important reason for this rejection. The most basic fact of human plurality is more primordial than abstract Heideggerian *Dasein*,[17] or more precisely, it is not so much an anthropological fact as its ahistorical potentiality. Consequently, although humans are historically variable to the extent that makes it impossible to speak of their essence, the structure of human plurality remains constant. The actuality of this potentiality may be lost, as was the case with concentration camps, but it can always be regained.

What is at stake here in terms of Arendt's philosophy of history? The level of inquiry concerns the conditions of the possibility of historiographical discourse that Paul Ricoeur called ontological hermeneutics, noting that its task is to "occupy the place of a speculative philosophy of history."[18] At first glance, Arendt's historiography appears to be nothing more than a quasi-postmodern collection of stories, a cluster of fragments that don't necessarily fit together. However, this apparent lack of coherence is based on a higher order of coherence that is ultimately temporal. The concept of anthropology indicates that Arendt converts her insights regarding temporality—its "practical" emanations in the form of labor, work and action as well as "theoretical" emanations in the form of thinking, willing, and judgment—into fundamental and quasi-anthropological characteristics. As Paul Ricoeur aptly noted, Arendt's philosophical anthropology provides insights into the "most enduring features of the temporal condition of man."[19] Arendt's thought is also hermeneutic to the extent that it departs from philosophical fundamentalism and takes consciousness to be secondary to the practice of life.[20] Such a hermeneutic perspective shares the historiosophical scope of reflections because history as a whole is the horizon of all horizons.[21] The remainder of this paragraph shows how Arendt's notion of the human condition, understood as phenomenological hermeneutic anthropology, redefines the more traditional metaphysical and transcendental levels of inquiry.

Arendt's well-known assertion that her profession is the theory of politics should be understood in this context.[22] This theory was never supposed to be about political science—its intent was, much more fundamentally, to provide the foundations of political science. *The Human Condition* obviously does not present any specific political philosophy, let alone any political program. Young Arendt stated quite outright that she was interested in the "formal structure of human existence" beyond its specific historical appearances—and her primary interest had not changed, it had only evolved.[23] While Arendt's theory of politics analyzes the condition of man as a political animal, it also reveals the relatively ahistorical conditions of human practice that structure, as she believed, all historical events.[24]

This is no less than an attempt at a redefined transcendental philosophy. Think of it in a similar way to the work of early Heidegger—a decisive point of departure for Arendt's thinking, despite her lifelong dispute with her teacher and lover. Undoubtedly, through his move to fundamental ontology, Heidegger left the question of the conditions of possibility of knowledge and the Kantian tradition behind. At the same time, however, he radicalized transcendental philosophy. Heidegger's *existentials* are no longer epistemic, but they move the search for primordial foundations even further than Husserl's constitutive consciousness.[25] Arendt's categories of *vita activa* are reminiscent of Heidegger's existentials because they are neither purely transcendental nor epistemic but bear a clearly ahistorical quality of being the conditions of human practice. At the same time, Arendt's attempt reaches a level of generality characteristic of metaphysics, thus—in Heidegger's words—revealing the horizon of possibilities in which being itself can be encountered.[26] Even if it does not concern the knowledge of being as such and in whole, Arendt's categorization remains characteristically general and ontological.[27]

Later in this book, this Arendtian "metaphysics of history" will be reconstructed from the perspective of philosophy of history—this is not in terms of what lies beyond the limits of the empirical but concerns what is most original in the sense of allowing the historical reality to emerge. The metaphysical entirety of being here is the whole of history—the horizon of all horizons. What are the conditions of possibility of history, which, at the same time, are the conditions of the possibility of historical knowledge? What is the source of both *res gestae* and *historia rerum gestarum*? Answering these questions will unravel the tension between the hidden essentialism of Arendt's view on this subject and her fragmentary method of reflection. This tension corresponds to the basic aporia—the contradiction between the intrinsic meaning of each deed and the meaning it assumes in a story, which, in the final reckoning, is the Grand Story of History.

What Is Arendt's Thinking?

Arendt's two favorite metaphors of thinking are the wind and Penelope's web. Like the wind, thinking makes things move while remaining invisible. Like Penelope's web, one that is continuously picked after it has been woven, thinking disappears without a trace, not leaving anything lasting behind.[28] Thinking is destructive toward its results.[29] For sure, Arendt is no nihilist, but she is an intellectual rebel, one that ultimately affirms thinking's potential self-destruction against submissiveness toward rules, regardless of their content. To take a closer look at Arendt's notion of thinking, an activity of the mind that propels the quest for historical meaning, this section differentiates several closely related concepts that, upon closer phenomenological inspection, appear quite distinct. These are psyche, consciousness, and cognition.

Arendt's notion of psyche covers the psychical apparatus that is structurally and physically identical for everyone thanks to the identity of organs sustaining bare life (*zoe*). Psychic internal experiences, such as emotions, are identical and passive for Arendt in the sense that they appear in reaction to external stimuli. Thanks to this identity, psychology can be a science, which is why Arendt is not interested in the human psyche.

Consciousness, on the other hand, denotes nothing more than the duration of the self, a mere sense of being the same.[30] When reaching to the world of appearances with the intent of asking whether something exists, consciousness becomes cognition[31]. Cognition is thus purposive and can satisfy its own cognitive needs by grasping the truth based upon the sensual apparatus.[32]

Arendt's notion of consciousness is phenomenological—it is always a consciousness of something. There is a fundamental difference inherent in consciousness—a difference that allows thinking to emerge. Thinking and consciousness do not exist alongside each other for thinking extracts the duality present in consciousness and thus actualizes the pre-reflective sense of the self into the form of an inner dialogue.[33] A silent, passive, and pre-reflective self transforms into the soundless speech reflection.[34] It is a process of **self-presentation**—a crucial concept for understanding the link between thinking and action.[35]

Arendt posits that a twofold transformation takes place here. The objects of the senses become images, which in turn become thought-objects (concepts), so that the mind transgresses sensory experience.[36] Concepts are "meaningful essences," albeit in a general rather than an absolute sense—which can be applied "everywhere" and which are spatially "nowhere."[37]

The crucial characteristic of Arendt's thinking is that it only asks what it means that something exists. Its criterion is meaning, and not truth, and it concerns "nearly everything that happens."[38] The criterion of meaning, in turn, is being consistent with oneself.[39] Arendt says that "thinking ... in contrast to cognitive activities ... needs speech not only to sound out ... it needs it to be activated at all."[40] At the cognitive level of truth, understood as *adequatio rei et intellectus*, speech is merely a translation of seeing. The metaphor of sight, which suggests constant presence and thus has advantages over the metaphor of hearing, does not apply to thinking.[41] The carrier of thoughts is speech—*logos*—but one that is not *apophantikos*, that is, whose criteria are neither truth nor falsehood.[42] Also, in contrast to purposive cognition, thinking does not have an end.[43] It leaves nothing behind that lasts longer than the activity itself. Thinking is *energeia*, a purpose in itself, an activity whose only metaphor is the feeling of being alive.[44]

Thinking thus goes beyond the limits of cognition, but at the same time, it conditions it. In Arendt's view, thinking is essential to understanding: "reason is the a priori condition of the intellect [understanding] and of cognition."[45] Humans ask questions to which they cannot find an ultimate answer, and their desire for certainty is founded upon unanswerable questions. Thinking thus preconditions ordinary cognitive activities, such as determining a historical fact, and is significant for comprehending the past in general.

In Arendt's reflections on thinking, one can easily sense an overtly existentialist tone. The need to think covers the whole of experience. It stems from the "existential interest" that transcends our cognitive capabilities.[46] Thinking seeks meaning in everything that happens to man.[47] It grows out of experience, which on its own lacks sense and coherence. Only thinking endows experience with meaning.[48] It is "in no way different from men's need to tell the story of some happening they witnessed."[49] Thinking—like storytelling—is an instrument of reconciliation with the world. As Arendt put it, "the sheer naming of things, the creation of words, is the human way of appropriating and, as it were, disalienating the word."[50]

The Temporal Structure of the Mind

Taminiaux is right in stating that the question of time was no less than "a topic central to (Arendt's) investigations."[51] However, it is not easy to determine in detail how Arendt sees the temporal structure of the mind, given the scarcity of her remarks on the subjects, mostly in *The Life of the Mind*. Nevertheless, she provides enough thought fragments to attempt to re-collect her view—a task that the final paragraph of this chapter undertakes.

The entire structure of the mind rests on temporal foundations, Arendt claims—the fundamental fact of human finitude:

> Man's finitude, irrevocably given by virtue of his own short time span set in infinity of time stretching into both past and future, constitutes the infrastructure, as it were, of all mental activities.[52]

The *ursprünglich* events that delineate lived time are appearance and disappearance, birth and death. This "finite life span ... determines ... time experience,"[53] as Arendt notes in passing in *Thinking*, meaning it is the most elementary structural condition of lived time. And finitude is accessible only to the thinking ego, for which it is the "only reality."[54]

There are scattered suggestions that owing to this finite nature, it is thinking that Arendt regards as the fundamental activity of the mind.[55] At the same time, however, Arendt tries to avoid appointing a hierarchy between these activities and, consequently, between their associated dimensions of time. As Robert Fine argued, the reification of the mind's activities into strictly separate faculties can be seen as a "potentially pathological product of the modern world."[56] For example, Arendt notes the futility of defending the purposeless activity of thinking from charges of its uselessness by arguing that it is the source of willing. Simultaneously, she claims that willing is determined neither by thinking nor by the power of judgment but is the cause of itself. Therefore, it would be far-fetched to conclude that Arendt sees thinking as directly affecting the faculties of judgment and willing—judging the past and willing the future.[57] The trouble is that Arendt is not consistent. Elsewhere in *The Life of the Mind*, she asserts that "it is hardly deniable that an order of priorities [between the activities of the mind] exists."[58] As far as temporality is concerned, it is safe to conclude that thinking is primordial, not because it determines judgment and willing but because it "prepares" objects to be given in a concrete form of "no-longer" or "not-yet." To quote Young-Bruehl, it has a "certain authority" over the two other faculties of the mind.[59] Since the latter are supposed to be autonomous, this is not a direct influence. Regarding judgment, for example, thinking brings about destruction that liberates one from common opinions. Referring to this issue in the context of political judgment, Arendt calls the power of judgment the "by-product of the liberating effect of thinking" that "realizes thinking, makes it manifest itself in the world of appearances."[60]

The broadly construed phenomenological-hermeneutic conception of time has far-reaching consequences for Arendt's understanding of the function of storytelling. The popular image of time—usually referred to as clock time—consists of a series of "now" points that follow each other: now—now—now—now—now, and so forth, toward infinity. Time is an empty structure of succession that can be represented by a numerical series of earlier and later "nows." All the now moments are equivalent, and the present is merely an elusive difference between an earlier and a later now. This is an abstract and simplified view of the reality of time.

By contrast with clock time, in phenomenal time every moment also contains, in Arendt's words, a "no-longer" and a "not-yet." The present is always extended, containing both lived past and future. Both views on time lead to paradoxes. There is no present in the clock-time view, while in the lived-time view, there is no independent past or independent future.[61] As Ricoeur noticed, this aporia is unresolvable, as each of these irreducible conceptions that he calls phenomenological and cosmological time introduces problems of its own.[62]

In the original phenomenological formulation, temporality is the original structure of the mind that allows us to perceive and experience the world continuously.[63] In his *Vorlesungen zur Phänomenologie des inneren Zeitbewußtseins*, Husserl considers the role of consciousness in constituting temporal experience. He distinguishes three phases of each act of consciousness, which he calls retention (primordial memory), perception, and protention (primordial expectation).[64] These are immediate and pre-reflective and together create a unity that assures the continuity of experiences.[65] From the phenomenological perspective, such a primordial time of consciousness precedes measurable clock time, which is its secondary objectification.

Husserl saw the continuity of time as directional. Although retention and protention overlap, time still flows toward the future. The loop in the temporal continuum was introduced only by Heidegger, for whom every diachronic relationship is secondary to the reciprocal entanglements of the three so-called "ecstasies" of primordial time. All three dimensions are intertwined in the common horizon of temporality (*Zeitlichkeit*). It is finite and primordial, and enables the order of the time of the world in which objects appear. Temporality forms the entire existential structure of Dasein.[66]

The phenomenological conception of time is far more complicated and nuanced than this brief overview, not to mention the differences between its many expositions. However, the above presentation suffices as a broad intellectual context for Arendt's thoughts on this subject. This is because Arendt shared Heidegger's view regarding the originality of the primordial character of ontological reflection against scientific enterprise, and consequently, the originality of primordial time in relation to world time. As Heidegger argues toward the end of *Being and Time*, the historicity of Dasein is the "existential origin" of the science of history.[67] In Arendt's terms, the human condition—her own "metaphysics" of being historical—preconditions the practice of storytelling and, subsequently, historical research.

The implications of this view are significant for Arendt's argument on the function of storytelling. If primordial time does not simply flow from the past toward the future, but instead progresses in both directions at once as if somehow entangled, one cannot talk of a simple causal relationship between earlier and later events. Consequently, in Arendt's historical writing, the relation of causality assumes a non-classical form. The past determines neither the future nor the story the future tells about it.

Access to the entirety of primordial time is given by thinking and thinking only. Thinking constitutes the fundamental "existential-ontological" condition of the possibility of whatever happens in history and whatever story one might tell about it. Arendt represents the experience of the finite time of thinking by citing two parables, by Kafka and by Nietzsche. In both, one witnesses a clash of the past and the future.[68] Both illustrate her view that finite time exists only due to the presence of the thinking ego (not consciousness and not *Dasein*). In *The Human Condition*, Arendt calls it an "interval."[69] The lived present is a knot in which "past and future are equally present." Time is lived as a "gap" in time, the in-between that "is called the present."[70] What man calls the present is:

> a life-long fight against the dead weight of the past, driving him forward with hope, and the fear of a future (whose only certainty is death), driving him backward toward "the quiet of the past" with nostalgia for and remembrance of the only reality he can be sure of.[71]

Arendt then draws the time of thinking as the diagonal force departing from the clash of past and future and the force that deflects the stream of time from its otherwise linear flow toward the future.[72] This force (unlike those of past and future) has a definite beginning at the place where the others cross and clash.

However, it does not have an end and points toward infinity. Arendt calls the diagonal force "a perfect metaphor for the activity of thought."[73]

Apparently, thinking is always tied to some historical point of departure, even though thinking itself—the condition of the possibility of breaking time into past and future—is ahistorical, so to speak. This would explain why Arendt says that the force that represents thinking is "limited" by its rootedness in the present. This rootedness determines the space for a search for meaning, which, for this very reason, is never final, i.e., never eternal or beyond time. In a word, it is historical.

Regarding time, thinking presents what is absent from both the past and future—Arendt makes this clear on several occasions. It abolishes temporal and spatial distance: it is both anticipation and remembrance, thus making the absent present.[74] Only thinking gives the fullness of time—future and past are equally present in it. The object of reflection is "what is absent—what has already appeared or what has not yet appeared."[75] As far as the past and future objects of thinking are concerned, thinking is "everywhere." With regard to space, however, it is "nowhere" and is, in this sense, "homeless."[76] This "nowhere" appears as such only from the external perspective of the world of appearances.

It follows from Arendt's scattered considerations that one can perceive the future and the past—entangled and indistinguishable from the perspective of the activity of thinking—in a twofold manner. On the one hand, past and future "as such" are forces directed toward the present, pushing it from both sides. They

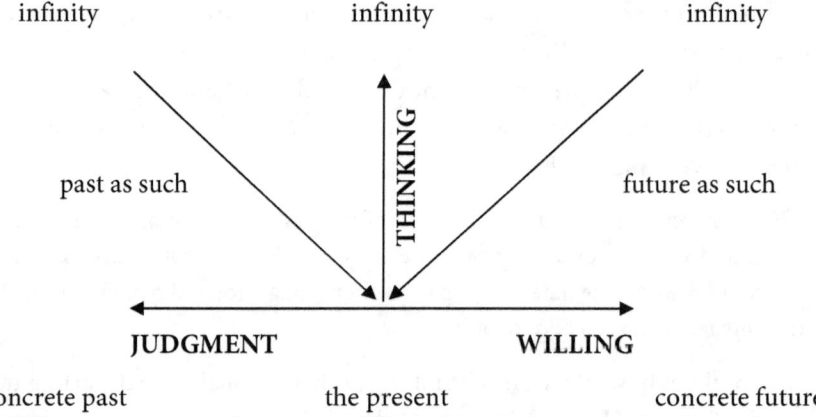

Diagram 1 The temporal structure of the activities of the mind.

manifest themselves "as pure entities."[77] When judging and willing though, one deals with concrete albeit still de-sensed objects from the no-longer-existing past or the not-yet-existing future that are now only indirectly dependent on the activity of thinking. From the point of view of the life of the mind, therefore, temporality assumes the following, mutually non-exclusive dimensions: (1) the temporality of thinking, a knot of the three dimensions of time; (2) the unspecified past and unspecified future as such; and (3) the concrete past of judgment and the concrete future of willing. Bearing in mind Arendt's schematic representation illustrating the activity of thinking, the Diagram 1 aims to comprehensively present the temporal relationship between the three faculties of the mind.

4

The Science of History as Ideology

The new logical movement in philosophy ... has a frightening affinity with the totalitarian transformation of the pragmatic elements inherent in all ideologies into logicality.

Hannah Arendt, *Understanding and Politics*

The Affinity of Totalitarian Ideology with Positive Science

Arendt defined totalitarianism as a form of government, the essence of which is purposeless terror pervaded by the fundamental existential experience of the superfluousness of men, and which is set in motion by ideology. Following Montesquieu, Arendt specified that in this type of political regime, ideology is a "substitute" for the principle of motion.[1] The analogous principle in a tyranny is fear, which unlike ideology, makes genuine action possible—people can still fight against political power and be guilty or innocent of their actions. Ideology is a substitute for action because totalitarian rule replaces actions with a movement of predictable behaviors—a collective of *animal laborans* that only reacts to external stimuli. This chapter explores Arendt's understanding of ideology in the context of historical cognition and demonstrates its implications for her project of fragmented and **non-ideological** historical writing.

Arendt does not use the notion of ideology in the colloquial sense of the "-isms"—racism, anti-Semitism, nationalism, etc. It is because the "-isms" make no pretenses to "explain the whole course of history" and are not complete "systems of explanation."[2] Ideology proper does, and when fully developed, it aims to simultaneously explain and set history into motion. For Arendt, the "idea" in the word ideology represents a law that is an "instrument" or a "premise" of explanation. This law binds historical events together in such a way that "the movement of history and the logical process [resulting from the idea] are supposed to correspond to each other, so that whatever happens, happens according to the logic of one 'idea'."[3] The law "promises to explain all historical happenings, the total explanation of the past, the total knowledge of the present, and the reliable prediction of the future."[4] An ideological movement for Arendt is literally the logic of an idea. As far as totalitarianism is concerned, Arendt views the difference between the Nazi and the Soviet ideologies (based on the supposed laws of nature or history) as being of secondary importance. From the perspective of ideological thinking, she claims, "ultimately the movement of history and the movement of nature are one and the same."[5] Nature is historical while history involves the development of natural predispositions.

Methodologically speaking, Arendt's view of ideology has much in common with the ideal of the unity of the natural and social sciences. Carl Hempel's classic nomological-deductive model clearly illustrates the belief that general laws function comparably in the natural and historical world.[6] According to the general law—an analogue of the idea of ideo-logy—"the logical structure of a scientific prediction is the same as that of a scientific explanation."[7] If the same conditions (event C) ever recur, concrete consequences (event E) will follow in a way specified by the general law. In other words, a successful explanation allows "rational anticipations," to use Hempel's term, which implies that even provisional and inconclusive explanation makes pretenses to anticipate the future. An ideal explanation discovers a general law, whose existence is assumed *a priori* (before it is discovered), and it shows that the explained event, the *explanandum*, was not random.[8]

Regardless of particular law or framework, Arendt harshly opposed the deductive model as such due to its coercive force of logicality. In her view, logicality is often accepted unconditionally out of the fear of incoherence of reality or the inconsistency of one's actions. And logicality boils down to a general model of "if A, then B" (or if P, then Q) that Arendt presents as the general model of conduct of the Nazi and Stalinist regimes, and which is also the general model of scientific deduction: "You can't say A without saying B and C and so on, down to the end of the murderous alphabet."[9]

One might notice that a logical alphabet need not be murderous and that the similarity to totalitarianism is purely formal. It is significant, however, that irrespective of its contents, it remains a logical alphabet for Arendt. She sees the specific idea contained in a given ideology (whose equivalent in Hempel's model would be a universal hypothesis) comparably to the axiomatic premise of reasoning, from which one can deduce indubitable conclusions. Thus, in her essay on understanding, Arendt explicitly notes the similarity between totalitarianism and logical positivism and asserts that "the new logical movement in philosophy ... has a frightening affinity with the totalitarian transformation of the pragmatic elements inherent in all ideologies into logicality."[10]

This most surprising formulation finds its justification in the context of Arendt's view of temporality. Logicality implies determinism, and historical determinism assumes that historical processes are regular causalities.[11] Therefore, it presupposes that the future is to an extent predetermined, which poses a fundamental problem for politics.[12] The implied fatalism is what is at stake here. It may be unspecified and independent of any concrete conditions but when realized, it may limit one's temporal horizon of action.

Again, one might soberly reply that even in natural sciences, general laws are only conditionally formulated. What kind of fatalism might they imply? Irrespective of their scope, the conditional laws necessarily assume a limited determinism related to the past being explained. Simultaneously, even if conditional, any explanation implies that if conditions (C) recur in the future (no matter how unlikely this is), then their results (D) will also take place. If, on the other hand, some unforeseeable and as yet unknown conditions (P) appear, they will necessarily lead to some logical outcomes (Q). Thus, the conditional nature of laws does not affect the issue of logicality, which is of Arendt's primary concern.

Once more, one could dispute this argument evoking the historically unique nature of laws involved in historical explanation. Karl Popper called them trends, which, unlike laws, are existential rather than universal.[13] The durability of trends always depends on the durability of their initial conditions. Nevertheless, accepting Popper's argument does not contradict the coherence of Arendt's reasoning reconstructed above. Explaining her methodological premises in *The Origins of Totalitarianism*, Arendt bluntly stated that her goal was to avoid "deducing the unprecedented from precedents,"[14] which meant keeping away from not only universally nomological but also historically limited explanations. This is not only about the error of transforming some of these infinite initial conditions into causes as Arendt firmly opposed the very historical conditionality as potentially affecting and limiting the political horizon of action.

As is evident from the points raised above, Arendt's response to totalitarianism is more radical than Popper's. Popper claimed that historicism is false by using a formal argument: since knowledge affects reality, and since one cannot predict future developments of knowledge, one is also unable to predict the actual future. For Arendt too, unpredictability is ontologically fundamental, but the whole problem of ideology, whose conception extends Popper's, is that it uses violence to establish a predictable reality. Thus, the question of its true value ultimately makes no sense. Popper's historical indeterminism turns out to have insufficient firepower to defeat the totalitarian interpretation of history.

Obviously, general laws must be empirically verified, which sets them apart from a pseudo-scientific idea. Ideology is similar to science in assuming that the explanation it proposes reflects the structure of reality, yet only scientific explanation is verifiable. The main problem of totalitarian ideology, however, is that it passes the practical examination of its effectiveness. Ideology in Arendt's view violently makes the historical world and thus verifies itself empirically. Through the movement of history and the logic of terror, the pseudo-laws of history or nature *de facto* prove to be true.

The Rational Mind of *Homo Faber*: Making the Historical World

In the context of Arendt's later writings from the 1950s and 60s, ideology exemplifies **metaphysical thinking** in the derogatory sense of the term. Metaphysical thinking traditionally portrays history in the image of a predictable act of making—the activity of *homo faber*.

Arendt's concept of work denotes all activities involving transforming the material world freed from the natural necessity of labor. Unlike *animal laborans*, *homo faber* clearly distinguishes a process from its product.[15] The end is superior, and it justifies the means—the violence that marks the path of production. In the act of fabrication, a model—*eidos*, idea—precedes the process of reification and it remains undisturbed after the work ends.[16]

The difference between the two types of activities is also temporal. The outcome of work is durable objects that despite undergoing a gradual material degradation endure as the same objects.[17] Arendt interchangeably uses various concepts that all suggest endurance over the course time, such as stability, solidity, and use (as opposed to consumption).[18] Contrary to the popular idea of nature being stable and the human world superimposed on it being the transient, human-made world, as opposed to the world of nature, is characterized by duration. The lasting effect of *homo faber* is the livable world that conditions the possibility of political action.[19]

On the other hand, although the process leading to a final durable artifact is a means that ultimately "disappears in the product," instrumentalism is inevitable.[20] *Homo faber* is dependent on the category of usefulness.[21]

Furthermore, since the chain of means is not limited *a priori*, *homo faber* allows for the generalization of instrumentalism, which brings the danger of degrading everything to the role of means.[22] From his perspective, the ready products become a transient and useful means toward further ends that are thus constantly escaping.[23]

The structure of work as presented above resembles the classic and commonsensical notion of action. It is a conscious activity geared toward achieving a goal in which the motive of an agent is the cause of a foreseeable end. Within Arendt's system, such actions differ from political actions proper, and shall be thus referred to as **actions of the structure of making**. These must be distinguished from behaviors characteristic of *animal laborans*. The distinction between the action of the structure of making and Arendt's concept of behavior corresponds to the traditional German differentiation, deriving from Max Weber, into *zweckrationale Handlung* (purposive-rational action) and *Verhaltung* (impulsive reaction). The utilitarianism of *homo faber* entails purposive-rational action—doing something in order to achieve something else.[24] Behaviors' definitional characteristic, on the other hand, is repetitiveness and reactivity, which brings them closer to labor, even if behaviors may present patterns that manifest in a similar manner to the model of making and are at least partially structured as work.[25]

Cognition as Alienation: A Story of Loss

If the theoretical equivalent of labor is the biologically established capacities of logical deduction and passive mental experiences, then the theoretical equivalent of work is cognition. In the hierarchy of activities postulated by Arendt, work and cognition are situated above the lowest rung of labor, logic, and the soul. However, they are problematic at the very least.

Arendt's story of the development of modern science is rather sentimental and sounds terribly traditionalist. It is focused upon progressing alienation resulting from doubt in one's senses and the concomitant production of sensory experience by instruments.[26] Natural-scientific experiments are viewed as producing artificial, non-worldly conditions and artificial, non-worldly products—which Arendt emotionally calls an alienation from the Earth.[27] A concomitant process marks the development of modern philosophy. Descartes's doubt signifies a departure from appearances so that truth is no longer given but must be made.[28] For Arendt, technology only proves that humans can **make**

truth according to the structure of their minds, even when it is the sole effect of an unpractical search for knowledge.[29] Descartes's fault in this respect is that he placed what Arendt calls the Archimedean standpoint within subjectivity, and thus made the mind the proper foundation of cognition.[30] Mathematics as a tool for the purposeful making of reality—be it the world of experiment or the human world—is also to blame. What is lost, Arendt posits, is the original meaning of the concept of theory, which became a hypothesis, the practical success of which became truth.[31]

But why should that be wrong in the first place? Arendt recalls that the Greek notion of theory comes from the word *theatai*, meaning the spectators in a theater, and denotes contemplation in the sense of pure intuition accomplished by the mind.[32] The temporal difference between contemplation and conceptual thinking is that the former silently perceives something eternally present, while the latter advances through soundless words toward infinity. The inner intuition is also a condition of making because every act of fabrication is enabled and controlled by a persistent model contemplated throughout the process. However, Arendt argues that making is more original. The source of ideas lies in the objects and not in the mind.[33] The philosophical importance of the activity of contemplation depends on the human practice that precedes it. In other words, and quite literally, a philosopher is a *"homo faber* in disguise."[34]

In the ancient times, as Gadamer argued, theory justified practice.[35] In modernity, on the other hand, "theory has to justify itself in the forum of practice."[36] Reliable knowledge only concerns what has been made and it is verified through making.[37] Scientific cognition takes advantage of contemplation, but it is a purposive process.[38] And purposiveness is what differentiates cognition from thinking.[39] Unlike thinking, cognition leaves an outcome in the form of knowledge that becomes part of the world—an object that can be accumulated. "Our desire to know ... can be fulfilled when it reaches its prescribed goal."[40] And like work, cognition is verified by its utility. Both rely on the categories of means and ends, and both are orientated toward making a concrete product. Science strives to rule nature. The truth of its purely theoretical aspects is verified through practice. Arendt argues that the instruments and force of *homo faber* enable modern lab science.[41] The outcome of this process is clearly practical: "The activity of knowing is no less related to our sense of reality and no less a world-building activity than the building of houses."[42] And there is nothing wrong with building houses. But it is wrong to attempt to create history as if it were a house—a purposeful product of making.

The Temporal Loop in the Production of Truth

In both *The Origins of Totalitarianism* and *The Human Condition*, Arendt attempts to show that science is a form of ideology, although of course, different from its totalitarian version. This is because comprehension and fabrication are two sides of the same coin.[43] Scientific rationalization creates reality according to a specific model. And totalitarianism is the culmination of the modern strive toward mastering the future and renouncing personal responsibility in the name of the science of history.

A substantive conception of history, which Reinhart Koselleck called the collective singular (*Kollektivsingular*), is one of the essential conditions of such fabrication. It belongs to a larger process of scientific rationalization, and preconditions the disposability (*Verfügbarkeit*) that is the purposeful management of history.[44] In Arendt's view, what enabled the belief in the substantive conception of history, with humans as the sole executors of its will, was "obsession with science which has characterized the Western world since the rise of mathematics and physics in the sixteenth century." Quoting Eric Voegelin, Arendt suggests that "totalitarianism appears to be only the last stage in a process during which 'science has become an idol that will magically cure the evils of existence.'"—thus underlining its continuity rather than discontinuity with previous historical elements.[45]

Speaking methodologically and more formally, it was shown how a model, according to which one fabricates a product, resembles the idea of a totalitarian ideology. This determines the necessary sequence between at least two events—a sequence governed by a deduction-like scheme. Both events are linked in such a way that movement in both directions is possible: from the cause (certain determining starting conditions) to the unknown outcome; or from the outcome to its unknown causes. *Homo faber* conceives reality as both made and explainable, and his models enable both prediction and explanation.[46]

The essential cognitive consequence of this view of ideology is that "comprehension is achieved by the mind's imitating, either logically or dialectically, the laws of 'scientifically' established movements with which through the process of imitation it becomes integrated."[47] In other words, comprehension integrates thinking with the movement of making reality—a processual version of *adequatio rei et intellectus* (the classical definition of truth understood as the correspondence between mind and reality). However, with the ideologically mediated fabrication, the mind corresponds to reality only because the latter has been violently and purposefully adapted to its models. It is the classical definition of truth gone awry.

Arendt's key insight is therefore that the question of the truth or falseness of ideology makes no sense because fictional (fabricated) ideas are incorporated into reality through violence. If reality is true, then ideology is also true. When Germany was transformed into a supposedly racially pure society, the Nazi ideology turned out to be true. The same was also the case with Soviet Russia becoming a classless society. The difference between ideologies and science proves to be merely a difference of scale and methods, which, in the case of totalitarianisms, are based on terror.

Arendt argued that totalitarian ideologies only radicalize modern scientific rationalizing tendencies as both strive for a total transformation of the world. Compared to science and older ideologies (such as the deterministic interpretation of Marxism), they are more ruthless in application. The key factor that enables the success of both science and ideology is, again, temporal. By first projecting and then fabricating the future, ideologies explain the future before it has happened. As with Popper's "Oedipus effect," what happens is exactly what was foreseen, except that the self-fulfilling prophecy is carried out through the means of terror.[48] Scientific prognosis, Popper explains in *The Poverty of Historicism*, "in a radical case can become a *cause* of the predicted event, which could have not happened if it was not predicted."[49] Although from Popper's anti-historicist perspective, predictions are doomed to failure, it is possible to fabricate the future based on its supposedly true anticipations, and the prophecies of totalitarian leaders indeed come true. They are their "retrospective alibis" and present "ideological scientificality."[50] The belief in determinism increases their chances of success. It is easier to implement the future when it appears inevitable.

Degradation to Logicality: Physiology over Politics

Ideological scientificality particularly speaks to the masses longing for a coherent picture of the world, one that is much more comforting that the contingent and uncertain reality:

> What the masses refuse to recognize is the fortuitousness that pervades reality. They are predisposed to all ideologies because they explain facts as mere examples of laws and eliminate coincidences.[51]

It is the masses, not propaganda, that are the subject and basis of an ideological regime. "The language of prophetic scientificality corresponded to the needs of masses," says Arendt, because the fictionally coherent world satisfied the desires of isolated minds detached from shared experience.[52] The capacity of logical thinking is independent of intersubjectively mediated reality. The truth of consistency, however, is empty, Arendt argues. "To define consistency as truth as some modern logicians do means to deny the existence of truth."[53]

The advantage of logicality is that it functions well in loneliness. *Animal laborans'* logicality, understood as the strength of the brain, thus attracts lonely, isolated individuals. In its detachment from experience, logicality is not false. Quite the opposite, it creates empty and evident tautological truths. Totalitarianism thus creates a world ruled by a logical "supersense." This supersense, the opposite of common sense, replaces contingency with "cogency, logicality, and consistency."[54] It creates a logical system in which events follow each other in the guise of historical necessity.[55] The principles of logical deduction, regardless of the model of inference applied, are seductive. They give the human animal a foothold and grant him a sense of security in an unpredictable world. What emerges is a "fool's paradise in which everything is known a priori."[56]

A more careful look at logicality as the main characteristic of a totalitarian system shows that the connection between totalitarian ideology and fabrication discussed so far is incomplete. A wider angle on ideology makes it clear that work undergoes an inevitable degradation. Looking at *The Origins of Totalitarianism* through the prism of *The Human Condition*, one may notice that totalitarian ideology and the entire totalitarian system are marked by the degradation of the ideals of *homo faber* to *animal laborans*. When the law guiding prediction and explanation ceases to apply, totalitarianism becomes an inexplicable labor. Ideology that is set in motion not by the idea but by its "inherent logicality" loses its original purposiveness and becomes a permanent movement to nowhere.[57] This logicality represents the opposite extreme, as it were, to the incoherent, chaotic, and pluralistic political reality.[58] Incidentally, even technology, one of the creative powers of the new world, is not merely instrumental, but speaking metaphorically, replaces intentional tools with the human automata that destroy the durability of the world. Although technology is not labor—after all, it contains an element of action—it appears like a biological process.[59] Work is annexed by labor and reduced to the process of life. Arendt thus presents a more radical version of Heidegger's falling (*Verfallenheit*).[60] A realized totalitarian system is the victory of physiology over politics.

Elements of Totalitarianism: Crystallization and Figural Causality

Arendt's methodological answer to these difficulties is the fragmentary method aimed at doing justice to the past in its contingent and discontinuous nature. Its goal, to use Walter Benjamin's expression, is "to blast open the continuum of history" while simultaneously redeeming the fortuitousness of the past.[61] In the introduction to the first edition of *The Origins of Totalitarianism* (1951), Arendt writes that she aims for an understanding that does not depend on "deducing the unprecedented from precedents" or "explaining phenomena by such analogies and generalizations that the impact of reality and the shock of experience are no longer felt." Instead, she is seeking an "unpremeditated, attentive facing up to, and resisting of, reality—whatever it may be."[62]

In an often-quoted sentence, Arendt explains:

> The book … does not really deal with the "origins" of totalitarianism—as its title unfortunately claims—but gives a historical account of the elements which **crystallized into totalitarianism.**[63]

Clarifying her aims to the Houghton & Mifflin publishing house while working on the manuscript, Arendt uses another metaphor referring to Nazism—amalgam—the meaning of which is similar to crystallization. The amalgamator of Nazism is anti-Semitism, which is, at the same time, an amalgam of its elements. This points to a multilevel structure of elements, which Arendt defines as "prepared in the form of historical cross-sections." Her intention is never "presenting history as a whole."[64]

Although Arendt uncovers and presents the elements or fragments of totalitarianism in the web of their historical connections, her narrative does not link them together in terms of continuity or any inherent logic. Not racism, imperialism, capitalism, anti-Semitism, liberalism, logical positivism, etc., directly impacts totalitarianism. Arendt planned that "the coherence of this book … should not be the coherence of continuity" and that "continuity in the historical sense of time is preserved only within the chapters—that is the pieces themselves."[65] In her private notes that appear to be the first version of the draft in question, Arendt also refers to the issue of coherence as a "very difficult and special problem." She expresses the intention to write a separate introduction devoted to it. Unfortunately, it was never completed.

The fragments of the past of totalitarianism are not its causes—"elements by themselves never cause anything," says Arendt, while crystallization itself is contingent and has no cause other than "the factor of freedom."[66] Crystallization marks an "event," understood as a set of particular actions (Arendt's example of an event is the "first world war"). Crucially, only from the crystallization perspective—the spectator's perspective—can its elements be discerned. As Arendt put it in the introduction to the German edition of the book, her intention was not to write a history of anti-Semitism or Imperialism but only a history of those elements that proved decisive at the end.[67]

In the notes on the draft of the book cited above, Arendt speaks of the "pieces" that are "put together by events" and comprise their "conglomeration." The notion of a historical event presented here is more than the sum of its elements. Its meaning exceeds the collective meaning of the elements and can be perceived only from the perspective of its further consequences. In this regard, every larger event that is the conglomerate of individual actions marks both an end and a beginning. It belongs to the past that it ends as far as the past conditions its possibility. It belongs to the present that it opens as far as the crystallization of elements deriving from the past is the outcome of free action, and not of this past—as far as this "crystallization itself can never be deduced from its elements."[68] Therefore, totalitarian crystallization constitutes a break in continuity and temporality, although it remains connected to the elements prior to it. The event of crystallization is unique, even if it consists of previously present historical elements.

Ágnes Heller rightly pointed out that the elements of totalitarianism that Arendt analyzed often survived the end of totalitarian regimes in an unchanged form, albeit in different configurations. What is more, as Heller put it, they "can contribute to the emergence of social tendencies quite different from, occasionally diametrically opposed to, totalitarianism."[69] This remark is not critical of Arendt's method but indicates that the crystallization of elements into totalitarianism was not unavoidable.[70] With the fall of totalitarian regimes, the elements did not cease to exist.[71] And moreover, in the more recent words of Richard Bernstein, "totalitarian 'solutions' have been—and continue to be—strong temptations."[72]

It rightly seems that Arendt would oppose any theoretical school of historical research and writing—be it Prussian factography, the Annales School, or Marxism. As she self-consciously observed, "One of the difficulties of the book is that it does not belong to any school and hardly uses any of the officially recognized or officially controversial instruments."[73] To Arendt, there are no pure facts, no long duration, and no deep foundations. In practice, Arendt presents fragments of totalitarianism in a piecemeal approach, composing something of a historical collage cutting across historical periods and layers.⁷⁴ In the words of Ingeborg Nordmann, Arendt's approach is not simply interdisciplinary, for she handles interdisciplinarity:

> Not like a historian, but like a philosopher who, moreover, has an extraordinary sense of the realism of the language and montage technique of the literary avant-garde.⁷⁵

This surprising composition has often been misinterpreted. For example, Robert Masters noted that "Arendt's theoretical premises are partly Marxist and partly existentialist and the shortcoming of these two schools produce odd blind spots in her thinking."⁷⁶ Robert Burrowes, meanwhile, reproached her for unclear differentiation between the means and ends of totalitarianism. However, Arendt's central point was that it was the collapse of this very distinction that defined totalitarianism.

In order to point to its fortuitousness, Arendt left the question of the causes of totalitarianism without an answer. She also avoided searching for any hidden developmental trends, believing that phenomenal differences are also essential. Even more so, Arendt objected not only to causes and influences but also to analogies and affiliations. She resisted functionalism, which would imply that she read historical phenomena as symptoms of hidden tendencies. All the way down, her goal was to give justice to the historically unique.

Regrettably, Arendt did not clearly specify the nature of her objections to social sciences in philosophical terms or elaborate on particular methods in detail. One may speculate that this was because her objections were highly general and concerned the very metaphysical foundations of scientific methods. In support of this claim, one may recall Arendt's criticism of any extrapolations of the experience of *homo faber* onto historical phenomena. In practice, Arendt is highly critical of the modern science of history with its theories of causality, logical positivism, structuralism, and of course, functionalism, which regards phenomena as symptoms of hidden forces.⁷⁷ Peter Baehr correctly observed that for Arendt, functionalism means normalization—considering any given historical phenomenon as a symptom of another being (regardless of its reach, let us add). Baehr agrees that "the danger of continuity types of argument is that they bring us back to where we theoretically started: normalizing a phenomenon **in advance of rethinking it**."⁷⁸

In her response to Voegelin's critical remarks quoted above, Arendt rejects the very distinction between essence and appearance. One should not reduce phenomenal differences to essential resemblance, she claims. Differences are only differences. There is no essence of totalitarianism other than the event of totalitarianism. Terror, understood as the essence of totalitarianism, is nothing more than an event. Similarly, Arendt opposes an ideal-typical approach that seeks to establish idealized parallels between diverse phenomena.[79]

In a similar vein, Richard Bernstein disagrees with the accusations of Arendt of her alleged ancient sentimentalism and rightly underscores the primacy of politics over history in her work.[80] One perceives the past from the political perspective of the present, and the aforementioned elements of totalitarianism—or any other historical phenomena—appear as such only after their crystallization.[81] Elements only constitute themselves as such thanks to later events. No matter how outrageous this may seem for more conservative academic historians, Arendt was never after an epistemic correspondence between her fragmentary narrative and the past. History, she claimed, only comes into being "whenever an event occurs that is great enough to illuminate its own past."[82]

Bernard Crick, who grasped the methodological design of *The Origins of Totalitarianism* exceptionally well, went as far as to suggest that Arendt "might have done better to be more digressive." He also noted that she "should have shown more instances of new lights that failed."[83] This is a fair point, as indeed Arendt only showed those elements that crystallized into totalitarianism and ignored those that led to nothing. In this sense, it is true that she narrated the history of the victors and not of the vanquished (despite being inspired by Benjamin).

This is not to say that Arendt's intention was affirmative with regard to this crystallization, quite the contrary in fact, as her purpose was to do away with totalitarianism. In her *Reply to Eric Voegelin*, she wrote:

> My first problem was how to write historically about something— totalitarianism—which I did not want to conserve but, on the contrary, felt engaged to destroy.[84]

Elsewhere, Arendt made a similar point:

> I felt as though I dealt with a crystallized structure which I had to break up into its constituent elements in order to destroy it.[85]

However, what was to be destroyed is not totalitarianism but rather the linear structure of explanation, which is comparable to the category of work. Not wishing to reduce historically unique phenomena to alleged causes, not even to conditions that precede them, Arendt's narrative aimed to break up historical continuity and to de-fetishize genesis (to play with Marc Bloch's term). The greatest paradox, which again stems from the foundational aporia of her work, is that in order to justify this approach, she boldly drew continuities between the modern science of history and the totalitarian ideology.

When it comes to ontology, however, History for Arendt is essentially and extremely discontinuous. **It is not made but enacted**. It is also fragmented to the extent that goes beyond radical indeterminism.[86] Arendt's favorite metaphor of this fundamental ontological discontinuity is natality—the act of human birth, the emergence of something new, unprecedented, and unforeseen.

The relationship between elements and the event of crystallization is figurative: the elements of the past of totalitarianism are chosen. Initially, before it is reduced to purposelessness, the event of totalitarianism fulfills its earlier "figures"—the past to which, through free action, one decides to relate. In the hands of a historian, on the other hand, most of these elements are "anti-figures"—to take advantage of Herman Paul's term—a past that is not chosen but which one should not forget.[87] The destruction does not concern the elements themselves but the connections between them and their crystallization. The latter presents a new, unprecedented quality, and not an outcome of previous developments.

Despite the above, the purpose of the fragmentary method is not solely destruction. It saves the elements of the past from forgetfulness, even if being highly critical of them. The example of Arendt's later book *On Revolution* reveals that they can be judged positively. *On Revolution* was also methodologically controversial. For example, Eric Hobsbawm, an influential British Marxist historian found it "metaphysical" and inhabiting a "vague terrain" between literature and psychology, a work with "occasional flashes of insight … [but] not particularly well-founded on evidence."[88] Although less fragmented than *The Origins of Totalitarianism*, *On Revolution* also presents history as consisting of elements—in this case of revolutionary tradition—and breaks in historical continuity. As in *The Origins of Totalitarianism*, destruction does not refer to the elements themselves, instead it concerns the links between the elements and their crystallization, which is mistakenly construed as their outcome, and not the beginning of something new. Though the subject matter is fundamentally different, and the attitude to the phenomenon is affirmative and not critical, the path Arendt takes in *On Revolution* mirrors that of her book on totalitarianism. It dispels the myth of revolution as a historical necessity. The premise that links these two historical works is the belief that, as Arendt put it in an essay *Understanding and Politics*:

"We know of no historical event which does not depend upon a great number of coincidences" and that the notion of the "a chain of events is, strictly speaking, a contradiction in terms."[89]

Social Sciences and Utilitarianism: Explanation as Justification

Arendt intended her unconventional historical method to escape the inevitable performative paradox that any attempt to explain totalitarian ideology and practice with potentially ideological tools would bring. The main difficulty that she encountered was that any scientific explanation of totalitarianism using a deductive-nomological model would have teleological implications. As Bernard Crick rightly noted, even mere historical continuity would bear ideological hallmarks for Arendt.[90] This is why, contrary to the beliefs of many historians and political scientists recounted earlier, Arendt had no wish to explain totalitarianism. She simply wanted to know how it became possible.

This problem went deep into the very matrix of social sciences and classical historical research in particular. Arendt believed that modern social sciences are unable to explain the concentration camps. She argued that existing studies stick to the traditional paradigm and display a basic and previously unquestioned assumption about the historical reality—the assumption on the utilitarian nature of human actions.[91] This assumption supposedly prevented these studies from grasping the true essence of the camps, specifically their deeply anti-utilitarian character.

In this Arendtian context, one should understand the notion of utilitarianism more broadly than the ethical concepts deriving from Jeremy Bentham and John Stuart Mill but instead as a presupposition of rationality. In *The Human Condition*, utilitarianism boils down to the very structure of means and ends— to the structure of "in order to" instead of "for the sake of." In *The Origins of Totalitarianism* and a few other early texts, Arendt also speaks of utilitarian common sense (not to be confused with *sensus communis*—the community sense).[92] It denotes the very subjective rationality of action, in the sense of its general and purely formal definition.[93] In other words, the assumption of utilitarianism comes down to the assertion that actions have a structure of work and the instrumentalist identification of ends with meaning. Utilitarianism for Arendt is the "philosophy of *homo faber* par excellence."[94]

If totalitarianism is a political system driven by ideological thinking and its concomitant actions, should these actions—means toward ends—be interpreted as the ultimate, non-reducible causes of totalitarianism? Arendt argues that this is not the case. The crux of the argument is that totalitarian terror—the essence of the system—is not a means toward something but has no end. A completed totalitarian regime falls under the category of labor, which is why the utilitarian presupposition of rationality precludes its comprehension. Totalitarianism presents a challenge for understanding since both traditional concepts of political science and classical cognitive tools, such as the key tacit presupposition of rationality, turn out to be insufficient when confronted with a happening that literally **happened**.[95]

This does not imply that Arendt finds all the elements comprising a totalitarian system purposeless. Specific totalitarian actions are purposeful, although they gradually lose their rational function. In this respect, Arendt again proposes a story that follows the trail of loss and shows how the practical ends, such as a crackdown on enemies (a constant important feature of tyranny) or gaining an economic advantage, slowly lose prominence. Ultimately, the series of actions that constitute the totalitarian whole is by no means purposeful. The victims turn out to be innocent, and the work of the camp unproductive. It is the whole that is purposeless and paralyzing to the utilitarian common sense.

One might take issue with this picture and point to the strictly ideological ends which totalitarian terror served. Although these ends might seem hard to conceive today as being rational, they would still follow the utilitarian model. The actions of totalitarian regimes would then be anti-utilitarian only from the ex-post rationalization point of view, which is seen with hindsight. Their purpose, in Arendt's terms, would be total domination—reducing the people to the species level, which would fulfill the behavioral ideals of full predictability. The goal of creating such an anti-utilitarian population, reacting identically to external stimuli, would nevertheless be utilitarian.

Why wouldn't that line of thinking be convincing for Arendt? Her key point is that the camps were only seemingly ideologically efficient. The ideological ends were never (and could never be) achieved since they were continually degraded to the role of means. While terror itself was the aim of the totalitarian movement, the workings of terror were essentially purposeless, labor rather than work—a meaningless, circular consumption.

Totalitarianism, a historical, unprecedented and contingent phenomenon, set itself the task of eliminating all contingency, novelty, and unpredictability. Margaret Canovan called it the "totalitarian paradox."[96] An analogous paradox guided Arendt's reasoning on the possible explanation of this phenomenon. Addressed with the positive methods of social sciences, totalitarianism was objectively and subjectively inexplicable. On the one hand, it was an unprecedented phenomenon that did not result from external factors. On the other hand, it did not serve any consciously designed aims. Simultaneously though, it created an entirely predictable and fully explainable camp population, and thus fulfilled the ideals of social sciences.

In her reply to Voegelin, Arendt notices that the main problem of historical research employing scientific methods is that "all historiography is necessarily salvation and frequently justification."[97] She responds to Voegelin's charges quoted in the first chapter by stating that her "chief quarrel with the present state of the historical and political sciences is their growing incapacity for making distinctions."[98] As a result:

> Everything distinct disappears and everything that is new and shocking is (not explained but) explained away either through drawing some analogies or reducing it to a previously known chain of causes and influences.[99]

In the general draft of *The Origins of Totalitarianism*, penned in 1946, Arendt was even more forceful in this point: "the inherent law of all historiography ... is preservation and justification and praise," while historiographical methods "presuppose a continual flow and an established tradition."[100] Is every explanation a justification? Arendt equates explanation with justification to underline that any explanation of the historically contingent imposes the guise of necessity upon the past—whether this concerns the totality of history (as in speculative philosophy) or more limited historical laws (as in scientific historical writing). Every conditional explanation presupposing the minimum of historical rationality contains the element of justification—it is not something that is limited to only conclusive explanations fulfilling the ideal present in Hempel's model.

Arendt's radical outlook was famously expressed by the following words:

> I parted quite consciously with the tradition of *sine ira et studio* of whose greatness I was fully aware, and to me this was a methodological necessity closely connected with my particular subject matter. ... To describe concentration camps *sine ira* is not to be "objective" but to condone them; and such condoning cannot be changed by a condemnation which the author may feel duty bound to add but which remains unrelated to the description itself.[101]

This, undeniably, is a strong belief. Karl Popper, like Arendt, wished to "[drop] the idea that the history of power will be our judge." At the same time, Popper said that since history has neither an inner nor transcendent sense, it "badly needs a justification."[102] And he argued that one should justify history through both retrospective explanation and political action aimed at building an open society. Arendt would agree that the judge should not be history but a historian. However, her verdicts pervert the traditional aims of historical writing. A proper judgment of the past ought to be not scientific but aesthetic.

5

Performative Self

Only by playing at what he really is, is man able to affirm that he is never identical with himself.

　　　　　　　　　　　　　　Hannah Arendt, *French Existentialism*

Playing the Who

One will recall that thinking involves a "difference in identity"—the split of the subject into two interlocutors.¹ The self becomes one only in a contact with the other. It is action that reveals **the who** of the actor, says Arendt. The activity of action occupies the top of the hierarchy of *viva activa*. It actualizes natality and corresponds to the existential condition of plurality. It is, however, the least practical of the two other activities. Following Aristotle, Arendt stresses that *praxis* and *lexis* are inseparable, coeval, and coequal.² A deed in a purely physical sense is not yet action—"Speechless action would no longer be action."³ And since the spoken word requires a listener—it is a communicative interaction. Arendt's key point is that language of action is not *logos apophantikos*, the criterion of which is the corresponding theory of truth, but a *logos* disclosing the speaker.⁴

But what is the who? It is apparently not tangible for the actor and appears solely and fleetingly to others in the discontinuities of language. Arendt uses the expression "disclosure of who," the literal meaning of which (dis-closure) recalls Heidegger's *Un-verborgenheit*, Gr. *a-letheia*, typically translated as unconcealment. Nevertheless, the apparent resemblance to Heidegger's account of the self from *Being and Time* can be misleading, for Arendt's notion of the who creatively transforms early Heidegger's idea of the self.⁵

In *Being and Time*, Heidegger famously stated:

> The who is not this one and not that one, not oneself and not some and not the sum of them all. The "who" is the neuter, **the they**.⁶

The they—a translation of the German *das Man*—represents an impersonal who, whom all primordially are. One can only become oneself (*Selbst*) by modifying this ordinary and average "They-self" (*Man-selbst*).[7] The move from the initial inauthenticity of the self to one's ownmost possibility of being, which Heidegger calls "resoluteness" (*Entschlossenheit*), entails becoming aware of finitude. In this respect, Heidegger opposes the substantial conception of the self as being present and unchangeable through time. As he puts it:

> Da-sein is **authentically itself** in the mode of primordial individuation of reticent resoluteness … In keeping silent, authentic being-one's-self does not keep on saying "I," but rather "is" in reticence the thrown being that it can authentically be.[8]

Jacques Taminiaux convincingly argues in detail how Heidegger's notion of authentic self reduces *Dasein* to a monad, which communicates neither with others nor with itself. The moment of insight into the ownmost possibility of being oneself is a pure intuition.[9] *Dasein* becomes a transcendental subject, whose "ultimate condition of possibility," in the words of Taminiaux, is "an isolated neutrality."[10]

For Arendt, meanwhile, the unique distinctness of the who is also an achievement, but it appears through communicative interaction with others. These others do not bear the negative characteristics of the they.[11] Although the concept of the spectator that figures so prominently in Arendt's late work does not appear in *The Human Condition*, the actors communicatively witness one another and thus play a similar role. The difference between the who and physical identity is that unlike the latter, it is mediated by language.[12] Its linguistic character makes revelatory action exceptionally transient—"as futile as life itself."[13] Arendt goes so far as to call it "the most futile" and "the least tangible"—a key point to bear in mind for the later discussion.[14]

The paradox and the greatest difficulty is that even though the who reveals itself through language, it remains intangible in language. Any attempts to grasp it linguistically will result in "a description of qualities he necessarily shares with others."[15] Arendt calls such qualities the what—psychological features that are essentially non-unique. Unlike the what, the who is a particular and irreducible way of being revealed through contingent, linguistic acts. Indicating what something is—pointing to its *essentia*—does not exhaust the fact that it *is*—its *existentia*.

The next difficulty, Arendt contends, is that "nobody knows who he reveals when he discloses himself."[16] The self does not exist before being revealed, and it remains hidden from the actor after being revealed. The who does not manifest itself as if it existed beforehand in a box that suddenly opens up. It only comes into being.[17] This also implies that the self cannot be given to oneself in the manner of a product.[18] Action needs another person and "is never possible in isolation."[19] Since one cannot "calculate" whom one will disclose, the consequences of action are already unpredictable at this level.[20] A spoken word, which is usually conceived pragmatically as a means to an end, is already an unpredictable action. The self it discloses is dependent on others and only visible to them.[21]

To give a sense of action's unpredictability and uniqueness, Arendt speaks of greatness, which she posits as a criterion of beauty.[22] Simultaneously, this concept leads to the nub of Arendt's view of history. In this context, the Greek, Aristotelian concept of *energeia* is crucial. In the case of *poiesis*, *dynamis* (possibility) is external to *energeia* (actuality). A work (*ergon*) forms when the potentiality disappears in a product. In *praxis*, meanwhile, *dynamis* and *energeia* overlap.[23] A given activity does not have an end other than itself (*entelechia*).[24] A disclosure of the who is a full actuality, neither preceded by any potentiality nor a potentiality for something else. The actors' motives and its consequences are insignificant—"the 'product' is identical with the performing act itself."[25]

In addition to the points raised above, greatness as the only aesthetic end of action implies standing out from (but still in front of) a crowd of equals, as conveyed by the theatrical metaphor of enactment.[26] Unlike the colloquial sense of the word, however, Arendt's enactment does not involve pretending. Quite the contrary, it means playing who one actually is. As Arendt puts it:

> By playing at what one is, one guards one's freedom as a human being from the pretenses of one's functions; moreover, only by playing at what he really is, is man able to affirm that he is never identical with himself.[27]

There is no model or pattern for a role. Playing the "who" is inconsistent and denotes donning the masks that conceal nothing but the naked life of *animal laborans*.

The Anticipation of Freedom

Arendt's later reflections on willing, especially in the second volume of *The Life of the Mind*, extend and complement the above remarks from *The Human Condition*. Willing is the faculty of the mind dealing with the future—it projects the future states of things.[28] And willing is the condition of possibility of action, even if the two are mutually exclusive. Willing anticipates but does not itself constitute freedom.[29] The relationship between willing and acting is problematic.

There are no doubts that in the 1958 essay "What Is Freedom?" Arendt opposes political and mental freedom.[30] By contrast, In *Willing*, first delivered as lectures in the early 1970s, she sees them as complementary. Willing constitutes a "spring of action," and thus a spring of political freedom. However, as Bonnie Honig rightly observed, the contradiction is largely apparent.[31] Starting from the earlier essay on freedom, it is easy to conclude that Arendt's approach to willing is essentially negative.[32] Arendt presents the conception of freedom understood as a product of willing as erroneous for it identifies freedom with sovereignty (an internal experience of willing). In Arendt's view, though, political freedom is not autonomous.[33] Freedom is possible only in communicative interaction. Politically, people are free without being sovereign. If sovereignty was a necessary condition of freedom, people could never be free. Freedom means both willing and being able. "Only where the I-will and the I-can coincide does freedom come to pass."[34] Nevertheless, the tension remains. If "Men *are* free ... as long as they act, neither before nor after," then the problem of willing as a capacity giving a semblance of freedom remains, even if Arendt expressly defends it as a necessary condition for action.[35]

Absolute Beginning—A Break in the Continuity of Time

In the volume dedicated to willing, it is not easy at times to distinguish Arendt's views from those of the referred authors. Fortunately, from the perspective of her work as a whole, it is evident that she draws her conception of willing from the creatively combined influences of St Augustine, Duns Scotus, and Immanuel Kant.

The first idea that Arendt borrows from Augustine is the dual nature of willing as consisting of willing and nilling—to be unwilling (*velle* and *nolle*). An act of willing contains both elements so that every nilling is also willing. The crucial characteristic of willing is that it has no cause other than itself. "In its sheer contingent factuality," willing "cannot be explained in terms of causality" because "it is ... precisely the will that lurks behind our quest for causes."[36]

The second idea is that willing constitutes a beginning. As is well known, Augustine rejects the ancient notion of cyclical time and replaces it with the Christian concept of linear time, which makes the notion of beginning theoretically possible. In *The City of God*, Augustine describes the beginning of the world and the beginning of time as the same—as the *principium*. He distinguishes it from the act of creating man, which takes place in time, from the *initium*.[37] Only men are aware of their finitude. They know that they have a beginning and an end. Having an absolute beginning in time, there are also capable of creating new beginnings. Thus, one of Arendt's favorite quotations is: "Initium […] ergo ut esset, creatus est homo, ante quem nullus fuit" which translates as "That there be a beginning man was created, before whom there nobody was."[38]

The first idea that Arendt takes from Duns Scotus is the idea of the superiority of willing over intellect. Unlike intellect that is compelled by reality, willing transcends being.[39] It is autonomous and undetermined (*indeterminata*) by existing objects. This does not imply omnipotence. Even if lacking any real impact on reality, the will is an unfettered choice of ends. It cannot be forced to will. The second and more significant thought of Duns Scotus that Arendt adopts is his original solution of the problem of the duality of willing. Scotus shows that the redemption of willing is not mental but happens through action.[40] As it transforms into action, willing loses its total freedom. Initially broken into two-in-one, willing and counter-willing, it becomes one actual act, part and parcel of the word.

Finally, there is Kant, essentially only a marginal figure in *Willing*. Nevertheless, it is from his *Critique of Pure Reason* that Arendt borrows the concept of an "absolute beginning."[41] In doing so, she quotes a passage from the third antinomy of reason, which refers to the human capacity to "spontaneously beginning a series in time."[42]

Notably, Arendt does not refer to the *Critique of Practical Reason*. Since, for Kant, willing is the power of desire determined by reason, Arendt equates it with practical reason and does not consider it to be autonomous.[43] It is limited to morality, conceives of freedom as subjected to the power of reason, and negates the spontaneity of beginning. In a slightly different context, Arendt contends:

> The inhumanity of Kant's moral philosophy is undeniable. And this is so because the categorical imperative is postulated as absolute and in its absoluteness introduces into the interhuman realm—which by its nature consists of relationships—something that runs counter to its fundamental relativity.[44]

What Arendt finds problematic is the rational—and therefore anti-political and anti-pluralistic—nature of the Kantian willing. Averse to all absolutes, like history, reason, or even man, Arendt takes a critical stance toward the idea of willing as subjected to reason. Rational willing sets itself against the diversity of the political world and, as Dana Villa put it, is "plurality-hostile."[45] What Arendt finds inspiring in Kant is not practical, but transcendental willing, upon which, the former is grounded, and thanks to which, one can free oneself from the causality of nature. In Kant's words from *Critique of Pure Reason*, the causality that "arises from freedom" is:

> the power of beginning a state **spontaneously**. Such causality will not, therefore, itself stand under another cause determining it in time, as required by the law of nature. Freedom, in this sense, is a pure transcendental idea.[46]

Regarding such causality, it is possible to "start a new series [of things or states] with all its natural consequences *in infinitum*."[47] Thus, a beginning is not only a beginning in time, but also a beginning of a particular time. It is absolute and not relative. There are a series of events that cannot be woven into some "time continuum."[48] Even if Arendt says in *Willing* that in historical reality "we seldom start a new series," it nevertheless happens, and is conditioned by transcendental freedom.[49]

To build her own argument, Arendt now compares such an understanding of beginning to Augustine's *initium*. She notes that if Augustine had wanted to be consistent, he should have defined the freedom of willing not as a freedom of choice (*liberum arbitrium*) but as the Kantian "absolute beginning"—the "freedom of spontaneity," corresponding to his concept of *initium*.[50] It is because the absolute beginning "abolishes the sequence of temporality" and the normal flow of time. It breaks the chain of cause and effect and opens up an "*abyss* of nothingness."[51]

Arendt's favorite metaphor to describe it is that of birth. An action is "the second birth," and to act means to begin something new.[52] The "function" of action is to "break" the continuity of automatic and predictable behaviors.[53] Action is like a miracle; it is "infinitely improbable."[54] Furthermore, this infinite improbability "actually constitutes the very texture of everything we call real."[55] The historical reality is marked with miraculous breaks and discontinuities. It appears continuous only in retrospection.[56]

The following conclusions emerge. The ontological foundation of unpredictable action is willing which is understood as pure spontaneity whose inner struggle ceases by acting. Willing allows breaking temporal continuity and establishing a new beginning. Therefore, resulting actions can be explained by neither external causes nor internal motives.[57] They are contingent since they potentially did not exist before their actualization and thus could well not have occurred. The only purpose of action is greatness—distinguishing oneself from the crowd of equals, and in doing so, an action resembles an original and unpredictable work of art. The Kantian concept of genius will throw more light onto this aesthetic quality of action.

Action as the Work of Genius

Arendt's action is like a stage performance. Its originality is of a value superior to consensus or rule-following. It is aesthetic rather than ethical.[58] What the aestheticization of action means, however, is unclear. For example, Julia Kristeva pointed to Arendt's resistance to implementing any permanent solutions into the fragile sphere of political plurality and stated that "political life resists its own aestheticization."[59] By contrast, Martin Jay criticized Arendt from the positions of critical theory precisely for her aestheticization of politics. Jay argued that autotelic politics renders the achievement of any practical aims impossible.[60] Richard Wolin, in turn, implicated Arendt in the anti-democratic effects of aestheticization, arguing that the theatrical qualities of action preclude interpersonal solidarity and drift dangerously close to fascism.[61]

These discrepancies are to a great extent apparent and result from the equivocal nature of the term "aestheticization," which relates to both *homo faber* and *zoon politikon*. Creative arts (such as painting) consisting in reification are more associated with work, whereas performing arts (such as music or dance) that involve spectators are closer to action. As Arendt notes, "in the sense of creative arts […], politics is the exact opposite of an art."[62] The similarity to performing arts, by contrast, is that politics also requires an audience, and that "accomplishment lies in the performance itself."[63] Performing arts, like political action, do not lead to the creation of tangible products, nor do they include an element of violence.

Arendt's interpretation of Kant's *Critique of the Power of Judgment* from the 1960s enables retracing the trope of the aestheticization of action and justifies this comparison further. The following section argues that the internal purposiveness of action is analogous to purposiveness without a purpose of the objects of beautiful art, as viewed from the perspective of spectators and taste. It describes and illustrates the performative nature of the Arendtian self with the help of the notion of presentation (German *Darstellung*), also referred to as exhibition—the product of Kantian genius. Such a depiction enables a better grasp of the relationship between the self disclosed through action (the represented or exhibited) and the action itself (the representation or exhibition).

Ultimately, the conclusions reached will enlighten the role played by judgment in historical understanding (see Chapter 8).

Arendt refers to the notion of genius (*Genie*) only briefly in her tenth lecture and only in the context of its relationship with judgment. This is surprising given that it is a foundation of her interpretation of the third *Critique*, the key to which is the subordination of genius to judgment/taste, which is comparable to the subordination of the actor to the spectator. The following examination of the Kantian notion of genius takes Arendt's analysis a step further by proposing that genius functions as a talent in the service of the "fine arts," which are analogous to political action, and that this resemblance had an undeniable, and possibly decisive influence on Arendt's reading of the third *Critique*.[64]

The Kantian notion of genius appears in *The Analytic of the Sublime* when the fine or beautiful arts are discussed. In the light of the *Critique of the Power of Judgment* as a whole, the fine arts are subordinated to the beauty of nature—they are beautiful insofar as they appear to be natural. Genius, the source of fine arts, is a natural gift, "the inborn disposition of the mind [*ingenium*] through which nature gives the rule to art."[65] Additionally, art differs from nature because "representation of it in its cause must have preceded its reality."[66] An act of willing is a *sine qua non* condition for the works of art, which are always the work of a human.[67]

The Kantian distinction between mechanical and aesthetic arts is crucial. Mechanical art is based on purposeful action that leads to a specific predetermined product. Mechanical art is "adequate for the cognition of a possible object" and "performs the actions requisite to make it actual."[68] The aim of aesthetic arts, in turn, is pleasure, which might be of a twofold kind. There is the pleasure of the senses that accompanies mere sensations (*Empfindungen*) and which one finds in pleasant art. And there is the "pleasure ... derived from reflection," which is "universally communicable," that we find in fine or beautiful art.[69] It is the latter that principally interests Kant.

The defining characteristic of fine arts is that they appear or seem to be natural. Despite recognizing that they are purposeful products, they appear to be "free from all constraint by arbitrary rules."[70] Thus, what is purposive (*zweckmäßig*) or designed (*absichtlich*) seems purposeless and not designed. One admires them neither with respect to concepts (in other words, their internal purposiveness) nor, as with pleasant arts, based on mere sensations. The fine arts appeal exclusively in the act of reflection.

Kant distinguishes four characteristics of genius, three of which surprisingly resemble Arendt's notion of action.[71] Firstly, there is **originality**—genius creates without any rules (*Regeln*) of creation, but at the same time "presupposes a definite concept of the product as the purpose."[72] Secondly, his products have an **exemplary** character. Their originality notwithstanding, works of fine art may provide standards and rules for judgment. Thirdly, the product of genius is **not purposeful**. The presentation of a given aesthetic idea surpasses the concept.[73] In other words, an artist does not possess the knowledge of his product nor accomplishes a purpose—he "does not know himself how the ideas for it come to him, and also does not have it in his power to think up such things at will or to plan."[74] Fourthly, genius is **grounded in nature**. Since fine arts are not based on concepts (and therefore follow no rules), and, on the other hand, cannot proceed without concept (and therefore operate with rules), Kant concluded that their source lies in nature. Fine arts seem natural since genius itself stems from nature.

Arendt does not mention this fourth characteristic. When reinterpreting the third *Critique*, she bears in mind human actions and not the beauty of nature. Thus, only the first three properties of genius are reflected in Arendt's profile of political action.[75] These include, firstly, originality in the form of action's **unprecedentedness**; secondly, its **exemplary character**, which may serve as an inspiration for future actors; and thirdly, **a discontinuity between willing and acting**, which is between the desire toward disclosing oneself in a specific way and the self being revealed.[76]

In summary, it is worth underlining the performative aesthetic qualities of action once again. Like the product of genius, action consists of breaking the chain of historical continuity and brings novelty, as such, it cannot be repeated but only "re-enacted."[77] It also does not exist potentially before it is actualized. It transgresses purposeful intention of willing (no one can design oneself as the self is dependent on others), and its meaning is supposed to be independent of its intentions and consequences—*ateleis*, i.e., to lie in the activity itself.[78] This is also why the disclosure of who resembles the presentation of an aesthetic idea by genius judged according to spectators' taste. In short, Arendt's action is a "performative work of art."[79]

The Autonomy of Self-presentation

There is another similarity between Kant and Arendt that is even more striking. The faculty of presentation in Kant is rooted in spirit (*Geist*)—the "animating principle" that is the "faculty for the presentation [*Darstellung*] of aesthetic ideas."[80] An aesthetic idea is the product of imagination, a certain representation:

that occasions much thinking though without it being possible for any determinate thought, i.e. concept, to be adequate to it, which, consequently, no language fully attains or can make intelligible.[81]

Kant points to the fact that such ideas exceed the capacity of unambiguous linguistic comprehension. Otherwise art would be dependent solely on concepts and would not resemble nature.[82]

This power to exceed is realized most of all in poetry that with its language surpasses its literal meaning: "It is really the art of poetry in which the faculty of aesthetic ideas can reveal itself in its full measure."[83] Poetry takes primacy before the fine arts expressed in sensory intuition, such as sculpture, architecture, and painting, as well as arts expressed through playing on emotions, such as music and the art of colors.[84] Is Arendt's action like performative poetry? The similarity is apparent. A deed is a linguistic expression whose meaning is never unequivocal and final. It presents the who of the actor, one that does not exist before its disclosure, and cannot be unambiguously grasped through concepts. The who is unique like the product of genius. It is an unprecedented, exemplary, and linguistic work of performative art.

The Kantian genius straddles the necessary world of nature and the contingent world of freedom, although ultimately, it is nature that plays the dominant role. Arendt also points to nature when saying in *Thinking* that the "urge toward self-display" characterizes all living organisms.[85] She follows the Swiss biologist Adolf Portmann's 1953 (1961) work *Animals as Social Beings* in asserting that matters of functional adaptation—especially the species capacity for survival—do not fully explain the diversity of appearances of the living world.[86] In her commentary, Arendt differentiates self-display (her translation of Portmann's *Selbstdarstellung*) from self-presentation.[87] In the self-display of both animal and human physical identity, presentation occurs by itself, as it were, without mediation by the will. Self-presentation, meanwhile, is intentional and involves a choice of what is to be revealed, even if without any final control. The notion of self-presentation in *Thinking* has the same meaning as the concept of self-disclosure from *The Human Condition*, which conveys the performative nature of the self.

What is the relationship between the self that is presented or disclosed and its presentation or disclosure? In his *Truth and Method*, Hans-Georg Gadamer considers presentation as "the mode of being of the work of art."[88] Like Arendt, he employs the Aristotelian concept of *energeia* and the notion of a game, which is a purpose in itself—game players perform their self-presentation

(*Selbstdarstellung*) in front of each other as spectators.[89] And like Arendt Gadamer cites Portmann and states that "self-presentation is a universal ontological characteristic of nature."[90] In Gadamer's philosophy, the opposition of reality and beautiful appearance is not voiced at all—representation is autonomous in regard to that which is represented. For instance, a painting is not a means serving the identification of the represented because its representation does not exist alongside the world but belongs to it.[91] There can be no one-directional relationship between the two (from the represented to its representation) because in the representation, "an increase [*Zuwachs*] of being" of the represented takes place.[92]

In expanding this analogy to Arendt's performative notion of action, it can be said that an action is not about a faithful adaptation of speech to some hidden and supposedly durable self of an actor, just as a painting is not about how faithfully the splotches on the canvas render the represented reality. Presentation does not exist alongside some substantial ego but establishes it. The language expressing the who is not an appearance superimposed on or imitating a hidden being. Comparably to an aesthetic being that enriches what it represents, action enhances its subject by adding to it through presentation and ensuring that there is more of it.[93] The represented (a particular self) would not exist without presenting action—it would remain split into the silently speaking two.

Public Appearance

In the introduction to her biographical collection of essays *Men in Dark Times*, Arendt cites a passage from *Being and Time* in which Heidegger claims that "publicness obscures everything." Other translations, and the original German text, have stronger overtones, including the original phrase "the light"—"Das Licht der Öffentlichkeit verdunkelt alles."[94] Arendt notes that this quote does not express an essential characteristic of the public sphere but rather signifies "the spirit of the times." In Heidegger's outlook, this sprit has to do with an inauthentic notion of time understood as a permanent presence.[95] Arendt, meanwhile, raises the essentially positive character of the public world, which is temporarily determined not by presence but by dialectics of temporal fragility and potential immortality.[96] Unlike in the thinking of Heidegger, people are originally private and not public. Only by satisfying all necessities of biological existence are they able to achieve public appearance and recognition. Arendt's reflection on the public space is a hidden polemic with a strong notion of subject, of which early Heidegger, in her view, was still a proponent.[97]

The strong notion of self hidden behind appearances (presentations) is a symptom of what Arendt considers one of the fundamental metaphysical fallacies of the Western tradition—the very dichotomy of being and appearance.[98] Arendt maintains that the world is essentially phenomenal—only appearances exist. The world and others appear in the mode of "it seems to me," which is an opinion, and not truth.[99] Every subject is simultaneously an object appearing to others.[100] In *The Human Condition*, the concept of the spectator only comes into view in the context of the retrospective glance of a historian. Nevertheless, its meaning is essentially the same as that of the spectators in the plural from the later *Thinking*, that is, all people appearing to each other. The actors who act together in the public sphere are spectators of each other, and thus each of them is both a spectator and an actor.[101]

Jürgen Habermas, who drew the basic framework of his theory of communicative action from Arendt, most accurately notes that the space of appearance simply means the *Lebenswelt*—everyday communicative discourse.[102] Habermas creatively adapts Arendt's ideas for his own needs, using her interpretation of Kant's *Critique of the Power of Judgment* for his universal normative project. However, Arendt's communicative model of action is by no means instrumental, not only in the sense of Weber's purposive action but even in the very Habermasian sense. In his more detailed reading, Dana R. Villa sets out why Arendt rejects all rational and universalizing models, pointing to the fundamental, performative dimension of politics.[103] The main reason is Arendt's refutation of teleology, including the teleology of consensus, which, even if it results from a rational discussion, involves domination over the future.

The space of appearance, and thus the world of everyday life, "precedes all formal constitution of the public realm."[104] It forms the basis of the institutionalized public sphere and maintains its social acceptance.[105] Seyla Benhabib accurately observed that this space is "institutionally unanchored," and in this sense it is ephemeral and transient.[106] It appears and disappears like communicative interaction. Arendt's concept of public space thus clearly suffers from generality as it is like an ocean in which all meaningful interactions and self-presentations take place. Moreover, it lacks specificity because public appearance is not only synonymous with freedom achievable through action as self-presentation but also with power. For Arendt, the concepts of power and freedom, like those of the public space and reality, are interchangeable. Both power and freedom belong solely to an acting group and never to an individual.[107] Power is the freedom and reality of man as an acting and self-presenting being.[108] And yet this lack of specificity only extends the aestheticization of action to power, freedom, and public sphere—all sustained by a performative self.

The Performance of Thinking

Arendt usually points to the differences between acting and thinking. In her *Introduction* to *Thinking*, she quotes Heidegger's maxim: "Thinking does not endow us directly with the power to act."[109] Incidentally, Arendt reproaches Heidegger precisely for equating acting and thinking. Her own philosophy is an apotheosis of action that takes a negative stance toward philosophers. Radically "private" thinking does not manifest the capacity to change reality: "in our world there is no clearer or more radical opposition than that between thinking and doing."[110] Almost paradoxically, in the very same passage, Arendt notices that action ultimately depends on thinking.

Arendt's comments on two historical figures, Socrates and Kant, exemplify their deep connection and show that acting and thinking are interdependent, in a similar manner to the interdependence of labor and logic as well as work and cognition, as discussed earlier.[111]

Bringing thinking to the public sphere lies at the heart of the Socratic revolution. Arendt contends that what Socrates did:

> was to make *public*, in discourse, the thinking process ... he *performed* in the marketplace the way the flute-player performed at a banquet. It is sheer performance, sheer activity.[112]

The metaphors used in this passage point to Arendt's notion of action. Thinking, like doing, requires practice—some exercise in thinking.[113] The key feature of Socratic critical thinking is openness to the judgment of others. In order to justify itself (*logon didonai*), it must reveal its own presuppositions.[114] For Arendt, making the results of thinking public is a necessary condition of thinking itself.

Arendt argues that the critical discourse of Socrates, that is, the discourse focused solely on the purifying activity of thinking, is brought to life by Kant. The key link between the two figures is the readiness to justify thoughts publicly. Kant not only advocated the public use of reason, but also performed—even if not literally—in front of the reading public. His "performance"—the word Arendt employs—was preceded by an exercise in a public sphere that was merely imagined. Even if performed in isolation, critical thinking:

by the force of imagination … makes the others present and thus moves in a space that is potentially public, open to all sides.[115]

Arendt describes such enlarged thinking as training one's imagination to "go visiting" other points of view. This does not indicate empathy but the representation of the perspectives of others through *sensus communis*.[116] In Kant's own words:

> It is said: the freedom to speak or to write can be taken away from us by the powers-that-be, but the freedom to think cannot be taken from us through them at all. However, how much and how correctly would we think if we did not think in community with others to whom we communicate our thoughts and who communicate theirs to us! Hence, we may safely state that the external power which deprives man of the freedom to communicate his thoughts *publicly* also takes away his freedom to *think*, the only treasure left to us in our civic life and through which alone there may be a remedy against all evils of the present state of affairs.[117]

Arendt refers to Kant's thesis in the affirmative: "the very faculty of thinking depends on its public use,"[118] that is on the possibility of communicative interaction. "The art of critical thinking always has political implications," because "critical thought is in principle anti-authoritarian."[119]

By raising the indirectly political, albeit politically conditioned dependence of thinking on a community, Arendt—like Kant, in her view—opposes the philosophical tradition of thinking detached from the world. Truth, be it scientific or philosophical, is dependent on communication. In the *Lectures*, Arendt states bluntly:

> Unless you can somehow communicate and expose to the test of others, either orally or in writing, whatever you may have found out when you were alone, this faculty [of thinking] exerted in solitude will disappear.[120]

The possibility of thinking is directly dependent on others and conditioned by human plurality: "thinking beings have an urge to speak, speaking beings have an urge to think."[121]

Hans Jonas emphasizes that thinking is oriented toward communication.[122] An expression or even publication of thoughts is already a political action. Thoughts that are expressed or proclaimed publicly in language become acts.[123] The radical opposition between thinking and acting disappears.[124]

The interdependence goes even further. As with the broad or primary and narrow concept of action, one can now identify two types of thinking. Villa calls these ordinary and extraordinary. There is expanded thinking that prepares for judgment and is potentially political. And there is thinking detached from the phenomenal world.[125] Richard Bernstein makes a very similar distinction based on the figures of Socrates and Heidegger and points to a "deep internal conflict" between them. In his view, it is a conflict that Arendt "never resolved."[126] There is thinking as a prerogative of everyone, and there is philosophical thinking of the few. It is only to this second kind of thinking that is destructive to behavior patterns that Bernstein assigns the power to prevent evil—the power that testifies to the practical significance of thinking for action.

6

The Temporal Conflicts of the Mind

Man's finitude, irrevocably given by virtue of his own short time span set in infinity of time stretching into both past and future, constitutes the infrastructure, as it were, of all mental activities.
Hannah Arendt, The Life of the Mind

The Clash between Thinking and Willing

In both the historical and the interpretative layers of *Life of the Mind*, Arendt pays close attention to what she regards as the fundamental inner conflict, or even "clash," between willing and thinking. This conflict stems directly from temporality as it is due to temporality that thinking and willing constitute mutually exclusive experiences of one mind. In thinking, the past seems to have been necessary, while willing sees the future as contingent and undetermined. Thus, the arising clash concerns things that are no longer in control and those that one can still affect. Arendt maintains that the arising tension between necessity and freedom is inherent in the lived experience of time.[1] Thinking cannot appropriate willing, and willing cannot refute thinking since it cannot will backwards.[2] Furthermore, not only are activities mutually conflicted, but each of them is comprised of parts of the self that are in a lesser or greater tension with each other. Thinking is a soundless, internal dialogue between one and oneself. Willing involves a struggle between the "I-will" and the "I-nill," and judging operates on the principle of the "enlarged thought" that makes the others mentally present in imagination.

As usual, Arendt is not being consistent. In *Willing*, she clearly associates thinking with the past and present. Earlier though, in *Thinking*, she had associated it also with the future and specifically with the experience of time, in which all its dimensions tangle together (as illustrated by a diagram she drew). In the second volume of *Life of the Mind*, thinking is juxtaposed with willing and stems from memory—all thoughts are presented as "after-thoughts." It is, therefore, no surprise that departing from the dichotomic view, Jacques Taminiaux regarded thinking as a capacity oriented toward the past. For example, Arendt contrasts thinking with willing, with the no-longer belonging to thinking, and the not-yet belonging to willing.[3] When aiming to underline the necessary absence of an object of thinking, she also states outright that "thinking always implies remembrance; every thought is strictly speaking an after-thought."[4] Nevertheless, if one begins with the final pages of *Thinking*, its "nowhere" will appear as actually assembling all the dimensions of time. Although it is indeed possible to speak of mutually exclusive activities, this does not deny that the function of thinking is fundamental, and the functions of judgment and willing are somewhat secondary.

The issue of temporal orientation also concerns judging. Some scholars consider it a practical faculty, and in this sense, future-oriented. Others, Taminiaux for example, see judgment as lying at the crossroads of all the conflicts of the mind.[5] Taminiaux correctly observes:

> With regard to the senses of time, it is as though each faculty of the mind was operating in terms of an exclusion of the tenses focused upon by the two other faculties.[6]

In his view, only in the case of judgment do all three dimensions of time acquire equal rights. When one recalls that Arendt explicitly presents judgment as a faculty for dealing solely with objects present or past, this claim appears to be at least problematic.[7]

Both judgment and willing stem from the gap in time created by thinking, from the temporal in-betweenness, and orient themselves toward the past and the future.[8] In *Eichmann in Jerusalem*, Arendt famously hypothesized that thinking might prevent evildoing. Without dwelling on this claim in-depth, there is one aspect of the link between thinking and judgment that is noteworthy in the context of Arendt's philosophy of history. It has to do with the preparatory character of thinking with regard to judging the past. Arendt's point is that thinking is originally and principally destructive—it breaks apart all fixed and socially binding rules of understanding reality and as such, it prepares one for judging objects without the mediation of any pre-given principles.[9] This weakens the automatism of the application of any general rules. Thinking does not bring rules to judgments, quite the opposite, it abandons and destroys all rules. When these are no longer binding, particular cases can be judged without their mediation.[10]

The Paradox of Counter-factuality

The above caveats notwithstanding, the antagonism between thinking and willing has several relevant side-effects. Arendt claims that this antagonism is the source of philosophers' aversion to willing, one of the main leitmotifs of her otherwise fragmented narrative.[11] What this aversion comes down to is either disbelief in the existence of will (which is treated as a metaphysical delusion—the case of Thomas Hobbes, Baruch Spinoza, and Gilbert Ryle in her view) or the denial of its freedom (an alleged result of the traditionally inferior ontological status of contingency).[12] While "philosophers" misinterpret willing from the perspective of thinking (from which it supposedly seems to be an illusion of consciousness), the same is true of the perspective of willing (from which thinking becomes equally unreal). Moreover, as Arendt puts it in *Willing*:

> The experience of willing is more real in a sense that we can simply prove freedom by refraining from doing something, whereas in the case of thinking, we can neither prove nor disprove the necessary character of the present moment.[13]

This is a critical issue as the faculty of willing enables Arendt to abolish both future and past fatalism, which clears the metaphysical ground for her fragmented historical interpretation. The real problem is that from the perspective of the present, the past that has taken place is indeed necessary regardless of whether it was previously contingent. Even if the past is an indeterminate future that has passed, it appears now "in the guise of necessity."[14] One cannot think otherwise, Arendt argues, for "there is no substitute, real or imagined, for existence as such."[15] This implies that one cannot consistently consider a different past—as historians do, for example, during counter-factual reasoning—without simultaneously denying one's present existence that is considering that different past. It would then be necessary to think about one's nonexistence, and therefore nothingness, which is indeed impossible. The past as it existed is thus a necessary condition for thinking about it in the first place. At the same time though, it is impossible to prove the necessity of the present—of one's own, historically shaped existence. To accomplish this, one would need to reverse the temporal process and prove that a different present was not possible. All that historians may know about the present is that it was not impossible, which does not mean that it was necessary. And this is abundantly clear from the perspective of willing.

Arendt uses Cicero's argument from *On Fate* for support, an argument that is comparable to that of Popper's. Fatalism is possible only from the atemporal perspective of an external observer (such as a God), for whom the entire process of history appears as present. Introducing an acting participant capable of starting a new series of events abolishes future predictions and, indirectly, the fatalistic view.[16] If one trusts the phenomenal evidence of willing, one cannot but conclude that the present is not an actualized potentiality. It is merely one of the many possibilities of the past, which (in contradistinction to those unrealized possibilities) is necessary only from the perspective of the self that came into being.

The Authentic Future

As noted earlier, in *Thinking*, Arendt distinguishes the temporality of thinking (containing all three dimensions of time) from past and future as "pure entities." In *Willing*, she additionally differentiates the concepts of future "as such" (an equivalent of the future as pure entity) and projected future of willing. Both futures are presented as hostile to the thinking ego. The future as such pushes the thinking ego from the front—its temporal arrow is reversed. The projected future, on the other hand, stands in opposition toward this pure entity as far as "the project negates the now as well as the past and thus threatens the thinking ego's enduring present."[17] Emmanuel Levinas expresses the very same conceptual distinction between two types of futures more succinctly, perhaps:

> Anticipation of the future, and projection of the future, considered as essential to time by all theories from Bergson to Sartre, are merely the present of the future and not the authentic future. The future is what is not grasped, that which befalls on us and lays hold of us. The other is the future.[18]

The present of the future—the future anticipated or projected in the present—is not "authentic," it is neither surprising nor unpredictable. Comparing Arendt's conception of time with Levinas is beside the point here—it suffices to use Levinas's opposition to elucidate Arendt's typically fragmented remarks. The future as such or "pure" is the authentic future, one distinct from the projected future of willing (the difference between them will prove significant for further arguments concerning historical judgment).

Arendt critically approaches the notion of the future as potentially contained in the present. By implication, she is wary of the idea of the present as potentially contained in the past:

> [T]he view that everything real must be preceded by a potentiality as one of its causes implicitly denies the future as an authentic tense.[19]

However, rather than problematize the relationship between potentiality and actuality further, Arendt only quotes Aristotle (several times), comparing this relationship to the act of fabrication (*poiesis*), in which the future product potentially exists before it is materialized. Willing as the conflict between I-will and I-nill implies the potentiality of actualization or non-actualization of a given future. After all, willing is undecided and wills mutually exclusive things until its internal dualism is overcome by action. Irrespective of this, the future projected by willing does not happen. The future is not a purposive outcome of the present. It is only in a state of isolation characteristic of *homo faber* that there does indeed exist a predictable future (an intended product whose realization is not inhibited by the other). The authentic future that Arendt mentions in both *Thinking* and *Willing* is one of a community, in which a constant encounter with others hampers any predictability. The face of the Levinasian Other is a community—the future as such happens through an encounter with plurality.

It appears that Arendt argues in favor of a radically open future, which is not merely the future of willing.[20] The issue at stake is the link between willing and action and the confusion of willing and political freedom—one that results in the illusion of sovereignty and the possibility of self-determination. Willing as the source of what man becomes is "the last of the metaphysical fallacies" of modernity, as Arendt mentions in *Thinking*.[21] Man is not a *homo faber*, a creator and producer of himself. There is an undertone of the critique of Marxism and existentialism (and Heidegger himself) in Arendt's fragmented narrative. Self is always dependent on others, even if it is conditioned by willing.[22] Besides, Arendt regards the potentiality of self-determination—which she calls a "solipsistic freedom"—as a terrifying thought.[23] Her criticism of the modern paradigm of production from the perspective of political action in *The Human Condition* points to the same problem:

> To act in the form of making, to reason in the form of "reckoning with consequences," means to leave out the unexpected, the event itself, since it would be unreasonable or irrational to expect what is no more than an **"infinite improbability."**[24]

This final notion leads to the very core of Arendt's metaphysics of history. For subsequent reflections, the following conclusions arise. The future is initially an undetermined and empty pushing force that transforms into a concrete and infinitely improbable moment happening now (the present is not one of the realized possibilities of the past). It turns into a past that from the perspective of thinking, appears in the guise of necessity. However, since the past, in its earlier form of the ongoing actuality, was an infinite improbability, it is actually the past infinite improbability—the past authentic future. The past authentic future is the past as one knows it—a past that no one wanted, and which no one can explain, yet which one must somehow face. It is this past that is the object of and a challenge for historical judgment.

Judgment—The Faculty for Dealing with the Past

Nowhere does Arendt present her general idea on the role of the faculty of judgment more clearly than in the *Postscriptum* to *Thinking*. Not for the first time does she express here the conjecture that "judgment is our faculty for dealing with the past."[25] As an etymological argument, Arendt recalls the oldest form of the Greek verb *historein* (from which "history" and "historian" derive)—from the Homeric noun *histor*, meaning "the judge."

In addition, her juxtaposition of Hegel and Kant offers the following alternative: the ultimate judge may be either History or man. To accept the former would mean to recognize whatever exists as right. The victors do not merely write history—they also create it. Acknowledging man as a judge would, in turn, mean recognizing one's independence from History and one's freedom of judgment—this is affirmation or negation of the past. In this debate, Arendt takes the side of Kant and expresses the hope that thanks to the faculty of judgment:

> We may reclaim our human dignity … from this pseudo-divinity named History of the modern age, without denying history's importance but denying its right to be the ultimate judge.[26]

The political principle of reclaiming human dignity is expressed by Cato's maxim, which can be found alongside the aforementioned *Postscriptum* on the first (and the only written) page of the otherwise unwritten third volume of *The Life of the Mind*—"Victrix causa diis placuit, sed victa Catoni": "The victorious cause pleased the gods, but the lost one pleased Cato."[27] As Elisabeth Young-Bruehl put it: "The political principle implied in reclaiming judgment's autonomy is freedom from Success."[28] In Arendt's private notes, the idea of associating the power of judgment with the past appears even more clearly, and in a more fundamental sense: "**Judgment constitutes the past**—also in the sense: what it wants to be remembered."[29]

Recognizing judgment as the faculty for dealing with the past, rather than, as some scholars would have it, a strictly practical ability will henceforth constitute the fundamental context for interpreting Arendt's *Lectures on Kant's Political Philosophy*.

Ronald Beiner, the editor of *Lectures on Kant's Political Philosophy*, argued that Arendt employs two conceptions of judgment that correspond to the early and late stages of her work. The first supposedly concerns the practical decisions of political life. The second, which Beiner calls ontological, is about a contemplative life distanced from politics. This thesis set the context for many later interpretations.[30] Although Beiner was undoubtedly right when suggesting that "the ultimate destination of *Judging* would be a return to the concept of history" (as the *Postscriptum* indicates), the question of whether there are indeed two theories of judgment is more problematic.[31]

The idea that the spectator's perspective is different and superior to that of the actor already appears in *The Human Condition*, albeit without a direct reference to the concept of judgment.[32] It occurs in relation to the activity of storytelling, which is inextricably linked to the power of judgment. Since an actor pronouncing a judgment will always become a spectator, it seems to make little sense to speak about judgment as an activity performed by an actor. The spectator and the actor are, as it were, the two possibilities of the same subject. For example, in the *Lectures* Arendt states:

> The public realm is constituted by the critics and the spectators, not by the actors or the makers. And this critic and spectator sits in every actor and fabricator; without this critical, judging faculty the doer or maker would be so isolated from the spectator that he would not even be perceived.[33]

The difference between a political and an ontological judgment (to which Beiner alludes) does not run along the actor-spectator line but rather along that between the spectator judging current events and the spectator judging past events. As such, it surely does not refer to early and late Arendt but maps the tension present throughout her work. In both cases, it is the same power of judgment at play, applied either politically or historically. In this respect, a judgment concerning current events, which became past anyway when the judgment is being pronounced, is just a specific form of historical judgment that may concern either the very near or the distant past.[34] Historical judgment, which is the product of the power of judgment as the faculty for dealing with the past, is primal in this sense.[35]

The Advantage of Hindsight

The terms "historical" and "political" are not mutually exclusive here. Arendt's historical judgment is itself deeply political because it is based upon *sensus communis*. Additionally, it is a product of a certain historical present. The boundary between two kinds of judgments rather runs along the line of the consequences of the actions being judged. All actions judged belong to the past, either nearer (just a moment ago) or more distant. However, in contrast with "political" judgment, in which no consequences of actions could have yet taken place, in "historical" judgment, these unintended consequences exert an influence upon its content.[36] Therefore, the historical spectator does indeed have an advantage over the political spectator:

> The advantage that the spectator has is that he sees the play as a whole, while each of the actors knows only his part, or, if he should judge from the perspective of acting, only the part of the whole that concerns him. The actor is partial by definition.[37]

The above quote remains characteristically ambiguous. Is the actor transformed into a spectator—one refraining from acting in order to pass judgment on the actions of others—watching the historical or a political play? A political spectator clearly lacks the advantage of hindsight. The historical spectator, on the other hand, watches the whole of the historical play from the perspective of unintended consequences. Ultimately, the distinction between the two types of spectators is crucial, but in a different sense than that initially proposed by Beiner. It also points to Arendt's fundamental aporia and not to her early and late work. It is also not a difference between the actor and the spectator but between the two types of spectators. Consequently, the "clash" explored by Beiner and others remains but only as a reflection of the basic aporia.[38] The advantage of both kinds of spectator is already evident in *The Human Condition* because the self disclosed in action depends upon others. When Arendt says in *Lectures* that the spectators constitute the public realm, she does not mean that the actors no longer determine it. After all, they have never constituted it. As she points out, "No one in his right mind would ever put on a spectacle without being sure of having spectators to watch it."[39] Arendt's notion of the communicative self implies that action makes no sense in isolation and takes place between actors who then happen to play the spectator's role. The image of a theatre auditorium with a clear division between the stage and the seats for the audience fails to do justice to this idea as the actors and spectators are constantly swapping roles.

All this has the following decisive consequence. The faculty of judgment should not be construed as a capacity directly translatable into political practice (an idea related to the concept of judgment attributed to actors)—at least not for Arendt. The power of judgment is not a kind of practical capability of deciding between possibilities (something like the capacity of *liberum arbitrium*), and it has no direct connection to willing.[40] The faculty of judgment metaphorically referred to as taste, pronounces judgments on the world in a disinterested way, which also means that it is not interested in morality. In Arendt's view, its reference to the future is limited.[41] The political aspect of taste lies in the fact that it unites people and not that it establishes purpose. Although thanks to the idea of humankind, "actor and spectator become united,"[42] and although theory and practice are mutually dependent for Arendt, there is no direct link between the faculty of the mind associated with the past (judgment) and the faculty of the mind for dealing with the future (willing). Arendt frequently emphasizes this mutual autonomy of the faculties, and the lack of the aforementioned connection is also justified by the fundamental notion of the gap in time from which all the faculties emerge.[43]

Primordial Time of Thinking and Action

It was argued above that as far as temporality is concerned, thinking is the most fundamental activity of the mind. Looking at Arendt's distinctions of both *vita activa* and *vita contemplativa* through the temporal lens, one may also notice that it is not only thinking that leads to the very core of temporality—to the primordial time—but also action.

It is almost surprising that while differentiating thinking from work in *The Human Condition*, Arendt does not compare it to action, although such a comparison suggests itself naturally. Arendt notices the uselessness of thinking, which she compares to the futility of a work of art and further to the process of life.[44] At the same time, she notices the comparable futility of action.[45] Despite this fact, Arendt clearly does not intend to compare thinking and acting with labor. At first glance, the temporality of action, like the temporality of thinking, appears to resemble labor. Action does not leave anything durable behind, and its products are even less stable than consumer goods. Actions are frail because they constantly disappear like the products of labor. Moreover, the lack of distinction between means and ends might suggest a labor-like repetitiveness. However, the temporality of thinking and acting is far from the eternal recurrence of labor.[46] The only recurrence involves starting the activities anew. The fact that thinking broadly construed is coeval with life as the "in-between" of birth and death does not imply that like labor, it has no beginning or end.[47] In *Thinking*, Arendt writes that every thinking process begins where the past and future clash, and strives toward infinity. In *The Human Condition*, she notes that thinking has no purpose outside of itself, which is a feature of political action.[48]

If one emphasizes the beginning involved in every political action, it appears as a break in the continuity of everydayness. Actions are like miracles— "interruptions of some natural series of events."[49] Remember that thinking takes place in the temporal "in-betweenness," in the gap that allows one to perceive the forces of past and future as antagonistic and not continuous. It is no different with action that occupies a "hiatus" between the no-longer and the not-yet. In *Willing*, Arendt speaks of "gaps of historical time,"[50] which she associates with radical breaks of continuity, such as revolutions. Actions split time understood as an indifferent change. Without considering the analogy between action and thinking, Kathrin Braun gets right to the core of the problem when she argues that the temporal dimension of action is that:

> it ends one time and opens up another; it disrupts the time of the process and opens up the time of the interval. It brings the current time to a close insofar as it stops time's race towards the future and breaks open a time span in the present, a time between limits.[51]

As Barbara Skarga put it:

> Events tear and change the flux of time ... They strike us without reasons, they surprise and incapacitate us, they show the meaninglessness of the course of the world and the absurdity of our seemingly rational projects ... they uncover the limits of rationality itself.[52]

Through thinking (a soundless dialogue) and acting (a speech that others can hear), one creates time as a stream both rooted in the clash of past and future, a given historical present, and directed toward the in-between of past and future (and not the future). One could render the temporal nature of action with a diagram comparable to that which was sketched by Arendt to represent thinking. From the point of view of clock time, action is a beginning in time; more fundamentally, however, it is the beginning of time. Viewed from the outside, speech can be objectified to follow the linear order of clock time. As an analogy to the temporality of "thought-train," it forms a narrative action-train that can be seen as a sequence of phases. However, its immanent temporality forms a whole that is different from the sequence of moments, in which it does not make sense to separate any successive past, present, and future.[53] In the actuality of action, the future and the past permeate each other. Seen from the inside, various phases of action form a whole—an extended and lasting now, the *nunc stans* of action. Unlike willing, action is a beginning without a purpose. Unlike work, it is not aimed toward a product. It is only aimed toward self-disclosure, which like thinking, is situated in the in-betweenness of time, marked off on both sides by the pressing forces of past and future. Actions create *bios*, a unique, personal story composed of breaks and discontinuities, and further on, a political history marked by the priority of the lasting present.[54]

Acknowledging the deep temporal connection between acting and thinking does not automatically cancel their opposition, as Arendt outlined it. Unlike acting, thinking takes place in solitude, it is a sequence of soundless words. Thinking involves withdrawing from the world, even if it remains in metaphorical contact with it.[55] Notwithstanding the similarities enumerated above, thinking is not action, and apart from exceptional situations, it is not directly political. It is a condition of the possibility of action, although in the same way that publicly presenting the outcomes of thinking is its condition of possibility. The main difference between thinking and action boils down to visibility. It is a difference between a language that appears in action and disappears in the process of thinking. Appearing and disappearing are two sides of the same process: the interplay of identity and difference, appearing fleetingly and intangibly in action, and disappearing in the domain of invisible thinking. Arendt never settles the potential order of priority between them, perhaps on purpose.

To summarize, both thinking and acting are *logos*—speech that discloses meaning, either through internal or communal dialogue.[56] Both thinking and acting are ends in themselves, leaving no durable product behind—both are performative and not creative. The frailty of action mirrors the frailty of thoughts. Both have a clearly defined beginning but no end—they point toward the infinite. Finally, primordial temporality is referred to by Arendt as the gap that underpins both. Both thinking and acting create and take place within a gap in continuous time, except that in acting, in addition to the temporal in-betweenness, there is a spatial in-betweenness of the public sphere that is absent from the de-spatialized process of thinking.

7

The Contingency and Decline of History

History, in contradistinction to nature, is full of events; here the miracle of accident and infinite improbability occurs so frequently that it seems strange to speak of miracles at all.

Hannah Arendt, *What Is Freedom?*

History as a Web of Contingencies

Arendt's standard approach to the topic of history is to distinguish its proper and improper conception. The former, derived from politics, is "a story of action and deeds."[1] The latter is social, behavioral, or vulgar.[2] Arendt's primary speculative point is that proper history is an ahistorical potentiality. Even if it remained hidden, it can always be retrieved. The focus of this chapter is such proper history, and the goal is to disentangle its essential characteristics from Arendt's scattered remarks and, most importantly, from her concept of action.

In *The Human Condition* Arendt observes that the spatial in-betweenness, in which all human actions take place, has a twofold character. On the one hand, it is the objective in-betweenness—the world of things. On the other hand, it is the web of relationships consisting of the actions of others. The latter emerges during a conversation between people and is virtually identical to the public space as discussed above.[3] Just like actions, it is frail, futile, and intangible.

The metaphor of a web points to the complexity of relations between particular actions. All unique self-disclosing speech acts not only fall into this web of linguistic relationships, but the web makes them possible in the first place.[4] The clash between the web of relationships and individual actions results in a "unique life story."[5] Arendt's key notions of "life story" and "real story" refer to individual life history—the sequence of actions mediated through webs of relationships stretching from birth to death. This story, unlike life in a biological sense, is linear and not circular.[6] We are "engaged" in it for "as long as we live."[7] As Arendt puts it, action mediated by the web "'produces' stories with or without intention as naturally as fabrication produces tangible things." Her use of inverted commas indicates that action does not produce the stories in the sense of purposive making but only unintentionally. Nobody is the author of his own life story.

A life story mediated by the web of relationships is thus resultant of actions and their unintended consequences. It is marked by numerous discontinuities and not planned. Since Arendt's life stories compose history as a whole—one may recall that she defines history as "a story of action and deeds"—so it is marked by discontinuities. Unlike fictional history, history as a whole has no subject capable of projecting and achieving the ends. In short, history is not made but enacted.[8]

Arendt's adversary in these reflections is the philosophy of history in a substantive sense—in her terminology it is identical to the philosophy of politics. The concrete and practical expression of such philosophy is, in her view, the modern science of history. It is oriented toward explaining the past and overlooks the fact that it is an inexplicable "mixture of error and violence." Scientific historical writing aspires to abolish the "melancholy haphazardness" of facts and replace contingent actions with predictable products, presenting the structure of the past as mirroring the order of making.[9]

Arendt's notion of a real story may be succinctly illustrated by Duns Scotus's doctrine of contingency. This doctrine is the second most important thought that Arendt borrowed from Scotus, whom she considered to be the first and last philosopher in history to have described it.[10] In Arendt's reconstruction of Scotus's historical conception, which she calls the "theory of partial causes," contingency is the price paid for freedom.[11] Since Arendt presents Scotus's beliefs as "speculative conditions for a philosophy of freedom," the argument is also helpful in describing her own conception of history.[12] The argument is that any historical change occurs as a result of a multitude of concurrent, fragmentary, and coincidental causes. It is not only individual acts of willing that are contingent (in the sense that they could have been otherwise) but also their resultant actions, and thus the whole of history is contingent. Arendt claims that Scotus's conclusions contradict Western philosophical tradition in placing particularity over universality and defending the ontological supremacy of contingency over necessity. This supremacy also translates into Arendt's view of the historical process as a whole.

One might also look at this view from the angle of Arendt's postulate of Heidegger's third turn, *die Kehre*, and her criticism of his concept of history, which she privately called "pitiful."[13] In Arendt's reading, the first turn consists in Heidegger's rightful rejection of willing and the "self-assertion of man" in the late 1930s, when in the second volume of *Nietzsche*, he moves from understanding willing as "creative" to understanding it as "destructive."[14] The second turn is Heidegger's interpretation of the original turn in his 1946 *Letter on Humanism* and the official rejection of subjectivism as still pervading *Being and Time*. The third turn, which Arendt calls a "fascinating variant of his philosophy," is localized in 1946 *Anaximander Fragment*, and it allegedly marks a departure from the idea of the "history of Being" [*Seinsgeschichte*], which is unambiguously interpreted by Arendt as a new incarnation of the invisible hand of the market representing the hidden mechanics of historical developments. This third turn presents a new notion of Being as always concealed and devoid of history. The actual history, meanwhile—and this is where one might read of the projection of Arendt's own view—has no subject. It is "the realm of error."[15]

Predictable Unpredictability

Arendt's speculative radical indeterminism rests of three conceptual pillars of unpredictability, purposelessness, and irreversibility. They combine and form what in *The Human Condition* Arendt characteristically describes by a metaphor of the "threefold frustration."[16] This frustration brings about an insight into the essence of the historical process. History as a whole is predictable only insofar as "the unexpected can be expected."[17] Or, as Arendt puts it in her later essay *On Violence*, historical events,

> by definition, are occurrences that interrupt routine processes ... every action ... destroys the whole pattern in whose frame the prediction moves.[18]

Arendt speaks of unpredictability in three different (even if related) senses, without clearly distinguishing between them. First, any action is already an unpredictable consequence of willing. Second, the consequences of action are also unpredictable and arise

> directly out of the story which, as the result of action, begins and establishes itself as soon as the fleeting moment of the deed is past.[19]

These latter consequences are not only unintended and unpredictable but also boundless. Action unleashes processes that form a life story that is devoid of any conscious human control. This may concern any single action, as Arendt maintains by saying that "sometimes one word suffices to change every constellation."[20]

Hegel's *Lectures on the Philosophy of History* provide a good demonstration of the consequences that Arendt has in mind, without sharing Hegel's beliefs on the meaning of history. As Hegel famously put it, universal history has meaning precisely because

> … something else results from the actions of men than what they intend and achieve, something else than [what] they know or want. They accomplish their interest, but something else is accomplished which was implied in it, which was not in the consciousness and the intentions of the actors.[21]

Hegel then uses the example of a person who sets a house on fire to destroy it, only for the fire to escalate out of control and burn other houses. The consequence of action that Arendt speaks about also, to some extent, occur in an automated, reactive, and inevitable way akin to the uncontrolled spreading of the fire. In the contingent web of language, everybody suffers from the actions of others. As Arendt put it:

> Action has no end. The process of a single deed can quite literally endure throughout time until mankind itself has come to an end.[22]

However, there are also non-automated consequences that present the third sense of unpredictability. These are other actions (as distinct from behavioral reactions) that are themselves breaks in historical continuity. In Hegel's metaphor, they would be putting out the said fire—an intended break of continuity conditioned by the fire—that would be impossible to accomplish if there was nothing to extinguish. A more concrete example from Arendt's historiography is the crystallization of elements into totalitarianism, which is not explicable in terms of a simple causal-effective relationship and is accomplished through the "factor of freedom."[23] Every genuine reaction to an action that falls into an existing web of relationships simultaneously exemplifies the third type of consequence—it is an element of the process initiated by the original action.[24] The combination of three types of unintended consequences forms the unpredictable reality of history.

The crucial caveat, however, is that when speaking of the unpredictability of history, Arendt only points to the constant and essential possibility of unpredictability. Predictability is a fact in a consumer society in which people cease to act. The predictability of a totalitarian society, on the other hand, results from the use of violence. Remembering that fabrication rests on action and violence on power, the conclusion to be drawn is that any predictability of history is enabled by unpredictable action. It is action that lies at the heart of history, whether, at a given moment, it is unpredictable or not. History is predictable only to the extent that it is essentially and thus (from the point of view of critical philosophy of history) speculatively defined by the predictable unpredictability of actions.

One must complement this picture with the irreversibility of all processes. Contingent, unplanned, and unpredictable consequences become a given historical reality and thus a necessity of the present—an unintended consequence of a now irreversible past.

Progress and Decline—The Hierarchy of Temporalities

Apart from the metahistorical insights into its nature, Arendt also discusses history as a whole in more objectified terms. Read together, *The Origins of Totalitarianism* and *The Human Condition* rest on a simplified framework of decline—a "basic eschatological structure" as Annette Vowinckel put it, with Greek antiquity as a period of political action and European modernity dominated by work and gradually degenerating into labor.[25] Meanwhile, Arendt's contemporaneity marked by totalitarianism and the consumer society demarcates the end of history.

This ultimately leads to a paradox between the objectives set for the fragmentary method and a somewhat schematic representation of the entire course of history in *The Human Condition*. The paradox reflects the fundamental aporia of the two types of meaning—meaning in itself, to which the fragmentary method is supposed to do justice, and historical meaning, which in the final reckoning is the domain of the speculative philosophy of history. Arendt represents this decline on two narrative levels—a description of real past events and a description of past interpretations of these events (the history of modern science and the history of its historiography). Examining Arendt's constructions from a conceptual angle of temporality, the decline of the West, which she principally presents in *The Human Condition*, appears as being ultimately based on three normative conceptions of time.

To begin with, there are some significant and usually overlooked temporal nuances concerning the activity of work and the associated category of progress. Ricoeur noted that the temporal character of work and cognition is mainly defined by durability.[26] Similarly, Taminiaux connects cognitive activity with presence.[27] Cognition is both directed at present, existing objects, and leads to the creation of present, durable products. The temporal difference between work and labor amounts to the difference between time as duration and time as indifferent passing. Duration involves the relative presence of things that resists the all-consuming process of the indifferent circulation of matter.

One should, however, differentiate the two aspects of fabrication: the product and the process leading to it. Consequently, one must supplement the above image with time understood as change—the succession of particular phases of the process of production (within labor, the differentiation between an activity and its product makes no sense). This distinction into process and product does not undermine the essential continuity of work, in which the end is contained in the beginning.[28] Making is a purposive process in which every moment is a direct consequence of its predecessor. Temporarily speaking, there is a fluid succession of phases through which the production process passes, where all the instances of this process are subordinated to the end of the final product. Thus, any change involved is governed in advance by the progressively reified model. Time as change is subordinated to time as duration. In the forward march of time, things that come later result from those that came earlier in a linear, causal-effective manner.

It follows that for *homo faber*, the future is a purposive outcomes of the present. It is "contained" in the present as a potentiality of a projected end. The future is the fulfillment of a present. Progress is very much real when it comes to production. It only becomes problematic when finite production becomes infinite.[29]

Arendt intends to show that in the development of modern science, a degradation of the above model takes place. She does not specify precisely when this occurs, yet this transition is the most important event of her narrative on modernity. Examined strictly conceptually, it is a transition from the "proper," finite process of making to an "improper" and infinite process devoid of the final product.[30] The steering of cognition toward a purpose can follow a similar degradation of this purpose to the role of means as exemplified by the modern notion of infinite scientific progress.[31] Progress itself is not a problem for Arendt—the problem is only its infinite character.

Arendt presents the *Zeitgeist* of modern times as marked by the primacy of the future, which equates to the loss of truth.[32] All that remains is an infinite chain of quasi-truths. The belief in the infinite progress of science then transforms into a belief in the infinite progress of history, in which actions lose their intrinsic meaning. As another member of the Heidegger's circle, Karl Löwith, observed:

> The bearing of the eschatological thought on the historical consciousness of the Occident is that it conquers the flux of historical time, which wastes away and devours its own creations unless it is defined by an ultimate goal.[33]

With infinite progress, there is no such limitation. The "eschatological compass," to use Löwith's phrase, is lost. Instead of falling on the present (as in Arendt's picture of a reversed time arrow), the future is getting increasingly far away. Infinite progress is a "permanent annihilation."[34]

The faculty of willing understood as a negation of the present is partly to blame. Arendt's view in this respect can be best read from her critique of Hegel's early concept of time as based on the power of negation. This critique is largely based on Alexandre Koyré's interpretation but in contrast to the work of Koyré (and unlike Hegel) Arendt considers this power of negation to represent willing. If time is constituted by the negation of the present, Arendt argues, willing cancels itself out by transforming the future into "anticipated remembrance" and thus into an object of reflection for thinking.[35] For Arendt it is "evident" that Hegel did not reconcile willing and thinking, but only annexed the former by the latter, a conclusion contradictory to the infinite character of negation. The interpretative scheme of infinite dialectics, in turn, enables inscribing every crisis into progress *ad infinitum*—again, a permanent annihilation.

As early as in *The Origins of Totalitarianism*, Arendt used the argument from finitude to argue with the idea of the accumulation of capital as a foundation block of a political community. She criticized the image of infinitely progressing time as representing the bourgeois liberal ideals of the endless pursuit of profit and wealth. Warren Buffett's alleged saying that his favorite investment horizon is infinite is a contemporary example of this quest. In defiance of the beliefs of capitalists, Arendt claimed that infinite time is a deception:

> Property owners who do not consume but strive to enlarge their holdings continually find one very inconvenient limitation, the unfortunate fact that men must die. Death is the real reason why property and acquisition can never become a true political principle.[36]

Arendt localized the origins of the notion of infinite time in the eighteenth century. It made it possible to count time starting from zero in both directions until infinity.[37] Such a notion was alien to Christianity, whose sacred temporality had a clearly defined beginning and end. The classical speculative philosophies of history represented a typical *homo faber* way of thinking, and they were still following the sacred pattern. The process of history was imagined as finite and purposive, and thus culminating with a product (absolute cognition for Hegel or emancipation for Marx). Karl Löwith saw modern philosophies of history as secularized theologies of history and substitutes for salvation. Arendt's take on this issue was much more down-to-earth. The concept of infinite progress for her marked the disastrous degeneration of the self-image of modernity. In *The Human Condition* its appearance is presented as the "turning point."[38]

Arendt's claim that the "only conceptual guarantee" of infinite progress is the notion of "organic" development may also be read through the temporal lens. Arendt obviously finds the latter notion deeply false for it implies that every present contains the seeds of the future.[39] With the framework of such a "pseudo-scientific" approach, as she calls it, "nothing altogether new and totally unexpected can happen."[40] Every present is more perfect than the past and less perfect than the future—unlike in the process of making, in which the author always surpasses his product.

Arendt's speculative narrative on the temporal foundations of the speculative philosophies of history more often arbitrarily states than proves these essentialistic claims. However, it is for this reason that it may be taken as representing Arendt's own views on the hidden mechanics of history. The narrative reconstructed here on the basis of Arendt's scattered thoughts on the subject is again a narrative of decline.

Even if infinite progress is linear (and not circular, like labor), it is unlimited and thus excludes both the authentic (unexpected) and the projected (purposeful) future. What remains is the process alone. The ideals of *homo faber*, the durability of his products and the temporal boundaries imposed upon the production process are lost. Structurally speaking, not surprisingly, the resultant temporality is closely related to totalitarian thinking. In such a distorted experience of *homo faber*, finitude is replaced by infinity. Infinite linear time is still directed toward the future, which distinguishes it from the indifferent circular temporality. However, the future never comes about as ready and durable. The product lies in infinity, and so infinite progress is qualitatively different from the finite progress of production.

Ultimately, a complete reduction of *homo faber* to *animal laborans* occurs. Arendt calls it the "second reversal."[41] This involves raising labor and life itself to the highest position in the hierarchy of activities. It is with such a bitter diagnosis of modernity, the victory of *animal laborans*, that *The Human Condition* concludes. Overstated as this diagnosis might be, there is no doubting its astuteness. In the society of labor, individuals function in an automated way corresponding to the automated processes of nature. Functional objects become objects of consumption. The pleasure of life itself is a substitute for usefulness. The ideal of mass society is not permanence but abundance. Political history is abandoned for the sake of the simultaneously pre- and post-historical pleasures of a purposeless life.[42]

To summarize, based on Arendt's normative arrangement of temporalities, one may distinguish the following levels of historical development: (1) the proper, finite temporality of thinking and acting (*zoon politikon*); (2) time as duration and the finite change it contains (*homo faber*); (3) time as an infinite yet still directional change (the degraded *homo faber*); and (4) time of indifferent, natural change (*animal laborans*).

With the victory of the indifferent temporality of *animal laborans*, the division between subject and object disappears. Life in a purely biological sense, not individual but a species life, in which labor of the body and of the brain, and consumption and exchange of matter with the environment are one, becomes the highest value.[43] Despite the fact that it contains an element of quantitative acceleration, because of its endlessness that recalls the repeatability of labor, the infinite process of history can now be conceived as indifferently circular.[44]

Table 1 Hierarchy of dimensions of time

Time concept	Practical activities	Theoretical activities	Relation to the concept of purpose
Circular	Labor *Animal laborans*	Logic	Purposelessness
Linear	Work *Homo faber*	Cognition	Purposiveness
Hermeneutic	Action *Zoon politikon*	Thinking	Purpose in itself

8

The Beauty of the Past

If judgment is our faculty for dealing with the past, the historian is the inquiring man who by relating it sits in judgment over it.
                                        Hannah Arendt, *The Life of the Mind*

Reflective Aestheticization of Historical Cognition

Arendt's point of departure in *Lectures on Kant's Political Philosophy* is the surprising or even "dead wrong"[1] contention that Kant never wrote proper political philosophy. His nominally political writings are treatises in the philosophy of history approached from a naturalistic standpoint.[2] In both cases, Arendt claims, Kant speaks of humankind as a species whose history is infinite progress governed by the ruse of nature. In his *Critiques* of pure and practical reason, Kant deals with man as a rational being with universally construed reason.[3] The *Critique of Aesthetic Judgment* brings about an entirely different matter, Arendt maintains. It concerns people living in political communities and needing each other. This observation, which, as Robert Dostal observed, is likely to be "simply wrong,"[4] or to put it more mildly, whose historical accuracy is debatable, nevertheless establishes Arendt's original reading of Kant. It is a reading focused on the concept of reflective aesthetic judgment. Despite Arendt's inaccuracies, and even if, as some scholars argued, "her turn to Kant is illegitimate,"[5] the following reinterpretation of Arendt's understanding of the Kantian judgment will prove to be significant for her conception of fragmented narrative discussed in the remaining chapters.

Arendt's reading is also guided by what she intentionally disregards, namely the *Critique of the Teleological Judgment*, and its notion of purposiveness. To appreciate this disregard, it must be emphasized that in Kant's philosophical system, judgment plays a mediating role between the theoretical philosophy of nature and practical moral philosophy. On the one hand, it applies to appearances (albeit not in a cognitive sense), on the other, it points to the supersensible—to nature's purposiveness and practical reason with its *a priori* principle of the final purpose (*Endzweck*).⁶ The purposiveness of nature leads one to consider oneself as purposeful, and in a twofold sense: being the ultimate purpose of nature (*letzter Zweck*), and being capable of establishing purposes. This is because one does not find the purposiveness that one perceives in nature anywhere else but in oneself. Purposiveness, therefore, points to the moral vocation. Kant is thus ultimately concerned about the purposiveness of both nature as a whole and oneself. The aesthetic power of judgment plays a merely preparatory function.⁷ Arendt, on the other hand, is interested solely in reflective aesthetic judgment in which purposiveness is purely formal and thus without a purpose—a fact that has grave consequences for her theory of historical interpretation.

The Kantian judgment is the power to think the particular, whether as subordinated to the general (some rule of the intellect), under which the particular is subsumed, or without the mediation of the general. In the former case, judgment is determinant (*bestimmend*); and in the latter, it is reflective (*reflektierend*). Only in this second case does the power of judgment appear as a fully independent faculty of the mind. This is because it then establishes the general rule or law needed for judging the particular.⁸

Furthermore, unlike a logical judgment, an aesthetic judgment does not state anything about the object (it is not cognitive) and refers solely to the feelings of pleasure or displeasure (*Lust, Unlust*). Kant divides aesthetic judgments into empirical and pure types. The former, so-called material aesthetic judgments, are based on sensibility and define the object as gratifying. The latter, formal aesthetic judgments—that is the judgments of taste—define the object as beautiful.⁹ The judgment of taste

> affords absolutely no cognition (not even a confused one) of the object ... [it] relates the representation by which an object is given solely to the subject, and does not bring to our attention any property of the object.¹⁰

The quality of beauty does not belong to the object but stems from the free play of the mind's faculties, imagination and intellect.

When discussing reflective judgments of taste, Arendt does not limit herself to judgments of beauty and ugliness. Instead, she expands the notion of judgment to include all judgments of the particular, such as: "This is beautiful, this is ugly; this is right, this is wrong."¹¹ Such judgment is not moral in the Kantian sense, as it is a judgment proceeding from the particular to the universal. If Arendt is suggesting something in here it is rather that the criteria of moral rightness are ultimately aesthetic and thus dependent on "it pleases or displeases me."

Secondly, Kant was mostly concerned with the pure beauty of nature, and not, except for products of genius, human actions. Arendt's intention, however, is evidently to transpose these reflections into the domain of history, which she presents as an issue of "eminent political significance."[12] The primacy of reflective judgment identified by many scholars is due to the fact that it provides a primary understanding that precedes any natural-scientific cognition.[13] Notably, Arendt also notices the reflective moment of determinant judgment. Even if the rule under which to subsume the particular is readily at hand, there is no rule on how to proceed with this subsumption. Any general rule application requires this very application—and thus the guidance of reflective judgment—to be defined as a rule.[14] For example, in jurisdiction, the particular case always specifies the legal rule and supplements the knowledge contained within it. In the words of Gadamer, the distinction between determinant and reflective judgment "is not absolute."[15] The indeterminacy of judgment is appropriate for historical interpretation due to the particularity of historical phenomena. Owing to their uniqueness, concrete political events, by definition, resist inductive generalizations. Arendt's remark that the subject of the third *Critique* is "the particular, whether a fact of nature, or an event in history" clearly shows that she views historical phenomena as valid objects of aesthetic judgment.[16] The relationship with the fragmented past appears as a question of taste.

Historical Judgments: Impartial and General but Not Necessary

As was shown earlier, there are numerous similarities between the Kantian concept of genius and Arendt's notion of political action. Regarding the moments of the judgment of taste, though, Arendt's interpretation markedly differs from Kant's.

Kant distinguishes four moments of the judgments of taste, which refer to the table of logical judgments introduced in the *Critique of Pure Reason* and concern quality, quantity, relation, and modality. Therefore, the judgments of taste are: for quality, **disinterested**; for quantity, **universal**; for the relation of purposes, **purposive without a purpose**; and for modality, **necessary**.[17] Regrettably, Arendt's treatment of these moments is not systematic. Explicitly, historical judgment is only disinterested.

As far as the first moment of the judgment of taste is concerned, beauty is an object of disinterested satisfaction (*uninteressiertes Wohlgefallen*). Interested satisfaction has an interest in the existence of a given thing. In the case of the pleasant (*angenehm*) and the good, satisfaction is interested owing to the senses or reason. One wants something because it pleases the senses or the faculty of desire (willing) determined by reason.[18] In both cases, one is interested in the existence of a given object and desire it—"Not merely the object but also its existence pleases."[19] In the judgment of taste, meanwhile, one is not interested in the existence of the object of judgment either through the senses or through reason. Therefore, nothing forces one to find satisfaction in the object, and more precisely, in its representation in relation to cognitive faculties.

In Arendt's work, the disinterestedness of aesthetic pleasure assumes the form of the historian's "impartiality," as opposed to her objectivity.[20] Arendt sees Kant's disinterestedness as not absolute, but instead as constituting a "relative impartiality."[21] Any interest in disinterestedness appears after the disinterested judgment of taste has been impartially pronounced.

The definition of beauty based upon the second moment of the judgment of taste says that beauty is an object of universal pleasing *a priori* without the mediation of a concept. This brings a universal validity of judgment. Something that pleases only one person cannot be called beautiful. One speaks of beauty as if it were a property of an object rather than merely its perception—as if one's judgment was logical and not aesthetic. Regarding what is pleasant, everyone has their taste and everyone may enjoy different things. As for what is good, there is a universality similar to that of the beautiful, albeit based upon a concept. However, the universality of the beautiful is not based upon a concept. It is aesthetic, that is, purely subjective, although it gives the impression of a logical judgment. The pleasure concerning a particular, beautiful object is thus universally imputed.[22]

Kant argues that it is not pleasure that precedes the judgment (for this would mean the object is merely pleasant) but the opposite. The source of pleasure is the capacity of the universal communicability of the state of mind—the free play and mutual stimulation of the cognitive faculties, imagination and intellect. One finds pleasure not in the object itself but in the harmony and the proportional relationship of one's cognitive powers involved in judgment, which one regards as applying to everyone. "The capacity for the communication of the state of mind ... must ... have the pleasure in the object as a consequence."[23]

This is why Kant argues that judgments of taste are synthetic *a priori*. They add the predicative "beautiful" bound with the feeling of pleasure to the concept, but it is not the pleasure that is given *a priori*, but its universal validity—the pleasure is imputed to all who possess cognitive powers. What is assumed *a priori* is the accordance of representation with the conditions of cognition as valid to everyone: "the subjective condition of all judgments is the faculty for judging itself."[24]

There is no trace of such universal pleasing in Arendt's interpretation. This is visible in her translation of the German *allgemein*, among other places, which she renders with the adjective "general," rather than "universal," the latter being the standard choice from J. H. Bernard's translation.[25] Arendt thus intends to "detranscendentalize" Kant's aesthetics as Ronald Beiner put it.[26] The Kantian "universal communicability" (*allgemeine Mitteilbarkeit*) becomes "general communicability." It will be shown later that the most important issue for Arendt is sociability (*Geselligkeit*), which is empirically (and not synthetically *a priori*) involved in the judgments' claim to generality.

According to the definition of beauty based on the third moment of the judgment of taste, it entails the perception of a given object's purposiveness, without an idea of any specific purpose. Kant defines purposiveness as the causality of a concept with regard to its object. A purpose is "the object of a concept insofar as the latter is regarded as the cause of the former."[27] Every object made according to a concept is therefore purposive, where the idea of an effect is its determining cause. Purposiveness without a purpose, on the other hand, denotes a situation in which the possibility of the object "does not necessarily presuppose the representation of a purpose" but in which we "can only make an explanation of its possibility intelligible to ourselves by deriving it from a will."[28] Such is the encounter with the "free" beauty of nature apprehended by pure judgments of taste.[29] One perceives nature as both inherently purposeless (not caused by a will) and, simultaneously, as if there was an acting power of desire determined by concepts purposefully acting behind it. In other words, to make purposeless nature comprehensible, one derives it from some unknown willing. Purposiveness without a purpose is a subjective formal purposiveness, in other words the form of purposiveness contained in the representation of a given object. It is not the property of the object but of its mental representation. Experiencing this formal subjective purposiveness is a source of pleasure.

Arendt does not pay particular attention to the third moment of the judgment of taste. In the thirteenth lecture, she notes the importance of purposiveness without a purpose for Kant but contends that a far more valuable criterion is "exemplary validity."[30] Nevertheless, the concept of purposiveness without a purpose fits particularly well into the spirit, even if not to the letter, of Arendt's reading. It will be shown later how this notion applies to both particular actions and the relations between them.

The definition of beauty referring to the fourth moment of the judgment of taste states that it is the object of necessary pleasure without the mediation of a concept. Not only may the beauty arouse pleasure—it must do so. As Kant mentions, this necessity is not an *a priori* necessity but neither can it be derived from experience. Its source is an internal community sense (*Gemeinsinn*):[31]

> A subjective principle, which determines what pleases or displeases only through feeling and not through concepts, but yet with universal validity.[32]

Arendt does not refer to the problem of necessity to any degree. In the broader context of her writings, it is evident that the pleasure of reflection is not necessary.

In summary, in Arendt's reinterpretation of the Kantian aesthetic judgment, the first moment of the judgment of taste—disinterested satisfaction in beauty—becomes the historian's impartiality. The second moment—the *a priori* universality of this satisfaction without the mediation of a concept—ceases to apply since the satisfaction is merely general. The third moment—the perception of purposiveness without the idea of a specific purpose—will prove to be the most important when explored in detail later in this chapter. The fourth moment—the necessary character of satisfaction in beauty—loses all significance, except for the role played by common sense in judging the past, although this role is also different than in Kant, as it shall also soon be shown.

Infinitely Inaccessible Spectacle of History

A key distinction for any historical interpretation is that which exists between the actor and the spectator. Arendt introduces this issue in *Lectures* starting with Kant's ambiguous assessment of war and revolution. Even if, from the perspective of practical reason, war and revolution deserve condemnation, the external observer might view them as progressive. In Arendt's reading, Kant interprets this progress dogmatically, as a ruse of nature in which the subject of history is humankind viewed as a species.

> The spectator, because he is not involved, can perceive this design of providence or nature, which is hidden from the actor. So we have the spectacle and the spectator on one side, the actors and all the single events and contingent, haphazard happenings on the other.[33]

Being "outside" of events allows the onlooker to see the "whole." The actor is partial, the spectator impartial like a judge.[34] It is the observer that occupies a privileged position, enabling the interpretation of past events from the perspective of the whole. His being outside is "the condition of understanding the meaning of the play."[35]

Even if the spectator's judgment is final, it should have no impact on the maxims of action. Morality should remain unaffected.[36] In the fifth lecture, these two perspectives stand "somehow in opposition" to each other,[37] and in the final lecture, even in "contradiction."[38] Both perspectives, incidentally, serve to overcome the problem of the contingency of the particular, either by granting it a value within the historical whole or within itself.

The Kantian spectator discovers the meaning of events on account of the future, not the present, and thus of the consequences that have not yet occurred. He may therefore pronounce upon progress or the lack thereof. He is guided by the hope of achieving the ultimate purpose of a perfect cosmopolitan system. For Kant, Arendt notes, the progress of the whole (alongside the self-destructiveness of evil) is a necessary presupposition.[39] A backward glance defines the future. As Kant put it in *Idea for a Universal History with a Cosmopolitan Intent*, "a guiding thread will be revealed ... for giving a consoling view of the future."[40]

For this reason, Arendt sees Kant's approach to politics as belonging to the old philosophical tradition initiated by Plato's *Republic* and disregarding plurality.[41] Kant's progress of the whole concerns the species, whereas the reasoning and moral duty are played out within the individual distanced from the community. Progress serves as the escape from the particular and the contingent. The ancient topic of the superiority of the contemplative way of life returns here in a new format. The withdrawal from the world is not absolute, but partial—to the "position of the judge." On account of the role that sensibility plays in cognition, Kant does not entirely turn his back on the world. The spectator, both a philosopher and a historian, no longer looks at the world of ideas but at the dynamic historical reality. Despite her fundamental hostility toward philosophical tradition, Arendt quotes Kant affirmatively, even if her position differs in some crucial aspects. Seeing how she constructively merges Kant's and Hegel's perspectives will help in the understanding of these differences.[42]

Arendt juxtaposes Kant and Hegel in the following way. For Kant, history means perpetual and infinite progress, the subject of which is the human species. History can be judged in advance, as it were, by considering the consequences that are yet to occur, yet predetermined by nature's hidden intentions. Therefore, the meaning of the future can be revealed in advance, before the completion of a chain of events.⁴³ For Hegel too, history means progress, although this time it is finite. Its subject is not the species but the spirit and it can be judged only from the perspective of the end, which is that of the current, unintended consequences of past events.

Arendt sees History—with Kant—as infinite. Nevertheless, she thinks—with Hegel—that it can be judged solely from the perspective of consequences—a perspective that from this angle is perpetually inaccessible. The play being enacted before the spectator is an infinite story of history, which, as a whole, remains forever intangible. The motif of the lack of the end of history is crucial. Arendt excludes both the final destination and the possibility of a final judgment on the whole of history:

> The story never has an end. The end of the story itself is in infinity. There is no point at which we might stand still and look back with the backward glance of the historian.⁴⁴

Although Arendt rejects the future-oriented perspective of judgment, she clearly affirms the perspective of consequences, which is alien to Kant's moral philosophy: "Kant condemns the very action whose results he then affirms with a satisfaction bordering on enthusiasm."⁴⁵ It is only the perspective of the consequences unintended by the actors that reveals "the meaning of the whole."⁴⁶

Comparing Kant to the Greeks, Arendt writes:

> The Greek spectator ... looks at and judges (finds the truth of) the cosmos of the particular event in its own terms, without relating it to any larger process in which it may or may not play a part. He was actually concerned with the individual event, the particular act ... Its meaning did not depend on either causes or consequences. The story, once it had come to an end, contained the whole meaning. This is also true for Greek historiography ... The story may contain rules valid for future generations also, but it remains a single story.⁴⁷

In this quotation, a particular event is equivalent to a singular story, which is yet another manifestation of the fundamental aporia. Although Arendt does not agree entirely with Kant, it would be a mistake to identify her position fully with the Greeks as presented above. Arendt describes the Kantian judgment concerning revolution as both aesthetic and reflective, even if it is a teleological, and not merely an aesthetic, judgment. The spectator interprets the revolution as a sign of progress—the future is of significance for him.⁴⁸ Arendt's notion of judgment is indeed aesthetic and reflective. Unlike the teleological judgment that refers to the purposive relations between the events of nature comprising a whole, aesthetic judgment merely reflects on the object's form in relation to the subject. It only involves purposiveness without a concept. Aesthetic judgment only gives us a "hope" that nature as a whole makes sense.[49] Each of nature's objects is then perceived as an "individuated system," which is a kind of "microcosm of the overall order of things."[50]

The next section demonstrates how, in Arendt's view, historical events can create indeterminate wholes that are comparable to parts of nature. In historical narratives, these parts appear purposive on account of these indeterminate wholes. Sets of events—such as the French Revolution or the Second World War—then comprise subsystems of history, comparable to the subsystems of nature, bringing the hope that history as a whole makes sense. The condition for the possibility of joining particular events into a whole is the temporal distance—a "withdrawal" to the position of the spectator.[51]

The final positive element of Kant's reflections that goes against tradition is the idea of the spectators in the plural. In the classical Platonic distinction between the political and the contemplative and solitary life, ordinary citizens are cave dwellers contrasted with the chosen few, namely statesmen or philosophers. For Arendt, on the other hand, everyone, regardless of their intellectual level, is capable of aesthetic judgment (although not everyone is endowed with genius, the capacity to create beautiful objects of history). A few actors are now contrasted with multiple spectators. Moreover, Arendt's spectators are not solitary. Arendt repeatedly emphasizes the principle of equality.[52] Historians are not distinguished from others. Judging is a possibility and need shared by humans, and it does not divide communities into the many and the few. With this enlightened rejection of the old hierarchy (which will return with Hegel's philosophy), the tension between philosophy (or history) and politics disappears. A philosopher (or a historian) no longer needs to write a political philosophy (or a philosophy of history) to tell the majority how they should act. Moreover, spectators not only appear in the plural but are also dynamic and historically variable. As Arendt contends:

> Even Kant ... could conveniently forget that even if the spectacle were always the same and therefore tiresome, the audiences would change from generation to generation; nor would a fresh audience be likely to arrive at the conclusion handed down by tradition as to what an unchanging play has to tell it.[53]

In summary, for Arendt, as for Kant, history is infinite, but as for Hegel, it can only be judged from the perspective of the consequences. The spectators exist in the plural and their judgments change over time. The Kantian tension between the perspectives of the actor and the spectator remains, but it is no longer a tension between what has meaning in itself and progress. It is now a tension between political action meaningful in itself and the indeterminate and changing reflective wholes, within which, from the perspective of the beholder, particular events play a role.

The Interpretative Function of Free Imagination

The play watched by the spectator is the story as a whole and not particular actions, and "it is the whole that gives meaning to the particulars if they are seen and judged by men endowed with reason."[54] Arendt's spectator, like Kant's, perceives this whole "by the eyes of the mind," and is able "to see the whole that gives meaning to the particulars."[55] But how is the spectator to see the whole of a story if every story is boundless and potentially infinite and therefore its whole is never directly given? The answer is through imagination. Imagination plays a fundamental role in judgment by enabling one to perceive wholes in a conceptually indeterminate manner.

Arendt construes imagination broadly. It is a condition of the possibility of memory, and in this sense, a "much more comprehensive faculty" than is usually assumed.[56] In conclusion to her essay *Understanding and Politics* from 1954, Arendt equates imagination with understanding, stating that "it is the only inner compass we have" to find the proper path in the historical world.[57] This is because imagination relates what is given to what is absent—the part to the whole, a fragment of a text to the entire text, the whole text to the context, and action to its historical circumstances. Not only the past but all dimensions of time constitute themselves through imagination. Imagination preconditions the "withdrawal" from the world, and thus all temporarily oriented mental activities.[58] Arendt's private notes confirm such a broad understanding. Imagination represents what is absent, whether from the past, present, or future: "imagination gathers the past and the future (all that is absent) into the present."[59]

Arendt distinguishes the function of imagination from the first *Critique*, where it serves cognition, from that of the third *Critique*, where it enables judgment.[60] The former is synthetic and cognitive; the latter is non-synthetic and reflective. The role of imagination in Kant's thought changes—it no longer solely serves the synthesis of representations.[61] And it is the reflective imagination that, owing to the free play of part and whole, proves useful in historical understanding. Comparing Arendt's notion with Heidegger's reading of the *Critique of Pure Reason*, will prove useful in elucidating her scarce remarks.

Imagination appears as the fundamental cognitive function when making any synthesis of concepts and intuition. This is because by providing the schemata (general images) for concepts, it enables the perception of objects and, subsequently, communication.[62] Kant differentiates between the schemata of empirical concepts (e.g., a cat), of mathematical concepts (e.g., a quadrilateral), and of pure concepts of the intellect (e.g., a substance).[63] Arendt only refers to the schemata of empirical concepts used in everyday communication. Only by producing schemata does imagination make images possible, and in this sense, it is productive. However, when Arendt writes that imagination "is something beyond or between thought and sensibility,"[64] she is likely referring to pure imagination *a priori*, which conditions empirical synthesis and is the supposed common root of sensibility and intellect.

In contrast to the above, in her New School seminar on imagination, Arendt writes that imagination represents an absent object that has been seen before. Thus, imagination is reproductive. Even artistic imagination produces novelty based on what was previously given.[65] Simultaneously, Arendt postulates that thanks to schemata, imagination produces a synthesis which lies beyond sensibility and intellect. The production of schemata takes place *a priori* and is thus productive. How should one make sense of this discrepancy? Heidegger's interpretation of Kant mentioned above is helpful.

As the tool of making present what is absent, imagination reproduces what has already been seen. It is reproductive because it creates images based on what has been sensibly given. Even if it "produces" something, it does so based on previous reproduction. However, this primal reproduction refers to an even earlier perception, and thus ultimately to a productive *a priori* imagination—to an imagination producing schemata. Does this mean that imagination is always primarily purely productive, that is, transcendental? Such is the conclusion of Heidegger's interpretation, although this is not to say that imagination can produce something from nothing. "Productive" here means shaping the horizon of objectivity. Purely productive, therefore, means enabling experience.[66] It follows that the secondary reproduction, recalling what is known, is also productive.

If reproductive means receiving something external, and productive means producing something out of itself, then imagination is neither. After all, it is supposed to stand between concepts and intuition. Even though it exists only in thought, a schema is neither a product of the intellect nor given in intuition. Imagination belongs to intuition, but it may watch an object without its presence. It is productive because it provides schemata to itself. It is both productive and reproductive. As Heidegger put it:

> If receptivity means the same as sensibility and if spontaneity means the same as understanding, then in a peculiar way the power of imagination falls between both.[67]

Imagination is the "unity of receptivity and spontaneity."[68]

Heidegger repeatedly underscores that Kant, in the second edition of *The Critique of Pure Reason*, abandoned this understanding of imagination, favoring the fundamental role of the intellect, which is now the source of pure synthesis. Arendt, meanwhile, points to another shift that takes place in the *Critique of Judgment*, in which imagination comes back as an entirely free faculty of the mind. In the aesthetic judgment, imagination is not reproductive but "productive and spontaneous." Furthermore, this freedom is supposed to be lawful, even if lawfulness belongs to the intellect. Kant speaks of "free lawfulness,"[69] which means that concepts do not control the lawfulness of imagination. Imagination is productive and free because it "schematizes without a concept."[70] Unlike in a determinant judgment, in which intuition is subsumed under concepts through the mediation of a schema, free imagination finds something general in the particular. This is why it is the appropriate source of historical understanding.

Historical Examples and Reflective Wholes

Arendt does not refer to schemata as being independent of concepts but instead focuses on examples. She stresses that an example is a particular that in the third *Critique* replaces the schemata of the concepts of intellect. An example, therefore, helps us to judge the particular without the mediation of a concept. It guides us in those situations in which there is no scheme available to recognize the given object. An example is not an objective standard, and the operation of judgment is not a logical operation of deduction or induction.[71] Pronouncing a judgment "seems logically impossible"[72] and examples, concrete intuitions rather than schemata, are provided by imagination.

At this point, one should distinguish two possibilities, which Arendt fails to do clearly in her seminar notes.[73] In the first situation, one already has an example from the past, which helps to pronounce a judgment. One thus refers to precedents that are "orientational" in nature but do not impose anything.[74] Arendt's examples representing good and courage are St. Francis of Assisi and Achilles. As in the case of genius, there is a continuation and not an imitation (*Nachfolge* and not *Nachahmung*)—a reference to the past that is inspiring rather than binding. The historical judgment does not move in a void but can draw examples from the past.

More challenging situations are those in which the judged phenomena are historically unprecedented. As in the case of totalitarianism, there are no previous adequate examples to hold on to. In these cases, one must determine the generality based on the unprecedented itself.[75] The example Arendt uses this time is Bonapartism, a concept derived from the particular example of Napoleon. Such a concept can then aid judgment of another, particular historical phenomenon and become an example for the first situation described above.

Most importantly, examples do not have cognitive status since nothing compels one to agree with a given judgment. Concepts deriving from particular historical phenomena are only exemplary and limited. As Arendt puts it in her seminar on imagination:

> Most concepts in the historical and political sciences are of this restricted nature; they have their origin in some particular historical incident; and we then proceed to make it "exemplary"—to see in the particular what is valid for more than one case.[76]

Thus, imagination also serves the construction of concepts in the historical sciences.

But what about the reference to the imagined whole? After all, it is the whole seen by "the eyes of the mind" that was supposed to give meaning to the particulars. It was in the mind of the spectator that "the particular instances and sequences are invisibly united."[77] In Arendt's reconstructed reading, the imagined whole is neither the whole of history nor the whole of nature as appealed to in a teleological judgment. In reflective aesthetic judgment, the whole concerns a particular object of nature that seems purposive, despite not having an internal purpose. One is dealing not with a single, but with many reflective and indeterminate wholes, whose parts do not fall under definite concepts. The same concerns historical concepts. The whole of the aesthetic form of a given historical object, such as the French Revolution, entails its parts being joined in an indeterminate way. The specific concept is only produced on the basis of the judged example. For Kant, such reflective wholes assure the possibility of subsystems of nature. In a comparable sense, they could enable the perception of subsystems of history, such as the French Revolution or Totalitarianism. These subsystems appear hidden behind concepts that organize and systematize the mutual relationships between their elements. This would not have been possible without free imagination[78].

Sensus Communis—A Historical Sense

What are the criteria of validity of such reflective historical judgments? Is it possible to define them universally, given that they are based on free imagination? Or are they just a matter of personal taste, "a fickle product of imaginative fancy"?[79]

A relative, albeit universally applicable criterion, is communicability grounded in common sense—*sensus communis*. In a tradition stretching back to antiquity, the concept of *sensus communis* has a practical character of *phronesis* directed against a purely theoretical philosophical attitude.[80] It is a practical sense with moral significance. By narrowing the concept of *sensus communis* to aesthetic judgments, Kant marks the beginning of the end of this tradition. Arendt follows Kant in not considering *sensus communis* as a practical faculty affecting the will, but also widens its applicability to the judgments of the past. Community sense becomes historical sense.

There are some ostensibly minor and scholastic but ultimately significant nuances regarding this concept. First of all, one should not confuse community sense with the colloquial understanding of common sense. In Paragraph 20 of the *Critique of the Power of Judgment*, Kant makes a clear distinction between two forms of common sense: *Gemeinsinn*—which makes judgments based on a feeling, yet in a universally valid manner—and *gemeiner Verstand* (which J. H. Bernard translates as "common understanding"), whose judgments are made based on concepts.[81] In Paragraph 40, Kant states further that we might designate taste as *sensus communis aestheticus*, and common human understanding (*gemeiner Verstand*) as *sensus communis logicus*.[82] *Sensus communis* is an internal sense, "the effect of the free play of our cognitive powers," and, as such, it is merely presupposed (Kant does not adjudicate here whether it really exists).[83]

Sensus communis must then be different from the German healthy understanding (*gesunder Verstand*), which, in turn (unlike the English common sense or Polish "zdrowy rozsądek"—literally, a healthy intellect), does not refer to morality.[84] Even if the metaphor of health evokes a distinction between the normal and the pathological, one that may also define the rules of effective conduct and suggest practicality, the notion of healthy understanding is merely logical. It is the capacity to subsume the particular under the universal, and it is not particularly relevant for Kant. As Gadamer notes, "the only significance of this sound understanding is that it is a preliminary stage of cultivated and enlightened reason."[85]

The matter is entirely different in the case of community sense. In Paragraph 40 of the *Critique of Judgment*, which Arendt quotes in her twelfth lecture, Kant clearly distinguishes the proper *sensus communis* from common human understanding.

> By *sensus communis*, however, must be understood the idea of a communal sense, i.e., a faculty for judging that in its reflection takes account (*a priori*) of everyone else's way of representing in thought, in order as it were to hold its judgment up to human reason as a whole ... Now this happens by one holding his judgment up not so much to the actual as to the merely possible judgments of others, and putting himself into the position of everyone else, merely by abstracting from the limitations that contingently attach to our own judging.[86]

For Kant, abstracting from contingent limitations consists of considering the form of judgment, the free play of imagination and intellect. For Arendt, who omits this caveat, it is more content-based and consists in the *a priori* consideration of the "possible judgments" of others.[87] Therefore, it is about pronouncing a judgment in accordance with other possible standpoints, which makes it potentially communicable as far as its content is concerned.

The word "possible" is decisive. The universality of judgment is not universal but postulated. Furthermore, it is not dependent on the actual judgments of others (which sets it apart from the capacity of conformism). The most important maxim of *sensus communis* is that of enlarged thought: to think by putting oneself in the place of every other person.[88] Judgments of taste acquire their specific, intersubjective validity from imagined communicability. In addition, Arendt excludes the supersensible element, through which Kant explains the antinomy of taste. In Arendt's words, "I judge as a member of this community and not as a member of a supersensible world."[89]

In the same paragraph, Kant introduces the concept of community sense (*gemeinschaftlicher Sinn*). It is taste, and not common sense, that is the actual *sensus communis*. The notion of taste is merely supposed to indicate the immediacy with which the outcomes of reflection impose themselves on a judge. Arendt also introduces a new concept to describe this sense—a community sense that differs from common sense. This results in the following interpretative puzzle.

Arendt distinguishes common sense, which is supposed to be the same for everybody, from community sense, which fulfills the function that Kant ascribes to *sensus communis* (*gemeinschaftlicher Sinn*). However, she presents *Menschenverstand* as its German equivalent and quotes Kant speaking of *gemeiner*

Menschenverstand. Slightly later, she uses the concept of *gemeinschaftlicher Sinn* to indicate the same thing, quoting a passage from Kant's *Anthropology* in which he refers to *sensus communis* as the equivalent of *Gemeinsinn*.[90] Furthermore, Arendt renders the maxims of common human understanding (*gemeiner Menschenverstand*) as "maxims of *sensus communis*," although only the second maxim—to think by putting oneself in the place of every other person—is ultimately the maxim of the power of judgment in her interpretation. The unavoidable conclusion is that Arendt does not distinguish between the German concepts of *gemeiner Menschenverstand* and *gemeinschaftlicher Sinn* as she does between English common sense and community sense. To avoid confusion the original English distinction will be treated as valid for her thinking.

In the practice of judgment, community sense is responsible for the communicability of judgments, and thus for their intersubjective character. Intersubjectivity has a fundamental status here. Arendt notes that even the effectiveness of logical procedures is dependent on community sense. Logical reasoning is only ostensibly independent from shared experience. When functioning in isolation, it leads to logicality or insanity, defined as a fully private experience.[91] For Arendt, therefore, community sense precedes theoretical reason. *Zoon politikon* preconditions *animal rationale*. As Kant asserts in his *Anthropology*:

> We have to attach our own understanding to the understanding of other men too, instead of isolating ourselves with our own understanding and still using our private ideas to judge publicly so to speak. This is a subjectively necessary criterion of the correctness of our judgments generally, and so too of the health of our understanding.[92]

This interpretation does not depart from the spectrum of other readings of Kant. Makkreel, for example, calls *sensus communis* a "transcendental condition of his critical epistemology."[93] Arendt's perspective is also quasi-transcendental since the mechanism is universally valid. However, it is also empirical in the sense that the specific content of the representations of others is now taken into account. As a consequence, the results are culturally and historically relative.

This does not change the fact that the value of the judgments of taste lies in their generality. The spectator is to reach the "general standpoint,"[94] even if this generality is ultimately relative. As Arendt puts it:

> The greater the reach—the larger the realm in which the enlightened individual is able to move from standpoint to standpoint—the more "general" will be his thinking.[95]

The spectator relates his private interpretation of an event placed in the imagined whole to the imagined community of judges. The "operation of reflection" based upon *sensus communis* makes use of imagination. It is imagination that permits one's thinking to be broadened: "imagining possibilities that are not merely variations of the self."[96] In her unpublished notes, Arendt puts the same thought even more directly:

> The more people I can make present in imaginative thought, the more *representative* is my thinking. Political thought is not universally valid (truth) but aims at *representation*.[97]

The representation of the possible points of view of others is the substance of *Bildung*, specifically self-formation or cultivation.[98] It expresses the need for the company of others. As Kant noted:

> A human being abandoned on a desert island would not adorn either his hut or himself ... and is not content with an object if he cannot feel his satisfaction in it in community with others.[99]

Whereas common sense stands on the side of authority and tradition, community sense presupposes critical thinking based upon communicability.[100]

If the value of judgment is directly dependent on its communicability, however, would potentially unique judgments not dissolve in the commonality of taste? Although one might at times get the impression that Arendt's postulate is for the greatest possible communicability, the concept of sociability is more appropriate. The intersubjective generality reached in judgment is not about empathy regarding fellow spectators. The judge is supposed to represent their viewpoints only in order to move between them. Kant defines sociability as "property belonging to humanity"[101]—a natural social drive. Humanity and sociability sometimes appear as synonyms, for example, when Kant states that they are "the universal feeling of participation" and "the capacity for being able to communicate ... universally."[102] The means of sociability is taste.

Arendt quotes Kant positively in the first lecture stating that sociability is the "highest end intended for man,"[103] and somewhat later saying that for men in the plural, the "true 'end' is ... sociability."[104] In the *Critique of Judgment*, sociability is the condition of possibility of judgment and a source of humanity.[105] Arendt emphasizes that the faculty of judgment already presupposes the presence of others. *Sensus communis* differs from empirical common sense insofar as it is both the condition and the outcome of community life. However, the prescriptive element of judgment is not so much its greatest possible communicability as communicability directed toward the society to which one wishes to belong. Communicability constitutes an imagined community. Thus, *sensus communis* is both a kind of preliminary communal understanding and a "possibility to be cultivated."[106] For Kant, the obligation of aesthetic judgment is conditioned, which means that one only "solicits assent from everyone else."[107] If it were unconditional, it would no longer be the judgment of taste. However, Arendt excludes not only the universality of judgments of taste but also the aspiration to it. One uses taste for "telling one's **choices**" and "choosing one's company."[108] The validity of judgments may be thus seen as secondary to the affirmation of freedom through it. In this vein, Linda Zerilli claimed that Arendt's notion of judgment reminds us "that our relation to others and the world is based on something other than knowing."[109] More recently, Jim Josefson argued in detail how Arendt's unorthodox reading of Kant emphasizes the freedom of the beautiful that is temporarily rooted in the moment.[110] Judgment decides whom one chooses to share one's world with, and a person with good taste "knows how to choose his company among men, among things, among thoughts."[111] Arendt illustrates this vividly with a quotation from Cicero: "I would rather be wrong with Plato than right with the Pythagoreans."[112] Taste distinguishes a given person and her ideal company among other social groups.[113]

Finally, the key move of Kantian aesthetics is that, unlike the pleasant, the beautiful pleases not in sensation but "in the mere judging."[114] Arendt distinguishes two stages in the procedure of judgment: the operation of imagination and the operation of reflection. First, thanks to imagination, the objects of the external or objective senses—sight, hearing, and touch—are "de-sensed" and internalized as representations.[115] This operation sets the necessary conditions for impartiality, as the objects no longer affect us directly. Following this operation of imagination, the proper operation of reflection based upon *sensus communis* takes place. Imagination enables one to mentally perceive wholes so that the meaning of judged actions is no longer contained in itself and is not, like Kantian beauty, autonomous. When one reflects upon the representation of action, one relates it to its context and consequences in a conceptually indeterminate manner. Furthermore, there is another imagined whole at play—that of a community. Through *sensus communis*, one's subjective historical representation linking a single event to a larger imagined whole is related to another imagined whole of a community. For the historian, this might be a *Denkkollektiv*—a community of researchers guided by the same research paradigm.[116]

The representation reflected upon now arouses one's pleasure or displeasure. Since the object of judgment—the past—is absent, it is the representation that affects, but somewhat paradoxically, as if it was an object of taste. To overcome the privacy of taste, the operation of reflection based upon *sensus communis* takes others and their judgments into account. As Arendt stresses, the operation of reflection is the proper operation of judgment establishing impartiality and communicability. Judgment is a far cry from the sense of taste, which is radically subjective, incommunicable, and cannot be expressed through language. Furthermore, in judgment, like in taste, "the it-pleases-or-displeases-me is immediate and overwhelming."[117] The operation of judgment entails the approval or disapproval of primal pleasure or displeasure. It is a secondary pleasure that occurs after.[118] What now pleases is neither an object nor its representation but the fact of pleasure or displeasure: "We are pleased that the world or nature pleases us" (or, one might add, we are displeased by the primal pleasure or pleased by the displeasure).[119] We reflect upon the sensation of the inner sense. The ultimate criterion of judgment is the communicability of this second-order pleasure stemming from the second-order representation and it is limited to the imagined community to which one aspires to belong. Therefore, as Jennifer Nedelsky showed, Arendt's somewhat relativistic approach has "little to offer" to judgments across diverse communities, including those with different historical sensibilities.[120]

Purposiveness without a Purpose

It was shown how Kant's distinction between mechanical and beautiful art corresponded to that between work and action, *facere* and *agree*. In mechanical art, just like in work, the object is purposive according to a concept constituting its cause. In beautiful art and the work of genius, meanwhile, just like the self in political action, the object cannot be purposively projected. However, beautiful art is supposed to be purposive without a purpose, while Arendt's political action was purposive in itself.[121] The analogy therefore seems false but actually it is not.

Kant claims that the pure beauty of nature manifests itself as purposive, in other words, produced on the basis of a concept, even if it is internally purposeless. Purposiveness here is merely subjective and formal; it is nothing more than a way of perceiving an otherwise purposeless object. With beautiful art, the situation is reversed. A purposive product of genius seems purposeless and thus resembles a product of nature. This is why Kant says:

Nature was beautiful, if at the same time it looked like art; and art can only be called beautiful if we are aware that it is art and yet it looks to us like nature.[122]

Apparently, purposiveness without a purpose may actually appear in two diverse forms. In the case of the beauty of nature, purposiveness is a way of perceiving an object devoid of internal purpose. In the case of beautiful art, an object is partly purposive (the genius projects but does not reach the purpose) and yet is perceived as being purposeless. In the former case, the purposeless seems purposive; in the latter, the purposive seems purposeless. If one uses the traditional phrase **purposiveness without a purpose** to describe the former case, by way of distinction, one should refer to the latter as **purposelessness with a purpose.**

There is another striking similarity between Kant's aesthetics and Arendt's philosophy of history, this time having to do with the relationship between works of beautiful art and political actions and how the continuity between them is established.[123] The relationship between two works of genius is that of continuation (*Nachfolge*) and not imitation (*Nachahmung*). Genius is not something that one can learn by following and imitating specific rules. As Kant puts it:

> The rule must be abstracted from the deed, i.e. from the product, against which others may test their own talent, letting it serve them as a model not for copying but for imitation. How this is possible is difficult to explain.[124]

Therefore, every work of creative genius is original, new and unprecedented, although it may draw inspiration from the previous work of another genius.

> The product of a genius ... is an example, not for imitation ... but for emulation by another genius, who is thereby awakened to the feeling of his own originality, to exercise freedom from coercion in his art in such a way that the latter thereby itself acquires a new rule.[125]

The artist applies specific rules—after all, the work of beautiful art contains an element of mechanical art—but these rules are neither abstracted from previous works (as this would be imitation) nor establish new mechanical rules to be followed. Kant explains this mystery of genius by the intervention of nature; Arendt obviously does not. But continuation (and not imitation) is what binds Arendt's political actions. These actions, by definition, are new and unprecedented. Additionally, however, they are inspired by past action, and historical actors may freely decide which aspects of the past they decide to refer to and reenact (cf. Chapter 10, esp. "Reenacting the past").

What ultimately adjudicates on beautiful art, however, is taste. Arendt explicitly refers to the subordination of genius to judgment in the tenth lecture. It is taste that knows the rule that "must be abstracted from the deed, i.e., from the product." Therefore, although the spectators do not need to know the material purposiveness of the judged products, they must assume some form of purposiveness. Kant, for example, writes:

> If the object is given as a product of art, and is as such supposed to be declared to be beautiful, then, since art always presupposes an end in the cause (and its causality), a concept must first be the ground of what the thing is supposed to be.[126]

For Kant, it is the genius who must possess this faculty of judgment—"a faculty for apprehending the rapidly passing play of the imagination and unifying it in a concept." This concept is "original and ... discloses a new rule, which could not have been deduced from any antecedent principles or examples."[127] This claim is critical as it suggests the possibility of new concepts, even if they do not do full justice to the aesthetic idea. Taste knows the rule of which genius is not aware.

The hierarchy between genius and taste may now be rendered in temporal terms and transposed into the hierarchy between the past and the judging historian—it is impartial, independent from, and privileged with regard to that past.[128] Incidentally, the temporal distance is also significant in Kant's aesthetics. Creative genius is future oriented, whereas taste is firmly retrospective in nature. For Arendt, the subordination of genius to taste goes beyond the relationship between two faculties of the same mind and signifies precisely the subordination of historical actors with their prospective attitude to retrospective historical spectators.

Pronouncing a judgment on beautiful art must entail a double movement of reflection. Firstly, one perceives something purposive (art) as not having a purpose (nature). As far as it is beautiful, art seems to be nature—it is purposeless with a purpose. Secondly, the power of judgment **discloses a rule *post factum*.** It thus perceives it as purposive while being aware that the object of beautiful art cannot be reduced to the project of genius. Genius as the capacity to produce beautiful art is subordinated to the power of judgment since it is judgment that ultimately decides whether it can be deemed beautiful. The power of judgment judges without having a concept of what the thing should be. However, the outcome of judgment may turn out to be a new concept, through which **what seemed purposeless with a purpose becomes purposive without a purpose.** The final purposiveness contained in the concept is just a form of perception of an act that is not wholly purposive (despite the presence of the element of purposiveness that is the element of mechanical art and which in turn does not occur in nature).

Beyond Truth and Beauty

This second shift rightly seems problematic. After all, was not a reflective judgment of beauty supposed to take place without the concept of the object of judgment? Would aesthetic reflective judgment ultimately have to make use of concepts? And not just in the paradoxical sense of the antinomy of beauty, according to which it is both based and not based on a concept?

Regarding the beauty of art and history, the antinomy of beauty may be softened to allow concepts to play a role in judgment. Since genius does not know what one is doing and is incapable of demonstrating, the power of judgment can only **create** these concepts afterward.[129] Arendt herself suggests such a possibility, stating that a reflective judgment (unlike a determinant judgment) "brings to a concept."[130] Makkreel notes that "most aesthetic judgments are at least in part conceptual," and that they may also "suggest new concepts."[131] These concepts are not determined; they are only orientational and constitute a proposal of how one could perceive objects. Although they cannot determine the next judgments, they can serve as examples.

In Kantian terms, the power of judgment does not refer to objects. Nevertheless, it has an indirect cognitive significance through affecting the intellect. Imagination that acts independently of concepts furnishes the intellect with "extensive undeveloped material for the understanding, of which the latter took no regard in its concept."[132] And let one bear in mind what the term "cognitive" means in this context—a fully cognitive judgment would be universally compelling. For instance, Arendt writes:

> If one says, "The sky is blue", or "Two and two are four", one is not "judging"; one is saying what is, compelled by the evidence either of one's senses, or one's mind.[133]

It is impossible to force anyone to agree with one's judgments—one can only "woo or court" this agreement. Aesthetic judgments are not cognitive in the sense that they add something to the knowledge of empirical facts. Their task is not to "schematize" but to "systematize" experience. However, this also means that even if they are not directly cognitive, they refer to cognition.[134]

In Arendt's nomenclature, reflective aesthetic judgment would have the status of opinion. It would not be a purely subjective opinion, but one in which intersubjectivity is inherent from the outset. Arendt notes that one arrives at an opinion by considering a given issue from various viewpoints represented in the mind.[135] Judgment is indeed supposed to be general, even if not universal. The cognitive content of historical judgment is aesthetic.[136] Although it does not involve a statement of fact, it is not a purely aesthetic play of imagination and intellect. One should not stick to a strict dichotomy of truth and beauty. It is debatable whether Kant himself was able to retain it.[137] Arendt's charitable interpretation shows the potential of the third *Critique* as fundamentally harmonious with the Gadamerian idea of the presence of truth in the experience of art.[138]

Consequently, intellect at the service of imagination is not irrelevant. It is simply no longer bound by determinate concepts. The power of judgment can produce new "schemata" and new concepts. The subordination of genius to taste in § 50 of the *Critique of Judgment* also points toward the role of the intellect (or understanding—*Verstand*) as the power of concepts:

> For all the richness of the former produces, in its lawless freedom, nothing but nonsense; the power of judgment, however, is the faculty for bringing it in line with the understanding. Thus if anything must be sacrificed in the conflict of the two properties in one product, it must rather be on the side of genius: and the power of judgment ... **will sooner permit damage to the freedom and richness of the imagination than to the understanding.**[139]

Seen in temporal terms, this subordination implies that the prospective attitude of genius (who cannot create their products according to a plan) is ultimately less relevant than the retrospective glance of judgment. The latter gives its verdicts with the benefit of hindsight, which considers the unintended consequences, and not just aesthetic ideas. The power of judgment beholds and understands more than the genius. It is thus able to develop a new concept, through which the product of genius will seem purposive (as based upon a concept) without a purpose (for this purpose is not the basis for the existence of the object, but only a form of its perception imposed by the power of judgment). Even if Kant claims that genius embodies taste as the element adjusting the free play of imagination and the intellect, this adjustment is only possible *post factum*, so that **a genius becomes something of a historian of his own art.**

Arendt thus radicalizes the Kantian aestheticization of aesthetics by moving it to the domain of history, which, in her view, has the nature of art. She might thus present a "misleading picture of Kant's aesthetics," her view being "partial and one sided," as Ronald Beiner argued, but such is her creative understanding that should be taken for granted.[140] The function of the temporal distance between actor and spectator is basically productive, becoming a condition of the possibility of exposing the meaning of past actions.[141] Not unlike in Gadamer's hermeneutics, where art illustrates the effective-historical character of understanding, what is at stake in Arendt's historical judgment is not the resemblance of representation (the concept that results from the judgment) to what it represents (the aesthetic idea or the past action). In the study of history, new concepts are constantly created. A historian does not remain at the level of purposelessness with a purpose (beautiful art/action seen as nature), and instead tries to view this art/action-nature as art once again (this time as a mechanical art involving purposive action). Political history is like beautiful art. It comprises particular actions that are purposeless with a purpose. Retrospectively, however, they appear as purposive, even if one is aware that this is solely a subjective formal purposiveness, and thus a form of historical perception.

The next chapter will return to this issue in the context of a historical narrative and relate such an understanding of retrospective purposiveness to Arendt's conceptions of a real and fictional story. To complement the subject of purposiveness, meanwhile, this chapter closes with the reconstruction of Arendt's view of teleological judgment.

The Perils of Teleology

Arendt does not actually raise the issue of purposiveness in *Lectures*, even though it is no less than fundamental. This is all the more surprising given her previous reflections on storytelling and the function of historical writing. Indeed, purposiveness, or the lack thereof, is one of the basic concepts (albeit not necessarily words) of *The Human Condition*. One should keep this broad context of Arendt's oeuvre in mind here when transgressing her reflections on Kant. The argument below does not concern what Arendt does in her interpretation but rather what she leaves out. Specifically, and crucially, Arendt does not transform the transcendental concept of the purposiveness of nature into the transcendental concept of the purposiveness of history.

Purposiveness in general is the transcendental principle *a priori* of the reflective faculty of judgment. A purpose, if defined in accordance with § 10 of the third *Critique*, that is, as the object of the concept that constitutes its cause, is objective and material. Subjective formal purposiveness as pertaining to the reflection on the purposeless objects of nature was also discussed in detail. These are the two fundamental, albeit not exclusive, notions of purposiveness in Kant.[142]

In the second part of the third *Critique*, Kant also introduces the concept of a natural purpose (*Naturzweck*), namely internal objective material purposiveness. This purposiveness characterizes living organisms that are both the effect and the cause of themselves. Even if objective (meaning not just purposive for the cognitive faculties), this purposiveness is merely regulative (and not constitutive) for cognition. This basically means that it is not knowledge.[143]

There is also a more relevant concept of external purposiveness (*Zweck der Natur*—the purpose of nature), which refers to the whole of nature in all its diversity and is expressed by teleological judgment. Such judgment assumes the unity of the particular causal laws of nature obtained in cognition and considers them as a purposive whole—the system of nature. This purposiveness belongs neither to the concepts of nature nor to the concepts of freedom—it is a concept of the faculty of judgment, constitutive to the pleasure that in this case stems from heterogeneous laws combined into a single whole.[144]

Despite firmly separating the two parts of the third *Critique*, Arendt notices that both concern the judgment of the particular. Why is she then not interested in how the particular is embedded in purposive relations? This may come as a surprise given that Kant speaks solely of purposiveness in a regulative and reflective sense. The purposiveness in the second part of the third *Critique* is reflective since one does not have a concept of the object under which to subsume it. The use of purposiveness by Kant is critical and not dogmatic. How then can Arendt's lack of interest in such reflective purposiveness be explained?

In her tenth lecture, Arendt observes that "Kant is convinced that the world without man would be a desert, and a world without man means for him: without spectators."[145] In the same passage, recalling the Kantian spectators of the French Revolution, she discusses the dependence of actors on spectators. However, Arendt's spectators are unlike Kant's, as their divergent attitudes toward teleology prove. In § 86 of the *Critique of Teleological Judgment*, Kant states that "without human beings the whole of creation would be a mere desert, existing in vain and without a final end."[146] And it is this final end or purpose that is Kant's primary concern. Neither cognition nor the feeling of pleasure makes it worth watching the world. "That it be created for enjoyment, or to be intuited, contemplated, and admired ... cannot satisfy reason ... "[147] This final purpose is good will, that is, the faculty of desire ruled by the *a priori* of pure practical reason. In Kant's view, the reflective teleological judgment concerning the ultimate purpose, and considering the world as a whole tied together by final causes (external objective material purposiveness), is ultimately based upon the determinant judgment of the pure practical reason concerning the final purpose.[148] Arendt's private notes on this subject also point to such an understanding of the Kantian teleology.[149]

Might not one simply reject this dependence on determinant judgment and focus exclusively on the regulative aspect of reflective teleological judgment? In the third *Critique*, unlike in *Perpetual Peace*, for instance, purposiveness no longer guarantees progress.[150]

Makkreel, like Arendt, sees the history represented by Kant in the essays *The Idea of a Universal History in a Cosmopolitan Intent* and *Conjectural Beginning of Human History* as subordinated to nature and its teleology. In the *Critique of Teleological Judgment*, Kant employs another, regulative and reflective use of purposiveness. History here is not purposive in an objective sense, and nature is not a providence directing human actions. Culture, meanwhile, as the ultimate purpose of nature, leaves room for the history of freedom that is different from natural history.[151]

Why does Arendt not allow for such a possibility? A likely reason is that her priority is to get rid of all teleological references for these would be incongruent with her political agenda to maintain the future in its authentic and indeterminate state.[152] Therefore, Arendt does not transform the Kantian transcendental concept of purposiveness of nature into the transcendental concept of purposiveness of history, even if only regulative. She maintains that reflective teleological judgment belongs to speculative reason and "has nothing to do with judgments properly speaking."[153] The unifying principle of purposiveness remains only in the aesthetic sense, which means without a purpose.

Nevertheless, even if there is a gap between the retrospective character of the aesthetic reflective judgment and the prospective attitude of the teleological judgment, if only reflective and regulative, teleology remains bound to the former at least in one sense. Ricoeur notes that political and historical judgment does concern the past only but "includes a prospective, even prophetic dimension."[154] This aspect exists in the agreement that the judgment proposes—in its potential communicability that, after all, refers to the future.[155] Following Makkreel, one might even call aesthetic judgment "normative" and "prescriptive."[156] For Kant, the projected agreement concerns the universal play of the cognitive faculties. For Arendt, it only concerns an imagined agreement on the past so that the future remains untouched. There is no direct transition from retrospective judgment to prospective willing that decides upon the course of action.[157] As Arendt insists, judgment is merely contemplative, and it only establishes a ground in which willing no longer needs to be constrained by resentments.

History as a Monumental Work of Art

The ontological ground of Arendt's aestheticization of history is her primary aestheticization of politics, a deeply "un-Kantian, anti-Kantian" move, as George Kateb called it.[158] Politics is not practical and does not serve the realization of purposes. Actions are unpredictable, and their outcomes are, to a great extent, unintended. The past was not created according to the intentions of past actors. Comparably to the free beauty of nature, it does not fit into any determinate concept, and like beautiful art, it does not represent anything concrete. It was indetermined, unpredictable, and infinitely improbable. And it was imperfect in the Kantian sense. If it was perfect, however, in the sense that its manifold was in accordance with a concept, it could not be beautiful.[159] After all, the pleasure that stems from the beautiful is meant to be independent from purposiveness. The past is beautiful only because it was not supposed to have a particular shape. If it had a "stiff regularity," it would be "contrary to taste."[160] The past is more reminiscent of an abstract painting in which the individual parts are related to the whole in an indeterminate way, without the unequivocal mediation of a concept.

The virtue for historians is that the past does not constrain their freedom of imagination, which would otherwise need to adapt to specific concepts. Unifying concepts do appear in historical narratives, but they are the products of reflective aesthetic judgment. As such, they represent the past as purposive only in a subjective and purely formal sense.

Drawing the ultimate conclusions from Arendt's interpretation, the past appears as a monumental work of art. The meaning of this work changes with ongoing events and the unpredictable consequences of past decisions. The past that is an object of historical judgment does not exist autonomously and in itself—it is dependent on the changing views of spectators and the unfolding temporal dynamics of unintended consequences of past actions. From a historical perspective, particular past events may appear as parts of greater sets, jointly creating the undetermined and merely imagined aesthetic wholes, but these are purposive only in formal and not material terms. No teleological wholes and no final purpose of history exist. The present is the past's contingent, unpredictable, and infinitely improbable outcome that exceeds the purposes established by past political actors. And yet, in a reflective historical judgment, the present is subjectively considered as the purpose of the past. Moreover, from the point of view of the present, the past seems necessary, even if one is simultaneously aware that it was merely not impossible. The subjective and aesthetic purposiveness of the imagined past cannot be projected into the future, except for the projection of the agreement of the company that one chooses, one's *Denkkolektiv* if you like, concerning one's preferred historical judgment of that past.

9

Redemption of Contingency

*Who says what is—*legein ta eonta—*always tells a story, and in this story the particular facts lose their contingency and acquire some humanly comprehensible meaning.*

Hannah Arendt, *Truth and Politics*

The Violence of Representation: A Fictional Story

The question remains of how judgment—the faculty for dealing with the past—relates to storytelling, how storytelling relates to the past, and what distinguishes Arendt's fragmented narrative from other forms of historical writing in this respect. Is a faithful narrative representation of the past that was lost after the totalitarian break in historical continuity possible and if so, under what conditions?

This chapter begins by placing storytelling within the structure of *vita activa* and re-interpreting it as a type of reification. Unfortunately, Arendt's reflections on narrative are disparate and scattered throughout various essays, almost like particular, discontinuous actions. Moreover, they mostly concern stories in the primal sense ("ontological" if you like) that precede proper historical narratives. Such primal storytelling is a condition of possibility of any professional historical writing, but only fragmented historiography is supposed to realize its radical postulates.

To break with the cyclical movement of the process of life, *animal laborans* needs the help of *homo faber*. To break the infinite chain of utility, *homo faber* needs the help of *zoon politikon*. And to give durability to his fleeting words and deeds, *zoon politikon*, in turn, seeks support from *homo faber*. Since frail and fleeting action lasts only a blink of an eye and disappears as quickly as it appears, acting and speaking man needs the help of *homo faber* in his highest capacity, that is, the help of the artist, of poets and historiographers.[1]

Arendt maintains that by making action immortal, fabrication attains its most profound meaning and transcends the banal sense of reification.

The works of historiography are unlike other products of *homo faber*. The significance of average fabrication products lies in their utility and resultant exchange value. The work of historians, however, lies outside of the realm of utility—it is "useless." Furthermore, it functions outside of the exchange market—it is "unique" and incommensurable with other goods. For a work of art in general, Arendt says in *The Human Condition*, the reification "is more than mere transformation; it is a transfiguration, a veritable metamorphosis."[2] Owing to its durability of a "higher order," it is the most "worldly"—it represents durability and immortality.[3] Finally, in the case of the reification of past actions, works of art, "by transformation and condensation, show some extraordinary event in its **full significance**."[4] Before having a look at how reification extracts such full significance from the past, the following paragraphs concentrate on an issue addressed quite explicitly, even if poetically by Arendt, which are crucial for the further argument—the loss of the real of the past.

When reified, fleeting words become a "dead letter"—their "living spirit" is lost.[5] This is the "price" that they "must pay" for their survival, says Arendt.[6] Nevertheless, the living spirit can be pulled out of the deadness of materialization by contact "with a life willing to resurrect it," that is an action reviving the past in the present. This present revival is equally fleeting, and the "resurrection of the dead shares with all living things that it, too, will die again."[7] The stories revealing who somebody is—the sequences of discontinuous actions mediated by the web of relationships—"may be recorded in documents and monuments, they may be visible in use objects or art works, they may be told and retold and worked into all kinds of material." However, stories reified and told are of an **"altogether different nature"** than the lived stories from the past.[8] The who is intangible in language and can only be described as the what. The "living essence" of a person can only "show" or "manifest" itself in a fleeting, extended moment of the present.[9]

Reification actually occurs on two levels. There is literal reification in a text or other type of material, as discussed above. There is also metaphorical reification that concerns the representation of a lived story. In *The Human Condition*, Arendt introduces an essential distinction between a real and a fictional story. This corresponds to the distinction between action and work and reflects the relationship between the past and its representation. Their juxtaposition enables the development of a context necessary for the immanent critique of Arendt's narrative theory.

A fictional story, unlike a real story, is made—there is a subject responsible for its course. Paragraph 25 of *The Human Condition* is crucial, stating:

> The fictional story reveals a maker just as every work of art clearly indicates that it was made by somebody; this does not belong to the character of the story itself but only to the mode in which it came into existence. The difference between the real and fictional story is precisely that the latter was "made up" and the former was not made at all.[10]

Revealing the maker of the real story (alternatively: life story) does not belong to the character of the story itself (the resultant of actions and the web of relationships), but **to the mode in which it came into being**. Although the subject of the story—its author or a ruling principle—is fictional, the story itself is not. People "make up" and invent stories by introducing their makers—authors, such as individuals or personified abstractions (states, social groups, or markets, etc.)—which do not belong to the real story.[11]

Arendt often compares historical writing to literary fiction, both of which are symbolized by the political function of the poet. This comparison is not about the fictional nature of historical writing but the realistic nature of literary fiction. The only fictional element of a story in this view is how it appears as a product explainable by its authorship. Analogously to work, a fictional story manifests a model—a principle or set of principles explaining how a given story emerged. Arendt implies that one may cognize a life story only by encapsulating it in the form of a product. And this de facto involves introducing a fictional element to an infinitely improbable past reality.

In this broad take on historical representation, Arendt does not question purposiveness, which is genuine as long as it belongs to the experience of *homo faber*, who indeed makes his products. Arendt also by no means questions fiction as an instrument for dealing with the contingency of past events. She only draws attention to the inevitable reductionism of such an approach and the peril of the ideological consequences implied in the representation of history as a product—"implications of violence inherent in all interpretations of the realm of human affairs as a sphere of making."[12] Why violence? Because without violence, one cannot fabricate the future analogously to the narratively "fabricated" past. The belief in fabrication, and in the extreme, historical determinism, is fundamentally totalitarian. This has been exemplified by such elements of the totalitarian worldview as the Russian deification of contingency, the Hassidic belief in divine providence, the Western belief in the laws of bureaucracy, and ultimately totalitarian ideologies themselves—the secularized speculative narratives of earthly salvation.

Given the scarcity of Arendt's direct reflections on the topic of the reifying function of narrative, the following analysis follows her suggestion on the structural correspondence between fabrication and the fictional story and extrapolate the former to the narrative level. By interpreting historical writing as work, Arendt's critical philosophy of modernity may be approached from a new angle. The "innermost belief" of modernity is, after all, as Arendt puts it in *The Human Condition*, and one that she methodically and consistently disputes, the conviction that **history is made**.[13]

Modernity is embodied by *homo faber*. It is science that produces its outcomes. It is an illusion of progress. It is the loneliness of the makers. And ultimately—although not in terms of a simple effect—it is totalitarianism. A conceptual opposition of action and work and their associated notions produce the following schema (see Table 2).

Does this set of antinomies apply to every historical writing and thus represent the opposition of past reality and narratives about it? Only to a certain degree it appears. It undoubtedly refers to the speculative philosophy of history, whose

Table 2 Real story versus fictional story

Action	Work
Real story	Fictional story
Past reality	Historical narrative
Actor	Author
Who	What
Revolution	Tradition
Discontinuity	Continuity
Intangibility	Reification
Illumination[14]	Commemoration
Disclosure	Closure
Autotelic	Purposive
Freedom	Sovereignty
Power	Violence

metaphysical elements are, nevertheless, contained in the modern science of history that Arendt wanted to part with. And these metaphysical elements are what Arendt primarily disputes, seeking to use her fragmented historical writing to disentangle herself from their fictional aspects.

Arendt's line of argumentation is that presenting history as a continuous and purposive process, having an author and a direction, characterizes the Western tradition of "substituting" work for action.[15] Arendt sometimes calls this an "escape" from the "inconsistency of the world"—from the unpredictability and discontinuity that define any genuine politics.[16] There is a "remarkable monotony" pervading the entirety of Western tradition in this respect, be it Plato (one of the leading figures held responsible for this situation by Arendt) or modern political philosophies.[17]

The common denominator of the latter, which for Arendt are no different from philosophies of history, is **the concept of rule**. And this boils down to the purposive structure of work and the associated notion of sovereignty—man in the singular, the author and the maker ruling over his predictable purposes. The belief in making politics, in other words ongoing history, goes hand in hand with the belief in the inevitability of violence. The representation of actions in the mode of making mirrors this belief and also involves violence, albeit violence in a cognitive form.

In *Thinking*, Arendt argued that the underlying foundation of this age-old belief is the metaphysical dichotomy of being and appearance. When it comes to causality, the dichotomy implies that every effect (appearance) results from a more fundamental and primal cause (being).

> The belief that a cause should be of a higher rank than the effect (so that an effect can easily be disparaged by being retraced to its cause) may belong to the oldest and most stubborn metaphysical fallacies.[18]

One must avoid drawing hasty conclusions, however. The opposite conviction—that the effect is of a higher rank than the cause—turns out to be another metaphysical fallacy, characteristic of the image of progress. The transition from the principle of causality to that of progress is a critical turning point in Arendt's speculative narrative on modernity,[19] although in neither case is this about the actual causality. There is nothing wrong with causality, nor purposive causality in this respect, which is real in any fabrication act: the maker as the cause is superior to his purposive products. What is true regarding fabrication, however, is not valid in the historical process, with the inglorious exception of totalitarianism.

Arendt calls the real author, the maker of the ongoing historical process, the "great unknown" not in the sense of not being sufficiently well known, but because this process as a whole is infinitely improbable—a contingent resultant of actions and the web of relationships. The great unknown applies equally to the whole of history, to a particular story and to each biography: "nobody is the author or producer of his own life story."[20]

Arendt's own speculative narrative on the speculative narratives of modernity is a history of decline. The end of grand narratives only leads to the disappearance of the *homo faber* ruling type of subject, one capable of achieving his purposes. He is replaced by a new "collective subject"—the process of life itself, a "worldless" consumer society and its global market.[21] The new subject—the "unitedness of many into one"—is no longer sovereign.[22] This change marks the degradation of *homo faber* to *animal laborans* as discussed above. The modern idea of history as fabrication is reduced to the naked process of nature. Humankind becomes a species, and political history comes to an end.

Nevertheless, in thinking, speaking, and writing about the past, the great unknown is necessarily replaced by fictional subjects that play the role of an author—a purposive cause of the happenings. These subjects are "personified concepts," which, as Arendt notes in *Willing*, result from a "veritable orgy of sheer speculation."[23] Their operation is easily noticeable in speculative philosophies of history. A subject can be more concrete—such as a nation or a social class—or more abstract and even metaphysical—such as Schelling's will or Smith's invisible hand of the market. All the grand emancipatory narratives—Christian liberation from sin, the Enlightenment's overcoming of ignorance, the capitalist conquest of poverty, or the Marxist abolition of exploitation—are based on the structure of work, the differences lying in the type of subject and the purpose to be achieved.[24]

The Abyss of Nothingness

The fictional features of a story that Arendt comments on represent two fundamental categories of Western historiography—genesis and change—along with the associated category of purposiveness.[25] In the practical experience of *homo faber*, purposive causality is real. What is pernicious is the generalization of this experience onto the whole of reality, which results in a representation of the past as purposefully constructed, and in extreme cases, as ruled by a single subject. Nevertheless, this generalization is not necessarily harmful when it has a smaller scope concerning particular historical wholes—larger than human actions, but smaller than the historical process.

Arendt critically comments on all "organic metaphors," as she calls them, which present human actions (the real history) "in biological terms."[26] These metaphors justify the evil and violence of history and reduce it to the self-preservation of the species.[27] Such history of the species, the history of *animal laborans*, is at the very least, not genuine. However, when it comes to *homo faber*, Arendt's attitude toward the fictional representation of the past on the model of making is far from unequivocal. As a matter of fact, it defines a crucial tension in her work. The characteristics of fictional stories reconstructed above are far from purely pejorative.

While Arendt distances herself from metaphysics and the principle of authorship, she recognizes the traditional Western reference to genealogy and despite her rather negative attitude, she emphasizes its various benefits. At the end of *Willing*, Arendt ponders the question of action as a beginning for the last time. When was the first beginning of all? The conclusion she reaches is surprising and "frustrating" to herself.

Arendt discusses two founding legends of the West. The Hebrew legend is the biblical history of the exodus and the arrival in the Promised Land. The Roman legend is Virgil's story about the wanderings of Aeneas that end with the foundation of Rome.[28] Both exemplify two types of freedom. First, there is liberation—negative freedom, and second, there is the establishment of freedom—positive freedom, a proper beginning. There is a temporal hiatus between the two—a hiatus now concerning action and not thinking. For Arendt, this hiatus proves that time is not continuous but fragmented. It is interrupted by events, which, regarding causality, are unprecedented and cannot be reduced to any previous series. In a quite affected phrase, Arendt posits that every genuine political action opens an "abyss of freedom," or even an "abyss of nothingness."[29] The beginning is unprecedented, arbitrary, almost mysterious, and crucially, **impossible to explain.**

The traditional way of coping with its arbitrariness is to reinterpret it in terms of continuity. This is achieved by referring to religious transcendence, to natural laws manifested in civil law, or, in the Enlightenment variant of the tradition, to universal reason, no matter how it may be construed. Arendt finds the most puzzling the fact that while looking toward the future, the revolutionaries looked back behind, sharing the surprising conviction that "salvation always comes from the past."[30] Even progress was often viewed as a return to the initial state.[31]

Arendt presents such an understanding of the new as a return or renewal of the old, a retrospective imputation of continuity, as a "device typical of the Occidental tradition."[32] And this device by no means satisfies Arendt's concerns. This is why, at the end of *Willing*, she once again cites St Augustine's concept of *initium* as well as her concept of natality. Both point to the fact that man, the beginning in an ontological sense, can establish further, absolute beginnings. Arendt's passage on the freedom of willing concluding her final book indicates an "impasse" of being "doomed" to be free—the necessity of freedom.[33] The impasse leads to the core of Arendt's fundamental aporia again. Seeking the solution to this impasse, Arendt recalls the power of judgment, which as the faculty of adjudicating between what pleases and displeases, provides a foundation for the absolute and unfettered freedom of willing. Without judgment referring to the past (although no longer based on simple genealogy), the beginning would remain arbitrary, and action would have to hang in the historical void.

Life Is Not a Story

Much earlier and in a different context, Arendt assigned to the story the function of redemption of contingency—the "transformation" of "sheer happenings" and reconciliation with the past.[34] A story establishes continuity and abolishes the arbitrariness of the beginning. As far as it "transcends mere learnedness" (the truth of past facts), this redemption is supposed to represent the most profound sense of historical writing.[35]

Arendt took the motto for the key part of *The Human Condition* devoted to action from Karen Blixen: "All sorrows can be borne if you put them into a story or tell a story about them."[36] In her 1968 essay on Blixen, Arendt cited the same sentence, adding: "The story reveals the meaning of what otherwise would remain an unbearable sequence of sheer happenings."[37] The concept of a story does not appear here in the sense of a life story but as its telling. Arendt repeatedly emphasizes the difference between life and a story. Another critical passage reads as follows:

> Life may contain the "essence" ... recollection, the repetition in imagination may decipher the essence and deliver to you the "elixir"; and eventually you may be privileged to "make" something out of it, to compound the story ... Life is neither essence nor elixir, and if you treat it as such it will only play its tricks on you.[38]

Incidentally, Arendt's own story about Blixen deciphers the essence concerning the very idea of bringing out the essence. Young Blixen, the future writer, was an actor in her life. Only as a mature woman, when she began to write stories about herself, did she become an author. In her first embodiment, despite not being the author of her life story, Blixen tried to embody and bring the story into life—to create her destiny. Arendt comments that Blixed committed

> the sin of making a story come true, of interfering with life according to a preconceived pattern, instead of waiting patiently for a story to emerge.[39]

Only in her second embodiment, when she was in her forties, did Blixen discover that "the chief trap in life is one's own identity."[40] This trap consisted of "taking oneself seriously," meaning ascribing oneself a stable self and attempting to actualize it in life. Identity, Arendt stresses, is the outcome of a spectator's retrospective glance. **Life precedes a story.**[41]

Rahel Varnhagen, the heroine of one of Arendt's much earlier stories, fell into a similar trap:

> To live life as if it were a work of art, to believe that by "cultivation" one can make a work of art of one's own life, was the great error that Rahel shared with her contemporaries; or rather, it was the misconception of the self which was inevitable so long as she wished to understand and express within the categories of her time her sense of life: the resolve to consider life and the history it imposes upon the individual as more important and more serious than her own person.[42]

As Arendt notes when commenting on Blixen's life, "you cannot make life poetic, live it as though it were a work of art."[43] Only in a story does life become such a work of art (a creative and not performative art that life essentially is). It is in a story that all "happenings" become "destiny."[44] The story is an instrument of reconciliation with reality because a narrated past ceases to be radically contingent and improbable. This is why it can "bear the sorrows" stemming from the haphazard nature of existence that every actor suffers in his or her life story.

For example, in her Blixen essay, Arendt states the following:

> It is true that storytelling reveals meaning without committing the error of defining it, that it brings about consent and reconciliation with things as they really are, and that we may even trust it to contain eventually by implication the last word which we expect from the "day of judgment."[45]

Judgment by implication occurs in every story as the last word is never final. And even if the meaning of life is disclosed in a story, this does not imply that life should be lived like a story. The anticipation of destiny was Blixen's sin—she lived her life teleologically. For Arendt, life remains in opposition to a story. One should not treat life as the essence or elixir of self, even if it ultimately forms a life story.

In *The Human Condition,* Arendt says that

> human essence ... the essence of who somebody is—can come into being only when life departs, leaving behind nothing but a story.[46]

In this quote, the notion of a story is, again, equivocal. Life here clearly means an individual, biological existence, while the notion of a story can be either a life story (the past biography as it really was) or a story told about it. In both cases, the whole of life can only be seen from the outside, and thus by the other, as a story.

Meanwhile, before life departs, it can be examined by oneself through an autobiographical story. Arendt shares Blixen's belief that

> without repeating life in imagination you can never be fully alive, "lack of imagination" prevents people from "existing."[47]

Autobiography affirms and reconciles one with the contingent past. One can safely infer from Arendt's scattered reflections that if the intangible who (in accordance with the caveats concerning the fleeting nature of the living spirit) is to become tangible in a story, it must be reified. Biographical storytelling thus involves essentialization and comprises all the elements associated with the category of work—a common denominator of metaphysics, production, and historical writing, except that operating on a personal level. Without such reification, the radically ontologically discontinuous self would not compose a continuous self out of the particular disclosed "whos." No doubt, Arendt justifies essentialization as long as it concerns the personal past and not the future. She does not renounce the unifying power of metaphysics ("fictional story") altogether, even if being aware of the potential risks. As far as storytelling imposing meaning on life is concerned, "the slightest shift of emphasis in the wrong direction will inevitably ruin everything."[48] The whole challenge of storytelling appears as telling the past while avoiding retrospective fatalism and simultaneous predictions of the future. The goal is not to delimit the future's horizon and, unlike Blixen, avoid becoming a slave to one's fate.

Even if declaratively fictional reification is restricted solely to retrospective biographical and autobiographical stories, in her broader, historical storytelling, Arendt employs cognitive instruments that clearly fall within the category of representing the past as being made. Almost paradoxically, in the words of George Kateb, Arendt "admires some of the very same characteristics in stories … that she deplores in ideologies."[49] The narrative universum of *The Origins of Totalitarianism* is not only inhabited by particular actors but also by many authors. These include states and social groups and other kinds of subjects—"personified concepts," to use Arendt's phrase, not participating in the enactment of the real story. *The Human Condition*, on the other hand, features a purely fictional structure of decline describing the history of the West.

Apart from these speculative aspects, to keep the violence associated with a narrative representation to a minimum, Arendt develops an original fragmented method—a way out of the impasses of a dichotomous structure of action and work.

Double-Edged Storytelling

Scholars disagree as to what Arendt's concept of storytelling implies. This is because, this paragraph argues, the inherent ambiguity of storytelling rests on the basic aporia of meaning pervading Arendt's work as a whole. The two functions of storytelling are, first, to provide redemption from contingency, and second, to provide redemption from necessity.[50] Commentators have generally recognized the latter function, in which the fragmented story redeems the illusion of the necessity of the past. There is a tension between these two functions as both types of redemption can turn into opposing forms of oppression.[51] Arendt's principal concern, redemption from contingency, may result in oppression by necessity, while redemption from necessity could similarly lead to oppression by contingency. The first function stems from the fictional aspects of a story, whereas the latter emerges from its real elements. It appears as if both narrative functions were dependent on reciprocal redemption.

The "ontological" foundation of this ambiguity is the double modality of the past, which Arendt explored in *The Life of the Mind*. On the one hand, the past is a contingent future that has passed, and, on the other, it is a necessity for present existence. In other words, the past needs redemption in both its contingent and its necessary modalities. This chapter already showed that as far as it refers to biography, redemption from past contingency is ontologically primary, while in the case of the illusion of a coherent life story, exemplified by Varnhagen and Blixen, redemption from necessity is more relevant.

Among those who noted the ambiguous status of Arendt's storytelling is Seyla Benhabib, who focused on the tension between storytelling, understood as Arendt's fragmented historical method inspired by Walter Benjamin, and the legacy of German philosophy preserved in Arendt's work through the structure of *Verfallgeschichte*. Benhabib was primarily interested in the fragmented approach, which she saw as epistemologically superior, even if the tension between the two remained unresolved. The function of storytelling, in this view, is anti-explanatory—it is the redemption from necessity through a break with chronology and historical continuity.[52]

Olivia Guaraldo offered a parallel view, also employing the notion of redemption. Storytelling guarantees redemption from continuity and progress and offers salvation from the fictional unity of history. Mark Redhead, meanwhile, emphasized that Arendt develops her notion of storytelling in contrast to modern forms of historical writing in which "particular events derive their individual meanings from a larger narrative."[53] Similarly, Annette Vowinckel saw the function of Arendt's storytelling as breaking with causality and revealing the general through the particular—in short, as redemption from necessity.[54] Ronald Beiner took a similar stand in claiming that historical judgment in the narrative form guarantees the "redemption" of action by enabling one to "experience a sense of positive pleasure in the contingency of the particular."[55] This is also redemption from fatalism and historical necessity.

Undoubtedly, the objective of Arendt's storytelling was to avoid the "retrospective illusion of fatality" in representing the past, to use Raymond Aron's expression.[56] Cato's maxim *victrix causa diis placuit, sed victa Catoni*—the victorious cause pleases the gods, but the defeated one pleases Cato—is, Arendt claims, the "political principle implied in the enterprise of reclamation" of the past after the break in tradition.[57] While History favors the victors, historians should favor the defeated. They should rescue from the past what is exceptional and extraordinary, what goes beyond the chain of standard and victorious accounts. By turning against the modern notions of history, they should liberate the present from continuity—a typical meta-interpretative instrument of the Occidental tradition.

Previous paragraphs showed that this function notwithstanding, storytelling was meant to perform another and more basic role. Arendt pointed out that the form of a story may coax out coherence and essence, which would otherwise be absent in the life story. Such a unification of life is ontologically primary, whereas the function of redemption from necessity discussed above is supposed to alleviate this former's potentially oppressive side-effects. In Arendt's nomenclature, a fictional story forces a straitjacket of fabrication on historical reality, thus creating a principal risk of transforming historiography into a philosophy of politics.[58] A fictional coherence is imposed upon the past first and foremost through an unnatural closure—a counterpart to the end of the finite process of fabrication. As Hayden White put it much later, teleological implications arise because of unnatural narrative endings, which present the historical world as finished.[59] Despite this risk, leaving past reality in its original and contingent state is equally dangerous as both extremities are paralyzing for action. The principal risk is where the tension between the two functions of storytelling lies.

Aporiae of Meaning

The discrepancy between the two functions of storytelling is founded on two concepts of meaning. It was observed earlier that the meaning of action lies in its performance and not in its ungraspable motives or effects. Arendt expressed that feature of action with the notion of **greatness**. She also spoke of the **innermost meaning** or **specific meaning** of each deed, one fulfilled in the performative disclosure of the who.[60] Seen from this angle, meaning rests neither with the intentions of the performer nor with the effects of the performance—"the innermost meaning ... must remain untouched by any eventual outcome."[61]

Nevertheless, when viewed from a historical perspective, an action, the meaning of which was to remain unchanged by its effects, needs to be deprived of contingency and provided with a new meaning. The **full meaning** of a life story may be given only by a backward-looking historian:

> Action reveals itself fully only to the storyteller, that is, to the backward glance of the historian, who indeed always knows better what it was all about than the participants. All accounts told by the actors themselves, though they may in rare cases give an entirely trustworthy statement of intentions, aims, and motives, become mere useful source material in the historian's hands and can never match his story in significance and truthfulness. What the storyteller narrates must necessarily be hidden from the actor himself, at least as long as he is in the act or caught in its consequences, because to him the meaningfulness of his act is not in the story that follows. Even though stories are the inevitable results of action, it is not the actor but the storyteller who perceives and "makes" the story.[62]

The above quotation from *The Human Condition* exemplifies most clearly that a life story is not equivalent to a story "made" by the historian. The latter may refer to a single biography or any other story that considers the unforeseen effects of past actions. As Arendt remarks a moment later, the meaning of the whole is hidden from the performer and is revealed only with a backward glance.[63]

In her later works, Arendt introduces the concept of the spectator, who stands outside events, which is a condition of historical judgment and understanding. Strictly speaking, the spectator perceives "the meaning of the whole"—the sense of action embedded in an imagined whole.[64] Due to the constant movement of history, which renders it unavailable in its totality, this meaning is never final. Nevertheless, as Arendt put it in *Thinking*, "the spectator and not the actor holds the clue to the meaning of human affairs."[65]

Since an unprecedented deed breaks historical continuity, meaning in itself relates to redemption from necessity. Historical meaning, on the other hand, imposes retrospective continuity (purposiveness without a purpose) and thus relates to redemption from contingency. Arendt's contradictory use of the concepts of **essence** and **melancholy** further exemplifies the tension between the opposing functions of storytelling, thus leading to the very core of the fundamental aporia.

On the one hand, Arendt speaks of "the living essence of a person," which is ungraspable and emerges through particular actions. On the other, she says that "the human essence" may be seen from the perspective of the end of life only, just like the life story as a whole.[66] Both types of meaning and both types of essence may be perceived only from the outside, in other words, by the spectators, where the distance distinguishing political from historical spectators is merely temporal.

Further on, in *Lectures on Kant's Political Philosophy*, Arendt notes that Kant deemed the idea of progress a "rather melancholy notion."[67] Additionally, Arendt cites Kant's opinion on progress in *On Violence*, underlining its "melancholy side effects."[68] She invokes a passage from *The End of All Things*, where Kant explicitly states that:

> The representation of an infinite progression toward the final end is nevertheless at the same time a prospect on an infinite series of ills which ... do not allow for the possibility of contentment.[69]

It is worth noting that neither in "The End of All Things" nor in "Idea for a Universal History from a Cosmopolitan Perspective," the essays by Kant to which Arendt refers, does the notion of melancholy *ad litteram* appear. Arendt employs the term to underscore the negative symptoms of progress when understood as necessary—closing the future horizon, inhibiting novelty, and thus paralyzing action. In a similar vein, Arendt refers to the concept of melancholy when critically commenting upon Nietzsche's attitude toward willing:

> Expectation, the mood with which the will affects the soul, contains within itself the melancholy of an and-this-too-*will-have-been*, the foreseeing of the future's past, which reasserts the Past as the dominant tense of Time.[70]

The link between the melancholy of progress and the melancholy of willing lies in the devouring of every present in favor of the future *ad infinitum*, and thus in anticipating the future's past. The usage of the concept of melancholy in this context makes sense precisely because in melancholy the sense of temporality is heavily distorted in a way that the past dominates lived experience. For a melancholic person, as Kristeva put it, "an overinflated, hyperbolic past fills all the dimensions of psychic continuity."[71] The meaning of the particular is lost in the totality of personal history.

Simultaneously, in the same first lecture on Kant's political philosophy, in which Arendt mentions the melancholy of progress, she also discusses the "haphazard, contingent melancholy" of history.[72] In the subsequent lectures, she uses the phrase "melancholy haphazardness" of the worldly affairs. This latter notion repeatedly appears in Arendt's works.[73] Kant's solution to this "deep-rooted melancholy disposition" in Arendt's view was an escape toward the whole. His gateway to a philosophy of history was the idea of the progress of humankind understood in naturalistic terms. Only in this way could history make sense to Kant, Arendt claims.[74] This usage of the term melancholy involves, contrary to the melancholy of progress, a loss of the whole that grants meaning to the particular. The melancholy of progress denotes a reverse situation—a loss of the particular for the sake of the meaning of the whole.

One is confronted once again with the most intrinsic contradiction of Arendt's thinking, and one that leads to its very core. Arendt argues that the impossibility of harmonizing the idea of human dignity and the notion of progress of the human species constitutes the main discrepancy in Kant's philosophy.[75] However, a comparable discrepancy pervades her philosophy of history. It is not the discrepancy between human dignity and progress but the discrepancy between the dignity or meaning of a deed in itself and the meaning that this deed assumes in hindsight. Arendt underlines the necessity of the "redemption from melancholy haphazardness" of political action. Simultaneously, she strives to liberate it from historical totalities, including the melancholy of progress and the melancholy of willing.[76]

One particularly striking exposition of the basic aporia appears in the last lecture on Kant's political philosophy, in which Arendt states that Hegel is right in claiming that the owl of Minerva spreads its wings at dusk. This is supposed to be true "for all stories" but not for the "deed in itself."[77] What does a story, and what does a deed in itself mean here? If the story is that of a life story (the meaning of which is not revealed until it is over) and a deed in itself is a particular action in this very story, then the meaning of this deed is supposed to, on the one hand, depend on the entirety of this life story and be visible only after it comes to an end, and on the other, to be entirely independent of such a whole. Alternatively, suppose this life story functions in a manner comparable to a deed in itself and thus has its inner meaning. In that case, the concept of a story in the above quotation may denote historical wholes (stories in the plural), while a deed in itself may well be a particular life story. This is how Arendt perceives a story in the Greek understanding, where it is always a "particular story."[78] Elsewhere, Arendt notes that when life ends, a life story becomes "an entity in itself."[79] Thus, a particular story (a story as an entity in itself) seems to be synonymous with a single act, which contains its full meaning, irrespective of any future consequences—a particular biography as it was lived and not narrated. Upon such reading, the owl of Minerva would grant meaning to stories in the plural, the effects and entanglement of which would change their inner sense. The perspective would depart from a single act and shift toward historical wholes. After all, what would a single act be if a particular life story also comprised a whole in itself? The tension in question would remain intact and become a tension between a single story containing all its meaning and larger stories in the plural, the sense of which, dependent on the unintended consequences perceived by the spectators of history, would never be final. In either case, the aporia of the two opposing functions of storytelling is not unraveled. Instead, its constitutive tension is emphasized.

Arendt's Narrative Turn

The next chapter returns to the theme of the constitutive tension. Meanwhile, the final section of the present chapter explores the epistemic discontinuity between historical reality and the story being told about it, which is a noteworthy feature of Arendt's narrative theory.

What connects both types of meaning representing the basic aporia is that both depend upon an understanding by the other—the spectator. Arendt calls understanding the "other side of action"—it allows political actors to situate themselves in historical time, reconcile with what had happened, and work out a context for further actions.[80] The result of understanding, Arendt says in *Understanding and Politics*, is "reconciliation" with the reality of actions—with "what we do and what we suffer."[81]

The desire to understand stems from willing, which cannot cancel the consequences of its past acts. To avoid resentment, willing seeks help from the intellect, which can explain the past by portraying it in the guise of necessity. From the perspective of thinking, the past seems necessary as it is a condition of every actual act of thinking, which in turn is a condition of the possibility of telling a story. The initial condition of the possibility of storytelling is the temporal extension of the mind, the Augustinian *distentio animi*, which enables the disparate elements of the past to be grasped in the form of a "coherent and continuous story."[82]

> Without an a priori assumption of some unilinear sequence of events having been caused necessarily and not contingently, no explanation of any coherence would be possible. The obvious, even the only possible way to tell a story is to eliminate from the real happenings the "accidental" elements.

The above quote from *Willing* explicitly presents the view that narrative organization abolishes contingency. As shown earlier, the ontologically primal function of storytelling is redemption from the contingency of past reality, which is creating continuity from discontinuous actions. According to Arendt, without an assumption of necessity, the story would lack any coherence.[83]

Would such an explanatory, coherent story—presented in *Willing* as the product of the intellect—not lead to oppression by necessity? Was it not what the pseudo-scientific philosophy of history and even totalitarianism was all about? Finally, was it not the reason why Arendt was ultimately more interested in the power of judgment than in the explanatory powers of the intellect? This is certainly so.

Arendt is apparently willing, and not for the first time, to sacrifice ambiguous meaning in itself, the infinitely improbable contingency of the past, for the imposed coherence of historical meaning. In *Willing*, she presents the idea that "no action ever attains its intended goal" as "the greatest riddle" of historical reality.[84] She does not conclude, however, that the meaning of action lies solely in itself, detached from intentions and outcomes. On the contrary, Arendt deduces that only a story presented "by the wisdom of hindsight" endows action with meaning.

This inconsequence is not a matter of supposedly "early" and "late" Arendt. Also in *The Human Condition*, invoking Aristotle's *Poetics*, Arendt distinguishes the disclosure of the "who" (taking place through particular actions) from the whole of the story, which has its own plot, regardless of these actions.[85] In line with the previous arguments presented in this book, Arendt makes a narrative turn, and substantially sooner than others.[86]

Arendt's claim from *Willing* that "not the record of past events but only the story makes sense" reads almost like Louis Mink's later narrativist maxim "stories are not lived, but told."[87] Considering the discontinuity between the world of experience and narrative, between life and a story, Arendt's theory of storytelling appears as a kind of discontinuity theory. Arendt is an anti-realist narrativist.[88]

Characteristic of a narrative turn is the conviction that the narrative form of understanding brings about specific *a priori* content. In his classic analysis of the similarity of historical writing and literary fiction, one of the most influential historical narrativists, Hayden White, treated both as discursive forms of the same kind—verbal artifacts representing reality.[89] As Herman Paul showed, White's premises were essentially existentialist—White claimed that historical reality lacks any intrinsic meaning and that humans are free to grant it with meaning.[90] Arendt's premises were, incidentally, quite similar to White's. For Arendt, the reality of everyday life is infinitely improbable, chaotic and unordered. Only telling a story about it combines its individual parts and endows them with a narrative coherence and essence that the experienced reality lacks.[91]

At first sight, Arendt seems epistemologically rather conservative—she never denies the truth of historical facts and considers them to be untouchable "brutally elementary data." Importantly for this discussion, however, is that despite assuming the existence of facts to be independent from interpretations, in *Truth and Politics* Arendt acknowledges that one needs a "principle of choice" to observe them and a "story" to grant them meaning. As Annette Vowinckel put it, "facts were interesting for Arendt only as a raw material for the interpretations of the past, which contained the actual meaning."[92] Although initially possessing an "annoying contingency" (since they might have been different from what they are), with time, historical facts become necessary, durable, and irremovable. They "stubbornly are," as Arendt puts it, as if they did not belong to the realm of human affairs but a higher order of things. However, there are no good reasons why they should be what they are, Arendt sustains. It is only through the retrospective "optical illusion" of modern philosophies of history that their original contingent character is distorted. The authentic contingency of facts "ultimately defies all attempts at conclusive explanation."[93]

The apolitical, factual past, however, cannot survive the encounter with the political world. By treating the truth of facts as opinion, power destroys and discredits it. A "factual statement … acquires political implications only by being put in an interpretative context."⁹⁴ A story is already political. As Arendt puts it in *Truth and Politics*:

> Reality is different from, and more than, the totality of facts and events, which, anyhow, is unascertainable. Who says what is—*legei ta eonta*—always tells a story, and in this story the particular facts lose their contingency and acquire some humanly comprehensible meaning.⁹⁵

Storytelling involves abandoning "pure" facts and entering political interpretation. And further on:

> To the extent that the teller of the factual truth is also a storyteller, he brings about that "reconciliation with reality," which Hegel … understood as the ultimate goal of all philosophical thought.⁹⁶

The aim of storytelling is neither legitimization nor radical criticism.⁹⁷ It is instead intended to reconcile one with historical reality. The political function of historical writing is to bring about a catharsis that enables acting in the present. It is not to master the past through an accurate and precise description but to accept everything that has happened. If one wishes to reconcile with the pain of reality, the past must be "resuffered." As a result of this experience, "the network of individual acts is transformed into an event, a significant whole."⁹⁸ The particular suffering or sorrows addressed by Blixen's quotation are then united into a whole, which allows the burden of the suffering to disappear. In this context, Arendt uses the example of a significant event of the First World War.

> The form for this is lament, which arises out of all recollection … The tragic impact of this repetition in lamentation affects one of the key elements of all action; **it establishes its meaning and that permanent significance which then enters into history**.⁹⁹

The source of historical significance is lamentation and recollection. Significance stems from the post-factum story, and not from the past life:

> No philosophy, no analysis, no aphorism, be it ever so profound, can compare in intensity and richness of meaning with a properly narrated story.¹⁰⁰

The story's specific plot is like *homo faber's* model—it rules over its course from behind, as it were, defining the whole process of its "fabrication," from the beginning to the end. Furthermore, as with *homo faber's* model, the end is already assumed and predicted in the beginning. A story in Arendt's sense brings about what Louis Mink described as a configurational understanding—comprehending events that could not be experienced as a whole. In a narrated story, Mink observed, the beginning and end are connected so that the beginning is a "promise" of the end.[101] It does not imply that *homo faber* reasons in a narrative fashion, but only that by grasping the model of past reality does one perceive the meaning of the whole story in configurational terms. One transforms its original temporal structure of succession and views it as if it was promised and made.

For Arendt, life itself has no narrative structure—beginnings, middles, or ends. The real stories that are the unintended consequences of action are unpredictable and open. Only fictional stories are finite, predictable, and closed. Since the significance of events may only be discerned in hindsight, historiography encounters a fundamental problem, as Arendt notes in her *Denktagebuch* in April 1953:

> Hence the paradox that history is a story that contains many beginnings, but no end, and therefore actually cannot be narrated … Thus every event presents itself historically as an end of a certain, so far hidden, beginning. In order to again reveal itself as a beginning, it requires a new event.[102]

What does it mean that history cannot be narrated? Or—to be more precise—that it cannot be conclusively narrated until it reaches its end?

Even a complete and exhaustive description of all historical facts would be merely a chronicle. And even if it was an ideal chronicle—to use Arthur Danto's term—it would, sooner or later, be no longer valid. A proper ideal chronicle would have to be written from the perspective of the final end, taking into account all possible outcomes of past actions. This is because, as Danto showed, later events affect the very description of their predecessors.[103] However, in the infinite historical process, the perspective of the final end is continuously escaping. The unintended consequences of past actions not only change their meaning but also, as was the case with the elements of totalitarianism, enable them to appear. History cannot be conclusively narrated since it must always be narrated anew.

In Arendt's reflections on storytelling, the *a priori* content of a story manifests itself in the redemption of contingency—it is the continuity imposed upon the broken thread of "real" historical time. Paradoxically, Arendt maintains:

> The need for explanation is nowhere stronger than in the presence of an unconnected new event breaking into the continuum, the sequence of chronological time.[104]

In other words, what most cries for a story is what is most unusual and improbable. Arendt is a narrativist because, just like later narrativists, she presents a story form as, to use Ankersmit's phrase, a transcendental condition of possibility of historical understanding in general, regardless of its specific type.[105] This is the condition of the possibility of the formation of historical meaning.[106] And Arendt, no doubt, is radical in this respect. The story's historicizing power penetrates so deeply into the fabric of reality that it touches the very narrating subject. It is the political animal, devoid of essence or elixir, that is in dire need of putting all the contingent puzzles of the self together. What maintains such a redemption of contingency and establishes a relatively stable foothold in the continually changing, contingent reality is *homo faber*'s creative power of fictional representation.

Totalitarianism: Purposive without a Purpose

How does this interpretation of storytelling correspond to the power of judgment—the faculty for dealing with the past? Surely, as George Kateb put it, "historians, novelists, and poets may show politicized aesthetic judgment … in their stories or accounts."[107] Or, as Lesie Thiele argued, "the narrative nature of judgment takes us beyond purely aesthetic criteria while at the same time preserving its crucial element of freedom."[108] Stories are certainly "critical to the enterprise of judgment" as far as they link events into comprehensible wholes.[109] Would Arendt's fragmented narrative share the essential characteristics of aesthetic historical judgment?[110] To address this question, this chapter ends by recalling purposiveness without a purpose—a concept of elementary significance for Kantian reflective aesthetic judgments and, by implication, for Arendt's reconstructed narrative theory.

It was shown earlier that Arendt excludes the objective purposiveness of history, regardless of whether it might concern individual actions, the relationships between them, or history as a whole. Although particular deeds are goal-oriented insofar as they originate in willing, self-disclosure is not an intended outcome. Ontologically speaking, actions are purposeless with a purpose. Historically, however, seen from the spectator's perspective and mediated by reflective aesthetic judgment, they appear as purposive without a purpose. The immanently purposeless relations between particular actions and history as a whole—the monumental example of beautiful art—may appear purposive without a purpose.

With the above point in mind, one may now adopt a new perspective on *The Origins of Totalitarianism*. The fragmented narrative of the first two parts of the book consists of particular stories that concern a wide array of phenomena that are often only loosely connected with anti-Semitism and imperialism, even more so with totalitarianism. As with the objects of beautiful art, they seem to be like nature, in other words, internally purposeless happenings that their participants did not plan. Simultaneously though, for historians viewing them with hindsight, they appear as formally purposive. Their purposiveness is initially manifested at the level of general concepts (such as continental imperialism or the Dreyfus affair) forming specific historic wholes—indeterminate reflective concepts of the power of judgment. Phenomena such as the Dreyfus affair could not be experienced as a whole by historical actors. When they are named—reflectively and indeterminately systematized in a narrative—they have already been historicized.

The particular stories of Arendt's narrative on the origins of totalitarianism compose certain individual narrative substances, to use Ankersmit's term, hidden under the concepts such as the Dreyfus affair. These particular stories are, of course, subsystems of the whole narrative of the book, yet this whole narrative, as was shown earlier in detail, is highly fragmented and incoherent. The concepts representing narrative substances are not theoretical since they refer to particular, historical phenomena—something characteristic of reflective judgments. Although these judgments dispense with the mediation of a concept of what a given thing should be, they can lead to the emergence of new concepts (such as the Dreyfus affair) that combine the scraps of the past into larger wholes. This is why these wholes (defined by the narrative sequences that make up a given story) are reflective and not determined. Although indeterminate, they appear purposive for the spectators.

Arendt's entire fragmented story about totalitarianism is purposive without a purpose. The continuity between the elements of totalitarianism and the particular stories represents no more than Kantian continuation (*Nachfolge*). The precedents accumulate and ultimately lead to a new form of government, but they are only an inspiration, not a cause, of totalitarian actions. Moreover, one can only perceive them as such from the perspective of their unintended consequences. The witnesses of history could not behold the elements of totalitarianism, and these elements cannot be discerned directly in historical sources (which is why David Bell compares them to hidden components of the subconscious).[111] In Arendt's words, the elements are the "subterranean stream" of the history of the nineteenth century, and they come to the surface only in hindsight with the triumph of totalitarianism—the seemingly purposive narrative closure.[112] Totalitarianism is no more and no less than an unprecedented event that throws new light on the whole of history up to its occurrence.[113] On closer inspection, the abnormality and exceptionality of the Holocaust appears as composed of typical elements of modernity, the totalitarian potential of which was yet to be recognized.

Totalitarianism thus marks a closure of the whole of Arendt's extensive story. This seems purposive despite the awareness of the contingency of the historical path that has prepared it. Events comprising narrative judgment are purposively related to its closure only in a subjective and formal sense since in the past reality, the events related to one another only in terms of succession.[114] Meanwhile, in a narrative representation, they appear as purposive and necessary, even though one knows that they were not, and that the purposive connections between them are merely fictional.

A well-known logical fallacy of *post hoc ergo propter hoc*, a confusion of consecution with consequence, relates to this phenomenon.[115] The fallacy exemplifies the explanatory power of narrative, in which events that come later seem to naturally result from previous events, which is also an essential asset of normal (not fragmented) narrative representation. With narrative fragmentation, like Arendt's, the explanatory power dissolves, but the "confusion" remains. It is ultimately thanks to purposiveness without a purpose that redemption from the contingency of the past may take place. The "lawfulness of the contingent is called purposiveness" says Kant[116]—contingency is now replaced with the illusion—but only the illusion—of destiny, which excludes any beliefs in future providence. As a result of the formal character of purposiveness, this redemption gives justice to the past in its real discontinuity and contingency—even though this past is already necessary for contemporary existence. Since the represented wholes are indeterminate, the past can be presented differently each time. It can be reported and narrated in many incommensurable ways.

10

Pieces of the Past

Whoever in the historical sciences honestly believes in causality actually denies the subject matter of his own science.
                                    Hannah Arendt, *Understanding and Politics*

The Irony of *The Origins of Totalitarianism*

The fundamental theoretical problem of Arendt's storytelling was: how can the contingency of the past be redeemed without resulting in projecting the future and thus oppression by the necessity implied in the historical narrative? This final chapter shows that Arendt was ultimately a proto-narrativist and that her fragmented method denied any direct resemblance between the historical narrative and the past. The chapter begins with exploring the links between storytelling and ideology with the help of Hayden White's tropological model. The analysis then proceeds to argue against the claim that Arendt's intention was to show the past as it really was. Finally, using a substitutive theory of representation, it develops a theoretical model of Arendt's fragmented narrative which provides a performative solution to the fundamental aporia.

In one of her first published articles—a 1930 review of *Ideology and Utopia* by Karl Mannheim, an influential German sociologist—Arendt followed the steps of Heidegger's fundamental ontology and accused Mannheim of "relationism"— the reduction of the ontological to the ontic.[1] Arendt insisted that thinking must not always be ideological as Mannheim's total concept of ideology postulated—it need not take the form of ideology or utopia.[2] Arendt's own notion of ideology that was developed later retained the negative Marxist sense of a false consciousness, which can and should be dispensed with, except that its subjects were not classes, but masses. *The Origins of Totalitarianism* was supposed to be non-ideological in this sense. Was it also non-ideological in the broader perspective that Mannheim's notion entails? After all, if ideology denotes a particular system of values professed by a historian as belonging to a particular culture or social group, then every historical narrative is in some sense ideological. As Jerzy Topolski, a Polish historical theorist put it, "no historiography can escape from ideology."[3] Would Arendt's fragmented narrative do?

In his influential *Metahistory* from 1973, Hayden White showed how the so-called tropological prefiguration of the historical research field imprints itself on the three levels of narrative that historians create—plot, formal argument, and ideological implications.[4] White postulated that the last level of ideological implications marks an inalienable ethical element of historical writing. He showed that narrative ideologies are simply convictions that concern social change, its preferred character, direction, and temporal orientation—and he did that by modifying Mannheim's classification from *Ideology and Utopia*.[5]

Looked at from the angle of White's tropological model, the first two parts of *The Origins of Totalitarianism* appear as prefigured in the metatrope of irony. Such prefiguration should lead to the plot of satire and to the argument relying on the contextualization of "synchronic representations of segments or sections of the process, cuts made across the grain of time as it were"[6]—the fragments of the history of antisemitism and imperialism. In most cases, the ideological layer that emerges from this configuration should be liberal. As White notes, however, irony is epistemologically self-critical, which means that these implications can vary. Moreover, the satirical form of narrative (for White represented by Jacob Burckhardt's method of contextualization, *Querschnitt*) is a model of "all putatively anti-ideological conceptions of history," which stand in the most extreme opposition to the speculative philosophies of history.[7] If the trope of irony were to be transformed into a complete vision of the world, it "would appear to be transideological." This is because, White contends, "Irony tends to dissolve all belief in the possibility of positive political action."[8]

Topolski's definition of ideology that no historian can escape invokes Heidegger's primacy of the future—"a dimension of time ... defining ideology."[9] However, Arendt's *The Origins of Totalitarianism* lacks such an implied future orientation and thus avoids the ideological dimension. It was shown earlier how Arendt's political focus on intangible disclosure in the gap in time manifests itself in her radical attitude toward teleology, which should be avoided at all costs. *The Origins of Totalitarianism* is anti-totalitarian because the book contrasts the coherence of the totalitarian world with a fundamentally incoherent and indeterminate "real" past. It is a fragmented and broken narrative. Arendt is ironic because all she projects is a radically open future, something new and yet unspecified, and thus no concrete project. The only quasi-ideological implication of her narrative is the break in historical continuity—a new beginning, an authentic, unpredictable future to come.

Reenacting the Past

In the introduction to *The Origins of Totalitarianism*, Arendt explains that her goal is not "deducing the unprecedented from precedents" and that she wants to preserve "the impact of reality and the shock of experience."[10] Arendt also notices that "comprehension, in short, means the unpremeditated attentive facing up to and resisting of reality—whatever it may be."[11] It seems that, as far as historical meaning is concerned, the notions of the unpremeditated facing up to reality and the shock of experience are clear indications that Arendt's aims are to do justice to the innermost meaning of action, and hence, fight ideology and redeem the necessity of the past.

Given that Arendt is speaking of past experience, how might this be possible? After all, she was explicit about the impossibility of retaining the meaning disclosed in action, not to mention that this action is now long gone. A few years later, in *The Human Condition*, Arendt made it clear that fleeting identity "can be represented and 'reified' only through a kind of repetition, the imitation or *mimesis*."[12] Like those acting in a play, political actors can re-disclose the identity of heroes only by reenacting their actions in the theater of politics.

Apparently, there is a contradiction between Arendt's belief that it is impossible to reify the self while at the same time allowing the possibility of its imitation through performative action. These ambiguities lead to the following question: is the purpose of reenactment an immediate manifestation of the past in the present or is it an imitation that does not involve resemblance? Moreover, even if an imitation were to recreate past action, this imitation would not yet comprise a historical sense of that action but merely its political meaning. After all, reenactment is not yet a story, even if it is performed from the perspective of the end. The key issue in the context of "facing up to reality" is whether Arendt is actually striving to fulfill the classical utopian ideal of historiography and **show the reality** of the past?

The main premise of Arendt's historical enterprise is the break in tradition and the resulting loss of the past. Is she then trying to resurrect this lost past? Is she like a nineteenth-century historian attempting to present what has really happened with the illusion so convincingly that the reader has a sense of participating in a bygone play? Is she like a taxidermist, whose success hinges on creating an illusion of life that has been irrevocably lost?[13]

The notion of repetition or reenactment is confusing. Regardless of other reasons, it immediately brings to mind the Oxford philosopher of history, Robin Collingwood, and his concept of reenactment—the postulated proper task of every historian to reenact the thoughts of historical actors in his own mind.[14] One might surmise that, comparably, Arendt's objective is to reenact the proper history of actions. However, it was shown that Arendt speaks of reifying the lived quality of action as a necessary condition of remembering. In other words, she excludes a representation as a direct making-present again.

Nevertheless, some maintain that Arendt's fragmentary technique was supposed to provide a kind of experience of the past. In this respect, a major influence on Arendt was Walter Benjamin and his fragmentary method, best expressed in the *Arcades Project*.[15] For example, Anabell Herzog argued that both Arendt and Benjamin dealt with fragments of the past that were not to be "narrated" but instead "shown" and "experienced." By recreating or "reenacting" these fragments, the past actions were to become present again. The function of storytelling upon this view is the redemption from necessity. The means to achieve it is breaking up the seemingly progressive movement of history into small fragments of the past.

Arendt's earliest historical work, the biography of Rahel Varnhagen, begun in Germany in the 1930s and intended to be her *Habilitation* (a postdoctorate degree) but not completed at the time, demonstrates this function of showing the past. In the introduction to this "experimental biography,"[16] written more than twenty years after the manuscript's completion, Arendt clarifies her method in the following way:

> It was never my intention to write a book about Rahel; about her personality, which might lend itself to various interpretations according to the psychological standards and categories that the author introduces from outside ... What interested me solely was **to narrate the story of Rahel's life as she herself might have told it.**[17]

Arendt then goes on to explain that her:

> point was not to assume to know more than Rahel herself knew, not to impose upon her a fictional destiny derived from observations presumed to be superior to those she consciously had.[18]

The method thus clearly neglects the spectator's perspective and aims to give justice to the inner meaning of past actions, mostly through Rahel's self-presentation through correspondence.[19] Arendt goes as far as to say that if she was "passing judgments upon Rahel from some higher vantage point," she had failed in her endeavor.[20] Seyla Benhabib thus rightly called Arendt's deep confidence in her claims about Rahel "astonishing."[21] Rahel believed in destiny and wanted to live her life as a story—and Arendt wants to remind the reader that life is not a story. Does this imply representing the past as it really was?

Annabel Herzog argued that the fundamental function of Arendt's storytelling is to illuminate the present rather than commemorate the past.[22] Stories are a "kind of political revelation" that is useful in "dark times" as a means of "illuminating" it. But why should commemoration and illumination be mutually exclusive? Could not the commemoration of the "glorious deeds" of the past serve the purpose of illuminating the dark present? Not within Herzog's interpretative framework, which represents the realist reading of Arendt's narrative theory. Herzog rightly maintains that storytelling is a kind of action, "one of the worldly realms of revelation." This revelation, however, does not concern the person who tells the story, whose task is merely to "expose" its protagonists to public view. It is these protagonists who are revealed and acquire a "phenomenal appearance on paper."[23] The narrator remains transparent, while her story gives a "faithful" account of the actions of the absent actor, who thus undergoes a second revelation.[24] The story performs an unmediated transmission of the past self to the present, just like Collingwood's reenactment performed an unmediated transmission of past thoughts.

Arendt's views are clearly inconsistent. The textual evidence for direct reenactment comes mostly from the early work on Rahel Varnhagen. Some statements from *The Origins of Totalitarianism* and even from *Eichmann in Jerusalem* are also confusing. Not only in her 1968 essay on Blixen discussed in the previous chapter did Arendt perform an apparent *volte face* with regard to her introduction to the biography of Varnhagen, as Eleanor Skoller contends, for the ambiguity persisted throughout her work.[25] An example can be found in the *Eichmann* book where Arendt points to the possibility of a direct relationship between past experience and storytelling, even though for her, as Kai Evers argued, "the proximity to the event and to personal experience poses a threat to storytelling."[26] This is why Herzog could view the purpose of storytelling as experiencing the fragmentary past, and attributed the power of redemption solely to the direct representation of particular "facts" from the past. Herzog is undoubtedly right that Arendt's method resembles Benjamin's "synchronic analyses of connections," yet the conclusions are one-sided. In *The Human Condition* and elsewhere the quasi-Benjaminian idea of preserving "the impact of reality and the shock of experience" from *The Origins of Totalitarianism* is explicitly denied. Arendt does not allow for the possibility of creating a faithful representation of the past.

These contradictions seem like yet another expression of the fundamental aporia. Similarly to Benjamin, Arendt rejected historicism understood as a synonym of historical continuity and pointed to its disruptions.[27] In doing so, she also assumed the point of view of the vanquished and was interested in establishing a redemptive relationship with the past through fragments. However, for Benjamin, the representation of the indeterminate character of every past moment was quasi-mystical. His *Jetztzeit* signified the fusion of past and present that provided redemption. For Arendt, meanwhile, messianic hope was an illusion. Despite the many methodological similarities, such as the focus on discontinuities and particulars, Arendt moved beyond Benjamin's quotations toward fragmented stories. Interpreting these stories in analogy to Benjamin's dialectical images may be misleading.[28] It is true that Arendt's historical work can be seen as an "imaginary museum" of stories that visualize the past, as Annette Vowinckel argued in detail, but ultimately it is a past that is not shown as such but narrated.[29]

Arendt's departure point was the loss of the continuity and coherence of the past. In 1954 she wrote:

> Whoever in the historical sciences honestly believes in causality actually denies the subject matter of his own science. He denies by the same token the very existence of events which, always suddenly and unpredictably, change the whole physiognomy of a given era.[30]

Arendt's method consisted of recollecting the past in narrated fragments, which was supposed to expose the traditional metaphysics of historical science focused on causality. In the introduction to the collection of Benjamin's essays *Illuminations*, Arendt quoted Shakespeare's *The Tempest* to illustrate the postulate of recollecting fragments of the past:

> Full fathom five thy father lies,
> Of his bones are coral made,
> Those are pearls that were his eyes.
> Nothing of him that doth fade
> But doth suffer a sea-change
> Into something rich and strange.[31]

In her essay on Benjamin, Arendt clarified this mysterious-sounding passage and the task of reclaiming corals and pearls. Here, she recalled the figure of the collector (also Benjamin himself, the collector of quotations). Starting from the "close affinity between the break in tradition and the seemingly whimsical figure of the collector who gathers his fragments and scraps from the debris of the past," Arendt posited that in her post-historical age, the collector is not a destroyer of tradition.[32] One does not have to tear out fragments from the past's continuous edifice since history itself has replaced him in this role. One is now left alone in a situation of an irrevocable end, in which one must "discover new ways of dealing with the past."[33] Moreover, since the past authority no longer tells one how to proceed, the collector's role becomes constructive. In the post-metaphysical epoch after rupture dealing with the past moves from being epistemic to being aesthetic and poetic. The past—the father from the Shakespeare quote—has changed its shape. It is no longer what it once was; it crystallized into something rich and strange. It now appears more valuable, as corals and pears, and therefore as beautiful objects.

Performative Storytelling

The previous chapter showed that the primal function of Arendt's storytelling was the redemption of the contingency of an individual past. Before the break in tradition, this redemption could be provided by history alone. Nowadays, however, to use Arendt's own words, "we are standing in the midst of a veritable rubble heap" of truths that before constituted the "pillars" of continuity.[34] We need to reclaim the lost fragments and redeem the past contingency without succumbing to the illusion of necessity. And this goal is no less than anti-scientific. As Koselleck put it, in the past studied by scientific history:

> [T]here appear structures which condition and limit room for maneuver in the future. History thus shows us the boundaries of the possible otherness of our future.[35]

From the point of view of scientific historiography, history is neither fully predictable nor entirely unpredictable—there are structural limits for what can happen in the future. The temporal orientation of Arendt's fragmented storytelling, meanwhile, follows the words of David Rousset, which she used as a maxim for the third part of *Origins* devoted to totalitarianism—"normal men do not know that everything is possible." Consequently, Arendt's narrative implies a maximally opened horizon of expectations. It shows that there are no limits of what can happen in the future.

Considering the epistemological difficulties associated with explanation through storytelling, David Luban came to the "disquieting conclusion" that "political understanding [by which he meant understanding of the political past—MM] is more closely related to political action than to *Wissenschaft* and demands qualities of mind that are political virtues."[36] In Luban's view, the purpose of storytelling is to disclose the meanings of particular actions from the past, confront the real stories of the past, and thus redeem necessity. However, such meaning of real stories cannot be represented directly but only manifested in appearance:

> The story is both the form and the content of explanation ... as it is both the form and the content of human action.[37]

It is the very act of narrating—the narrative action performed here and now—that endows the story with meaning.

Several scholars have noticed this performative dimension of Arendt's storytelling. One of the reviewers of the first German edition of *The Origins of Totalitarianism*, Ursel Hanau, rightly concluded: "It is not only history writing on a grand scale, it is also ... a large-scale attempt to help determine the history that is still in flux"[38] Ágnes Heller observed that "almost all Arendt's books are also acts of political intervention."[39] Seyla Benhabib spoke of the narrative nature of identity: "Who we are at any point is defined by a narrative uniting past and present."[40] Julia Kristeva focused on the particularity of the "who" in the act of telling and noticed that human life is human "as long as it can be represented by a 'narrative.'"[41] George Kateb likely observed that for Arendt "meaning is in the telling."[42] Olivia Guaraldo, meanwhile, maintained that suspending historical continuity in a contingent narrative is a "political gesture."[43] All these examples present Arendt's narrative as a political disclosure. What is the epistemic status of Arendt's storytelling as a narrative representation of the past?

It was showed that Arendt's fragmented historical writing was meant to eliminate the sense of necessity and inevitability from historical development. It was also underlined that it cannot grasp the reality of the past, whether it be through a simple description of facts or some mystical union with the past. Finally, it was noted that storytelling is a form of political action. There are some seemingly compelling arguments favoring the realistic narrativist interpretation of Arendt's storytelling, in which there is a continuity and overlap between life and a story. Not only is a story action, but also action is a story. Julia Kristeva assumes such a position in her book with the telling subtitle *Life Is a Narrative*. Similarly, for Guaraldo, unlike scientific cognition that is suppressive of contingency, storytelling is life itself, and it faithfully represents its complicated paths.⁴⁴ A fragmented story does not impose a fictional closure on reality but repeats the real structure of events. Storytelling is like life—fragmentary, discontinuous, and inconclusive. However, this is only partly true.

Arendt's conception suggests that even if a particular story is narrative action, it still imposes some sort of coherence on the world. The story's essentializing and fictional aspects are crucial since they allow it to play its redemptive role and give meaning to an absurd and meaningless life. The point is rather that this imposition of coherence need not itself be coherent. After all, since a story is an action, it can be told each time anew. Acknowledging the narrative character of action must not lead to the assumption that stories mirror life. Even if particular actions have a narrative structure, they must not be mutually coherent (like a story). Furthermore, even if people continually tell each other stories about the past, they merely become historians of their own lives. There is still a rupture between life and the story.⁴⁵

The stories that Arendt narrates are—just like the past events that they refer to—contingent and unresolved. They respect the contingency of action. Their closure can be different each time a story is told. However, while the contingency of representation is faithful to the contingency of the past, the past no longer appears as radically contingent. A story is not a pure reenactment. It is obviously impossible to present the past reality in an unmediated and faithful way. Guaraldo is well aware of this, as well as of the paradoxes that result:

> To narrate stories, to imitate the fleeting moment of action by re-telling does not mean to preserve the original structure of that action. It would be naïve to presuppose that there is a real correspondence between reality and narrative.⁴⁶

However, in her effort to preserve the realness of the past, Guaraldo comes to a paradox of faithful representation:

> In order for this uniqueness to be preserved … we must admit a paradoxical notion of an imitation that is always new.⁴⁷

Forced to admit the impossibility of an epistemically faithful representation, the conclusions that Guaraldo draws are indeed paradoxical.

A way out of this paradox of fidelity and resemblance—of a life composed of stories and yet not a story—is to distinguish two levels of storytelling—that of objective reference and that of its performance. There is a story being told and there is the very act of storytelling. Arendt herself does not make this distinction, but some of her ambiguous remarks point toward it, for example, when she says that stories "at least for ourselves, contain in a nutshell the full meaning of whatever we have to say," as if we **had to** say it.[48] Pointing again to the original aporia, "have to" indicates necessity and historical meaning and "say" the political and contingent dimension of storytelling. Thinking with Arendt against Arendt, one may conclude that at the represented level, ontologically discontinuous facts are linked together in a quasi-purposive way. The story is continuous and has closure; otherwise, a chaotic totality of infinitely improbable happenings and the past radical, meaningless contingency could not be redeemed. At the performative level, however, the story is already an open and discontinuous action. Telling a story becomes political when the story told builds on past discontinuities in a novel and non-explanatory manner. A story does not explain the past by applying coherent scientific models but solely through particular reflective wholes. It thus imposes (and not simply uncovers) the nutshell of meaning on past actions while simultaneously disclosing its agent—the storyteller.

Reenacting the Self

Arendt's fragmented historiography, contrary to modern, scientific historiography, encumbered with the legacy of metaphysics represented by the figure of *homo faber*, is not cognition but political action. It does not bring about the reality of the past. It is an action that contains a creative element of fictional authorship (*homo faber*) but which, unlike scientific explanation, maintains the primacy of the indeterminate present over the past and the future. Storytelling is a political act that performatively presents an acting subject, and thus directly transposes epistemology to ontology.[49] A closer look at the concept of representation in an ontological sense will provide a better understanding of Arendt's reenactment.

Conceived of in epistemological terms, the measure of the effectiveness of representation is the resemblance between that which is represented (the past) and the representation (the story). Meanwhile, an ontological representation is first and foremost a substitute for reality, something that replaces it rather than a mere imitation. Ernst Gombrich famously argued that a hobby horse, despite neither intended to be nor actually being similar to a real horse, is a better representation of one for a child playing with it than, for example, a table that resembles a horse more.[50] It is no different with an artistic presentation, which also need not be a faithful replica of what it represents.

Ankersmit showed that historiography is a similar case. Since the presentation precedes what it represents, it cannot be a direct manifestation of the past.[51] In a similar manner, the whole of the linguistic deed (regardless of whether it is transient speech or a text reified in a material of some kind) has an ontological and self-referential status. It does not resemble the past—it substitutes for it.[52] In Arendt's moderate view, the correspondence between the past and the narrative about it occurs solely at the level of descriptions represented by factual statements and not the whole of a story. This whole, on the other hand, is a kind of reflective aesthetic assembly of the past. Ankersmit calls the narrative wholes "narrative substances" and claims that they function like linguistic things—it is to these substances that one ascribes the properties that are seemingly properties of the past.[53] Narrative substances are not knowledge but "organizations of knowledge"—they bring unity and coherence to the otherwise incoherent past.[54] Ankersmit also calls these narrative substances "logical mannequins" since they **substitute** for a no longer existing reality. These wholes, postulated as being present in the past reality, are specific interpretive proposals for our perception of the past. They establish the past by substituting for it. As Ankersmit observes:

> Proposals may be useful, fruitful, or not, but cannot be either true or false; the same can therefore be said of historical narratives.[55]

Arendt's stories that present an assembly of historical facts in the web of quasi-causal and seemingly purposive relations (aesthetic judgment) are neither true nor false. Even if resemblance and substitution partially overlap, the story being a political action presents an opinion and not the truth. Truth, as Arendt would say, compels, whereas agreement with a given opinion is a question of free will and trust. For Arendt, the present is autonomous in its narrative perception of the past. As a result of this, a story can become a constitutive element of the public world. The presentation precedes and establishes what it represents. In Arendt's conception of performative self, the self does not exist before its presentation, but only as a consequence of it. There can be no resemblance between what one is and what one presents in action because these are one. By presenting oneself, a person "substitutes" for oneself, so to speak. On the other hand, telling a story about the past from a third-person perspective, as previously discussed in this chapter, presents the past in a novel way and thus grants it meaning. Simultaneously, the storyteller presents themself. These two modes of presentation overlap in the special case of an autobiographical story, which unites both types of substitution and both types of meaning. The last two sections of this chapter explore this particular case more closely and demonstrate why it does not ultimately abolish Arendt's basic aporia.

Revolutionary Conservatism

When introducing the notion of narrative identity in his *Time and Narrative*, Paul Ricoeur recalls Arendt as allegedly claiming that it is the story of one's life that answers the question of identity.[56] Is Ricoeur correct in proposing such an Arendtian genealogy? Does Arendt's storytelling present the narrative identity as a crossover of sameness and change? A story is supposed to solve the dilemma of the subject as, on the one hand, identical with oneself, and on the other, as fragmented and illusory. Narrative identity mediates between the objective qualities of identity known as the *idem* and the *ipse* qualities indicating the uniqueness of the who. It permits a simultaneous grasp of transformation and unity of the self.

Arendt's notion of who is considerably more fleeting than Ricoeur posits. The self was to be disclosed in the extended present and visible to others only in the fleeting moment of action. At the end of the crucial twenty-fifth paragraph of *The Human Condition*, in which Arendt states that the who is only disclosed through biography—the life story in which one is the hero without being its author—she also introduces the concept of reenactment, thus withdrawing from the possibility of knowing the identity through a biography alone.[57] Suddenly, Arendt is speaking of an intangible, political disclosure and enactment of the self somewhat comparable to what took place in the past. She is thus returning to the idea of meaning in itself that belongs to particular deeds, only that, in this case, it refers to the reenactment of a past story. Once again, the core of the fundamental aporia comes to the fore. If one treats Arendt's remarks concerning the impossibility of retaining the fleeting quality of the who seriously, one must acknowledge that, in a biographical story, the self of a past protagonist is reified and represented as a story, and that this story, as a kind of political action, only presents the self of the storyteller—it discloses her/his intangible who.[58]

The solution presented above enables the two functions of storytelling to complement each other. Representing the past as work imposes upon it an otherwise absent continuity. Simultaneously, the very act of telling marks a rupture in continuity and opens a temporal rift between the past and the future. As storytelling is a purposive work, it aims for the redemption of contingency. As it is also a political action purposive in itself, it discloses the storyteller's self and constitutes a new beginning. Seen from the perspective of outcomes, historical meaning belongs to what is represented, and political meaning, seen in the fleeting moment of action, belongs to representation itself—to the particularity of **this** presentation of the past. It permits the simultaneous redemption of contingency and necessity—the novelty that establishes durability. As *The Origins of Totalitarianism* showed, the more distant the essentializing component of the narrative (what it represents) is from the coherent modeling characteristic of the philosophy of history, the greater its political potential.

Referring to Nietzsche's well-known typology, Judith Shklar observed that Arendt's fragmented historiography bears the hallmarks of monumental history.[59] While critical history is supposed to describe and explain, the primary function of monumental history is to serve the present. This role is perhaps best epitomized in the 1963 book *On Revolution*, in which Arendt strives to preserve the grand revolutionary tradition while destroying the belief in its continuity, or worse, in its necessity. Arendt thus presents both a radical and a conservative position. Writing about revolution means citing acts of revolutionary action, which are acts of destruction that are simultaneously new beginnings (the revolutionary element). It also means establishing a new revolutionary tradition and founding continuity based on revolutionary experience (the conservative element).[60]

The dualism of revolution and tradition reflects the two corresponding functions of storytelling. Arendt does not seek the causes of revolutions but tries to resurrect the revolutionary spirit. She recalls the possibility of disruption in order to bring down the myth of historical providence. Her narrative is discontinuous and fragmented and unlike professional historical writing, it does without the metaphysical coherence of history. Furthermore, due to its originality, Arendt's narrative breaks continuity and thus establishes a new beginning while it commemorates and preserves the past. In an uncommon way, it constructs continuity based on discontinuity. As Arendt notes in *On Revolution*:

> Perhaps the very fact that these two elements, the concern with stability and the spirit of the new, have become the opposites in political thought and terminology—the one being identified as conservatism and the other being claimed as the monopoly of progressive liberalism—must be recognized to be among the symptoms of our loss.[61]

The rupture in historical continuity is a fact; continuity does not need to be broken but needs to be established. Furthermore, the established continuity is a condition of political action understood as a rupture. Revolution presupposes tradition, just like action presupposes continuity. Action requires tradition if only to have a background from which to distinguish itself.[62] Continuity must thus be rebuilt while ensuring that one does not get oppressed by history again.

Heller too discerns revolutionary conservatism here. The tradition established by Arendt is not tradition with a capital "T," but traditions in the plural, mediated by and dependent upon political action. Like Arendt's notion of narrative identity, they build on discontinuities without creating an all-encompassing permanence. Revolutionary identity is no more than fragmented revolutionary experience.[63] The history of revolutions reflects the development of the self on a macro scale; it is made up of small revolutions, just like the self is made up of mutually discontinuous actions.

A story is a type of action—an act of political intervention facing the past. It is an intervention into historical time, simultaneously breaking it apart and sewing it together. It can refer to both the past worthy of commemoration (revolutionary tradition) and the past that one does not wish to honor (elements of totalitarianism) yet that one should not forget and retain as a warning. In both cases, though, the objective is the same. It is the dual redemption of time that is obtaining a partial coherence of the past and broadening the future horizon for action. Arendt's fragmented story is thus both real and fictitious. If the latter element were to dominate, it might indiscernibly transform into the philosophy of politics. The redemption of contingency would turn into oppression by history and the horizon of the future would narrow down. To avoid this, fragmented historiography must remain incoherent. Fully coherent is the act of presentation only, a proper action that, rather than disclosing the selves of historical protagonists, presents the who of the historian—an intervening political actor.

The Odysseus Paradox: The Impossibility of Fulfillment

In her key essay on the concept of history, Arendt refers to the scene "paradigmatic for history" which took place in *The Odyssey* at a feast held by the Phaeacians, when Odysseus weeps while listening to a story praising his deeds at Troy told by the blind bard Demodocus. Since Odysseus knew the facts from his past, why does he cry? Had the story solely included facts, Arendt notes, he "would have been bored rather than moved." However, "what has been sheer occurrence now became 'history.'"[64] Odysseus weeps because he was not fully aware of the sense of his life while it was lived. He did not weep when he experienced what is now being told. "Only when he hears the story does he become fully aware of its meaning."⁶⁵

It is the blind poet that first discerns the meaning of Odysseus' life with the "eyes of the mind." Demodocus sees the whole that remains invisible for Odysseus engaged in the events. In his imagination, particular deeds or acts "fit together and produce a harmony."⁶⁶ The proper meaning is revealed only in a story being told and not in a life story. The *Odyssey* scene is paradigmatic for history since its epistemic value is not what is at stake. The image of the weeping Odysseus, who knows the facts of his own life better than anyone else, illustrates the principal motivation behind the writing of history. It is not knowledge but reconciliation with reality. The concept of "reenactment" from *The Human Condition* reappears here as linguistic "imitation" of action "transforming" the past.⁶⁷

Adriana Cavarero refers to this situation as "a paradox of Ulysses [Odysseus],"⁶⁸ a paradox that lies in the hero's identity being imposed upon him by someone else. Only upon hearing the story told by Demodocus does Odysseus realize who he really is. He is thereby able to begin his own autobiographical story about the adventures he experienced during his return from Troy, chronicled in the four stories of the *Odyssey* that follow. Much like Arendt, Caravarero notes that one's identity may be made known only through biography—through storytelling concerning a life story. The who then becomes visible as a "unity," and a pattern emerges that was previously invisible from the first-person perspective. As far as this remark concerns the what of the self, and as long as one remembers that it is impossible to capture the who as revealed directly in action, it is congruent with Arendt's thought.

Cavarero pursues the subject further, arguing that since one cannot see one's who, one's identity must be imposed by the other. She further claims that for Arendt, an autobiography would pose an "absurd exercise," as no one can know and recognize one's who.⁶⁹ In this way, Odysseus allegedly did not know himself. He only learned who he was in the story of Demodocus, which moved him to tears and, in a way, prompted his autobiographical story.

Caravarero rightly maintains that Odysseus, like every person, does not know himself and cannot perceive his own fleeting who. However, can Odysseus see himself through the story of the other? Whatever the story of Demodocus says, it does not present a real, but only an objectified and reified Odysseus. Could not Odysseus likewise objectify himself? And is such an objectification not a condition of the possibility of recognizing himself in the story of Demodocus? In both cases, Odysseus does not observe his political identity but rather its representation—a reified narrative self. Hearing the story of himself told by Demodocus, Odysseus has not perceived his past who, but the present who of Demodocus, revealed while he was objectifying someone else. Odysseus could have only seen the "innermost meaning" of the action of Demodocus and the historical sense of his own biography.

Long before hearing the story of Demodocus, Odysseus must have known who he was, insofar as he could tell his own story to himself. He is Odysseus of Ithaca, who wishes to come back home, to his previous life. Arendt is actually mistaken in claiming that Odysseus had never previously wept. On the contrary, he had cried often, perhaps too often, but such was the result of his frequent representation of himself to himself that is telling himself his own life story.

When held captive by the nymph Calypso, Odysseus' "heart strain[ed] with tears and groans and sorrow."[70] He suffered from being aware that he had lost his home—his "eyes [were] always full of tears, because his sweet life was passing while he mourned for his return."[71] While making use of both the love of the goddess and unlimited access to ambrosia, he simultaneously longed for his previous life and Penelope. Also later, at the court of Alcinous, Odysseus was aware of his plight. Even before Demodocus started singing, Odysseus had stated, with tears in his eyes, that he was the unhappiest of men. And he cried more than once after Demodocus began telling his story.

Interestingly, Odysseus was ashamed of his tears. Every time Demodocus started a song, he would hide his face in a cloak to not reveal his who as intensely experiencing the sight of his objectified self.[72] The next song of Demodocus, this time initiated upon Odysseus' explicit request, made him cry even more, which is probably the scene that Arendt had in mind. Homer compares his "face [which] grew wet with tears" to the cries of a woman who prostrates herself on her dead husband.[73] This marked the intensity of Odysseus' emotions, as if having witnessed the death of his older self, belonging now to the past, which he could perceive as a whole only from the perspective of consequences. The hero also wept on his arrival home—with his son Telemachus and then with his wife Penelope—as they all "shed tears."[74]

Asked by King Alcinous about the reason for his constant tears and sighs, Odysseus introduces himself as "Odysseus, son of Laertes," thereby revealing his what rather than his who.[75] What follows is a long autobiographical tale—a story describing the numerous adventures and "misery" of Odysseus. Earlier, though—also at the feast of the Phaeacians but before hearing the story about himself—Odysseus, when asked to "tell me your country and your people," answered with an autobiographical story about his seven years of captivity on

Calypso's island.⁷⁶ He also must have known who he was back then, otherwise he would not have been able to undertake action and set out on a journey. At a minimum, his tale proves that he had reported on his journey earlier, for instance, to the goddess Circe.⁷⁷ He knew who he was and was able to share his story with others.

By introducing himself to Alcinous as "Odysseus, son of Laertes," Odysseus objectifies himself, his name functioning now as a narrative substance, to use Ankersmit's notion. It is a linguistic thing, a what.⁷⁸ The name "Odysseus" does not refer to the past itself but to its representation—to the entirety of a biographical story. As Arendt observes, in the bard's story, Odysseus is an "object" that everyone, including himself, can hear and see.⁷⁹ This status of a presented object holds in the story told by Odysseus himself.

Expanding on Arendt's thought, the real Odysseus now attributes to the linguistic "Odysseus" some features, actions, and adventures, which strictly speaking, do not refer to the speaker's past self. This is because, in point of fact, there was no "Odysseus" in the past. There were only particular actions, disclosures of his who. In retrospect, and from the perspective of consequences only, a complete form of "Odysseus" now appears in the story.

Given that it is Odysseus, not Demodocus, who is now telling the story, the spectators see both the object—the what of "Odysseus"—and the narrating hero—Odysseus himself. The fullness of Odysseus' identity—his disclosing who presenting his reified past disclosures—can only be grasped by listening to his story about himself, the real aspects of which will forever remain hidden from himself. One discloses oneself solely to the other and never to oneself. Irrespective of whether it is a biography or an autobiography, this who remains concealed from the narrator. It is exclusively the spectator listening to Odysseus' autobiographical story who can grasp the two kinds of meaning—an innermost political (representation) and historical (represented)—united in a single extended act occurring in the gap in time.

The real Odysseus also reveals his who in the fictitious story he tells in disguise, not wanting to be recognized. Both the story he tells the swineherd Eumaeus, introducing himself as a newcomer from Crete, and the fake story told to Penelope disclose Odysseus' self, even though they are full of false facts and none of the listeners recognize the hero.⁸⁰ The words being told are a lie, yet they reveal the genuine Odysseus.

The significance of the detachment of the objectified and objectifying self, the what and the who, is similarly apparent when Odysseus is back in Ithaca. Telemachus, Argus (his dog), and Penelope recognize him as being the same and yet different. The nurse Eurycleia, who has known him since his childhood years, recognizes him when washing his feet, observing a particular wound.[81] Similarly, Penelope checks if Odysseus knows what he, being himself, should know. The physical recognition and the knowledge test, however, are not enough to determine his current self. Not knowing whom they have become in the time that has passed, Odysseus and Penelope cry. After they "had the joy of making love"—somewhat comparably to the feast of the Phaeacians, when Odysseus had to consume before listening, crying, and telling the story—Penelope tells Odysseus about what she had been through, and he tells her of his troubles and grief.[82] Even though they had recognized each other earlier as the same, they had to report to each other everything that had taken place since their last meeting. The story of the bard or anyone else would not suffice because they wished not only to get to know **what** they were (what was narrated), but also **who** they were as they were narrating what was narrated. They both desired to experience life as an act of storytelling, and thus the innermost, political meaning of action narrating the past.

If life consists of telling stories, if the line between the narrating and the narrated self is blurred, does the boundary between reality and fiction disappear? If everyone is a protagonist (actor) and, at the same time, a creator (spectator) of his own story, is life itself not a story? Ultimately not, rightly, even if not consequently, says Arendt, for her narrative anti-realism is also fragmented and not unequivocal. It is because narrative representation grants insight that can be considered only in retrospect. A story form is a universal condition of possibility for giving meaning to the past, regardless of whether it concerns historical epochs or the narrator's personal past. In the latter and more original case, the narrative splits life into two parts in the gap in time—the represented past and the representing story—and one becomes the historian of one's life. Furthermore, while representing oneself, one becomes someone else—someone representing the former lost identity that is objectified into a story about the previous life. In this role of a representative, one becomes more than what one represents and what one could have represented earlier.[83] One breaks the temporal continuity that usually accompanies everyday life and reveals oneself in a completely new way—as representing oneself in this, and not another, manner. What is represented in the story may be observed by the narrator. However, one cannot experience the very act of representation visible to the spectators of this one actor performance alone.

Notwithstanding these claims, the aporia of a story is never definitively overcome. In an autobiographical story, the two kinds of meaning do not completely overlap with one another. Although the other can experience the meaning of an act of representation, the self represented in this act never covers the entirety of one's life story. As long as life continues, it cannot be captured as a whole, and when it departs, it can only be told by others. Even if it objectifies the whole of one's life, a biographical story told by the other does not show the fleeting who of its hero. By contrast, an autobiographical story reveals the narrator's self, but what it objectifies always remains a step behind the act of representation, never giving an account of the whole life. No one is capable of seeing and telling the whole of one's life story. The gap in time remains in place. The yearning for ultimate meaning is never completely satisfied. The aporia of the story transpires as an irremovable feature of the finite human condition.

Conclusion: In Praise of Inconsistency

I would like to say that everything I did and everything I wrote—all that is tentative.

Hannah Arendt (Toronto, November 1972)

It is only now, having traveled the long interpretative path covering Arendt's speculative, critical, and applied philosophy of history, that one may give full justice to the motto of *The Origins of Totalitarianisms*, which comes from Karl Jaspers' 1947 sizable book *Von der Wahrheit—On Truth*. It is a motto that succinctly and accurately captures the epistemic and aesthetic aims of Arendt's fragmented historiographical enterprise.

> Weder dem Vergangenen anheimfallen noch dem Zukünftigen. Es kommt darauf an, ganz gegenwärtig zu sein.[1]

Give yourself neither to the past nor to the future. What matters is to be entirely present. The whole paragraph, which appears in the part of *On Truth* entitled *The contemporary task of logic*, actually reads:

> Therefore, the attitude must be: give yourself neither to the past, nor to the future. What matters is to be entirely present: in organizing the acquired truth to keep open the paths that continue.[2]

Curiously, it is only the latter part of this sentence—the one pointing to the need to keep the future open—that is marked in Arendt's personal copy of *Von der Wahrheit*.[3]

Arendt conceptualized storytelling as an instrument for dealing with the contingencies of the self and of the world. She also warned that every story is potentially catastrophic, which totalitarian ideologies illustrate in the extreme. This is because, while performatively creating and preserving narrative continuity indispensable for the political self, any interpretation of the past (including personal past) might easily turn into retrospective prophecy in which the past serves as a promise of the future. Such "prophecy in reverse," as Karl Löwith called it, demonstrates "the past as a meaningful 'preparation' for the future."[4] Its disastrous effect is the future perversion, which haunted Jewish prophetics, Christian eschatology, and by implication, the modern science of history that ultimately distorted the classical Greek *historein*. If one is to avoid this future perversion, Arendt argued, one must break the infamous tradition of substituting work for political action and get rid of teleology.

In the *Critique of the Power of Judgment*, discussing the subjective character of the purposiveness of nature in the reflective judgment, Kant illustrates the free formation of the beauty of nature by the sudden transition from a fluid to a solid state—the process of crystallization.[5] The process itself is purposeless, sudden and immediate, and it is only subjectively, through an aesthetic judgment, that it is regarded as being directed toward a purpose. *The Origins of Totalitarianism* provides an example of such an aesthetic judgment expressed by the act of narration. The book **presents** (and not represents) the past as purposive without a purpose. It shows the past as purposive insofar as totalitarianism—a **crystallization of elements** as Arendt metaphorically describes it, a crystallization grounded in free will but ultimately contingent and producing a new historical quality—**appears to be the purpose** of previous events. This aesthetic illusion is necessary to redeem the contingency of the past. Simultaneously, the book presents this illusion as an illusion, thus retaining the awareness that the historical path to totalitarianism was melancholic and haphazard, to refer to Arendt's favorite metaphors.

The notion of totalitarianism as used in *The Origins of Totalitarianism* is itself a reflective historical concept. It organizes the entirety of Arendt's story and forms a narrative closure that crystalizes the fluid nature of the genealogy of totalitarianism. The concept also lacks a definite status as it is further defined by its elements, which are reflective notions of a lower order. Ironically, it is only from the viewpoint of this closure that its elements, such as anti-Semitism, racism, and imperialism, become noticeable as puzzles of this larger whole. Considered separately, these elements of totalitarianism are also purposive without a purpose and likewise serve the existential function of the non-teleological redemption of past contingencies. The basic aporia of meaning rendered in terms of purposiveness—the purposiveness of work and cognition on the one hand, and the internal purposiveness of action and thinking on the other, is overcome by aesthetic purposiveness without a purpose.

The many critics of *The Origins of Totalitarianism* are undoubtedly right—the book is a perversion of scientific and scholarly endeavor. This perversion, however, illustrates in Arendt's view how to tackle history after the break with the past. The book is an example of a disclosing political action—it reveals the sympathies and antipathies of a historian, her subjective preferences, judgments, prejudices, and opinions. It is a book that itself breaks the continuity of time and separates present from the past. Ironically, Arendt would probably agree with Isaiah Berlin's diagnosis that *The Origins of Totalitarianism* is not a scientific work, but a "metaphysical free association," except that she would drop the word "metaphysical." It is a free association, indeed, but one that is supposed to dismantle the metaphysics of modern scientific historical writing. It is a work that draws conclusions from the loss of the past as a coherent whole and arranges fragments of the past into remarkable new constellations.

Arendt's historical *opus magnum*, a somewhat chaotic collage of microstories presenting the past as lacking any predetermined essence is a forerunner of historiographical postmodernism.[6] *The Origins of Totalitarianism* provides an excellent model of a disturbed narrative that escapes coherence and continuity.[7] Interruptions, the effects of disorientation, and uncertainty play to the strengths of the book, cutting it off from the academic ideals of non-contradiction and completeness. For Arendt, incoherence is an asset, not a failing. As stated at the beginning of this book and in the words of Arendt, "fundamental and flagrant contradictions rarely occur in second-rate writers; in the work of great authors, they lead into the very center of their work."[8] One may empathize with Arendt pointing to the interpretative value of incoherence, even if it is hard to define the exact boundary separating it from undesirable nonsense. Viewed from a theoretical angle, inconsistency implies a logical contradiction, but it also avoids fictional narrative coherence. As Polish philosopher Leszek Kołakowski once observed, total consistency is tantamount to fanaticism that precludes values incongruent with a given order of representation.[9] Arendt's fragmented historical writing, in contrast, praises interpretative inconsistency. Values implied in Arendt's narrative on totalitarianism are not based on binary logic—they often permeate and preclude one another.

As George Kateb put it, the difference between meaningful and meaningless story for Arendt is not "the difference between intelligible and unintelligible" but rather "between the aesthetically compelling and the aesthetically disappointing."[10] The same is true of Arendt's ambiguous reflections on storytelling. To deal with these, one must become a collector of quotations—one must reclaim often contradictory fragments and scraps of thought and present them as a story, a coherent story on incoherent and ambiguous storytelling. What Richard Bernstein stated with regard to Arendt's reflections on the Jewish question is no less true when it comes to her philosophy of history—"At the core of her insights are blind spots, and, indeed, that insight is achieved at the cost of blindness."[11]

Arendt's fragmented historical writing is thus undeniably closer to political action—it is closer to speaking in the public sphere comprising a reading and receptive audience than it is to the academic values of truth and intersubjective validity. This is why Peter Steinberger is right in asserting that "Arendt's work ultimately encourages or, at the least, presents no obstacles to a certain kind of intellectual anarchy," except that this anarchy must not amount to a failure.[12] Throughout her life, Arendt was a political animal. Her essays and books were acts of political intervention, conveying "the splendor or beauty and creativity or freedom of politics,"[13] and her political judgment was often "arrogant" in the sense of evading any preconceived theoretical models.[14] Arendt's historical writings neither express a longing for the past nor reflect its truth. They also do not anticipate future realities in the way scientific predictions do. They rather dwell in the space of meaning between the past and the future, which on the one hand, enables the redemption of the past and, on the other, leaves the autonomy of the future intact. Full of statements that are often arbitrary and judgmental, and frequently asserting rather than proving, these writings reveal not so much the past as Arendt—the *zoon politikon* herself.[15]

As a final note, action in the form of the narrative judging of the past, a narrative reconciliation with the past, is one of the possible forms of forgiveness.[16] Pointing to this similarity, Lisa Disch noted that reconciliation with reality through stories "effects a kind of forgiveness."[17] Julia Kristeva, meanwhile, directly associated the power of judgment with forgiveness calling the latter a "paradoxical modality of judgment."[18] A narrative forgives not so much individual actions or events, for it would be outrageous to say that Arendt forgave totalitarianism, as their sequence—the contingency of the whole. In *The Human Condition*, Arendt presented forgiveness as a form of action that enables liberation from the irreversibility of the past. Forgiveness brings "redemption" of the consequences of action, which were once unpredictable and are now irreversible. It pertains to the whole of a particular real story. Forgiveness "puts an end" to the past.[19] The function of forgiveness mirrors that of a story—both lead to liberation from the consequences of past actions. Both are a kind of action that breaks the mechanical sequence of cause and effect. A story is a form of forgiveness that puts an end to the past. It opens and maintains an indeterminate temporal gap between the no-longer and the not-yet, and thus implicitly brings a promise of a new, unknown and unpredictable political order.

Arendt's historical writing on totalitarianism is at once a diagnosis and a remedy for the crisis of modernity, which manifested itself in the break with tradition. The result of this break was a gap in time, and Arendt's fragmented narrative aims to sustain this gap and make oneself at home in the discontinuity of time. The more existential lesson of Arendt's ambiguous storytelling is that everyone is like Odysseus from her paradigmatic story—both aware and unaware of who he truly is. Constantly a step behind oneself, one strives, without any success, to catch one's shadows. And like Odysseus, one must not merely be aware of the path one has covered. Most importantly, one must be prepared to encounter the unexpected.

Notes

Introduction

1. HC, pp. 104–5.
2. J. Ring, *The Political Consequences of Thinking, Gender and Judaism in the Work of Hannah Arendt*, State University of New York Press, New York 1998, pp. 213–29.
3. S. Benhabib, *The Reluctant Modernism of Hannah Arendt*, Sage Publications, Thousand Oaks–London–New Delhi 1996. J. Habermas, "Hannah Arendt's Communications Concept of Power," *Social Research*, vol. 44, no. 1 (1977), pp. 3–24. Habermas's main objection concerns Arendt's failure to account for structural violence that can preclude this consensus.
4. D. R. Villa, *Arendt and Heidegger: The Fate of the Political*, Princeton University Press, Princeton–New Jersey 1996. B. Honig, "Toward an Agonistic Feminism: Hannah Arendt and the Politics of Identity," in: *Feminist Interpretations of Hannah Arendt*, ed. B. Honig, The Pennsylvania State University Press, University Park, PA 1995, pp. 135–66.
5. N. C. Moruzzi, *Speaking through the Mask: Hannah Arendt and the Politics of Social Identity*, Cornell University Press, Ithaca–London 2000.
6. R. Bernstein, "Judging—The Actor and the Spectator," in: idem, *Philosophical Profiles, Essays in Pragmatic Mode*, University of Pennsylvania Press, Philadelphia 1986, pp. 221–37. Later on, Bernstein argued that the problem of thinking permeated Arendt's entire oeuvre; see R. Bernstein, "Arendt on Thinking," in: *The Cambridge Companion to Hannah Arendt*, ed. D. Villa, Cambridge University Press, Cambridge 2000, pp. 277–92. L. Bradshaw, *Acting and Thinking: The Political Thought of Hannah Arendt*, University of Toronto Press, Toronto–Buffalo–London 1989, p. 100. Bradshaw, on the other hand, claimed that Arendt's main field of reflection was the relationship between theory and practice. Early Arendt, she argued, defended human practice from its "transcendent" rationalization, while late Arendt moved toward the analysis of thinking as a condition of responsible action. According to Jennifer Ring, the tension between theory and practice "characterizes," but does not "dichotomize" Arendt's work. Ring reduces it to the tension between the German and the Jewish legacy: Ring, *The Political Consequences of Thinking*, pp. 297–9.
7. BPF, pp. 17–40.
8. LOM I, p. 197.

9   Its applicability to past reality, however, remains out of the scope, even though from the political science perspective Arendt's works on totalitarian regimes, despite being partly superseded, cannot be ignored.
10 Some commentators detect the presence of Arendt's mature thought only in the text "Ideology and Terror," written in 1951 and added as a final chapter to later editions of *The Origins of Totalitarianism*. See M. Canovan, *Hannah Arendt: A Reinterpretation of Her Political Thought*, Cambridge University Press, Cambridge 1992, p. 62; R. H. King, "Endings and Beginnings: Politics in Arendt's Early Thought," *Political Theory*, vol. 12, no. 2 (1984), p. 244. Even Arendt's doctoral thesis, *Der Liebesbegriff bei Augustin*, which she defended in 1928 (English translation: H. Arendt, *Love and Saint Augustine*, ed. J. Vecchiarelli Scott, J. Chelius Stark, University of Chicago Press, Chicago–London 1996), contains the nucleus of some of her later insights on the hierarchy of the dimensions of time. See R. Beiner, "Love and Worldliness: Hannah Arendt's Reading of Saint Augustine," in: *Hannah Arendt: Twenty Years Later*, ed. L. May, J. Kohn, MIT Press, Cambridge, MA 1996, pp. 269–84.
11 E. Young-Bruehl, *Hannah Arendt: For Love of the World*, Yale University Press, New Haven–London 1982, pp. 276–80.
12 MDT, p. 201.
13 Arendt presents the fundamental activities as relatively ahistorical in nature; only the order of their mutual relations changes (BPF, p. 62). She also notices that they can change in the future (HC, pp. 3, 6, and 10). Paul Ricoeur notes that the activities are still historical—P. Ricoeur, "Action, Story and History: On Re-reading *The Human Condition*," *Salmagundi*, no. 60 (1983), p. 61. Moreover, some practical acts, such as artistic activity, can fall under two or even three categories. It should also be noted that the activities contained within one category might not have much in common. See B. Parekh, *Hannah Arendt and the Search for a New Political Philosophy*, Macmillan Press, London–Basingstoke 1981, pp. 108–10. Arendt admits that her division is not disjunctive. An element of labor, for example, is present in all activities as long as they serve to sustain the process of life. See Arendt, "Labor, Work, Action," in: *Amor Mundi: Explorations in the Faith and Thought of Hannah Arendt*, ed. J. W. Bernauer, S. J., Martinus Nijhoff Publishers, Boston–Dordrecht–Lancaster 1987, p. 34. Action, meanwhile, is necessary for commencing work and for the socialization of labor. The element of action "is inherent in all human activities" (HC, p. 9). However, Arendt's somewhat essentializing approach to the categories of *vita activa* made some scholars argue that her threefold distinction "has little value as a classificatory scheme" (B. Parekh, p. 110)—an argument this book disagrees with.
14 The volume devoted to thinking was first published, in three parts, in *The New Yorker* in 1977 (21 November, 28 November, 5 December), and one year later,

together with *Willing*, as *The Life of the Mind*—albeit without the anticipated third part, which was supposed to be devoted to the power of judgment. The latter was then reconstructed from lecture notes by Ronald Beiner, and published five years later. Both *Thinking* and *Willing* were prepared by Arendt but as lectures (delivered in 1973-4 in Aberdeen and in 1974-5 in New York). Consequently, the book edited by Arendt's close friend and guardian of her intellectual legacy, Mary McCarthy, cannot be claimed to be complete. See LOM I, pp. xiii–xiv, LOM II, pp. 241–54.

15 See the positive reviews by: E. Shorris, "In Praise of Sheer Nonsense," *Harper's Magazine*, vol. 257, no. 1539 (1978), pp. 84–6; I. L. Horowitz, "Open Societies and Free Minds: The Last Testament of Hannah Arendt," *Contemporary Sociology*, vol. 8, no. 1 (1979), pp. 15–19; T. O'Meara, "The Life of the Mind," *Theology Today*, vol. 36, no. 1 (1979), pp. 99–103; J. V. Schall, S. J., "The Life of the Mind," *Theological Studies*, vol. 40, no. 1 (1979), pp. 204–6; D. Donoghue, "Hannah Arendt's *The Life of the Mind*," *Hudson Review*, vol. 32, no. 2 (1979), pp. 281–8.

16 As Arendt explains in the introduction to *Thinking*, there were two factors that led her to write *The Life of the Mind*. The first was the experience of the thoughtlessness of Adolf Eichmann during his trial in Jerusalem, and the resultant hypothesis regarding the connection between thinking and evildoing. The second factor was Arendt's desire to add to her earlier reflections on the *vita activa* (LOM I, pp. 4–8). At times one might get the impression that it is the activities of the mind that condition practical activities. For example, Arendt writes that "the principles by which we act and the criteria by which we judge and conduct our lives depend ultimately on the life of the mind" (LOM I, p. 71). In a similar manner to the endeavor of *The Human Condition*, in which Arendt sought to investigate the internal diversity of the human praxis, her analysis strives to emphasize the internal differences within the activities of the mind that are far from serene and silent contemplation. Furthermore, on a declarative level there is continuity between early Arendt, as a philosopher of practice, and late Arendt, as a philosopher of the mind. In *The Human Condition*, Arendt clearly states that the activity of thinking, "the highest and perhaps purest activity of which men are capable," remains outside of her analysis, which is purposively "limited" to the three activities of the *vita activa* (HC, p. 5). And it is to thinking that Arendt returns in the last sentences of the book: "if no other test but the experience of being active (…) were to be applied" to the human practices, then thinking may "surpass them all" (HC, p. 325). The work is concluded by a maxim of Cato the Elder: *Numquam se plus agere quam nihil cum ageret, numquam minus solum esse quam cum solus esset*—"Never is he more active than when he does nothing, never is he less alone than when he is by himself." The very same maxim appears on the first page of *The Life of the Mind* (LOM I, p. viii).

17 Arendt gave an earlier version of these lectures at the University of Chicago in 1964, and later at the New School for Social Research in New York in 1970.
18 LKPP VI, p. 33.
19 See especially LOM I, § 9.
20 LOM I, pp. 69–76.
21 Parekh has made such a case, albeit without developing it, particularly regarding the most problematic relationship between thinking and action. See Parekh, *Hannah Arendt and the Search*, op. cit., pp. 103 and 123–5.
22 Temporality is metahistorical in the sense in which Koselleck uses the concept to refer to his own categories of the space of experience and the horizon of expectations; it defines both the conditions of possible histories and the conditions of their cognition. See R. Koselleck, "Space of Experience and Horizon of Expectation: Two Historical Categories," in: idem, *Futures Past. On the Semantics of Historical Time*, trans. K. Tribe, Columbia University Press, New York 2004, pp. 255–76. In its first role, temporality conditions not only the movement of history in general (which Koselleck calls the collective singular) but also postmodern stories in the plural—Arendt's "life stories." See R. Koselleck, "History, Histories and Formal Time Structures," in: idem, *Futures Past. On the Semantics of Historical Time*, trans. K. Tribe, Columbia University Press, New York 2004, p. 93.

Chapter 1

1 For more on the development of the book, see E. Young-Bruehl, *Hannah Arendt: For Love of the World*, Yale University Press, New Haven–London 1982, pp. 199–11.
2 D. MacDonald, "A New Theory of Totalitarianism," *New Leader*, vol. 34 (1951), pp. 17–19.
3 A. Alvarez, "Art and Isolation," *The Listener*, January 31, 1957, p. 183. According to Alvarez, the publication of *The Origins* initiated the 1950s in American literature, even though the book is nonfiction.
4 H. A. Reinhold, "The State as Monster," *Commonweal*, vol. 8 (June 1951), p. 218.
5 A. Darack, "A Plunge into Hell," *The Cincinnati Enquirer*, May 13, 1966.
6 J. Maier, "Über Flüssigmachung des Menchen," *Aufbau*, Friday, March 30, 1951, p. 11.
7 HAP, *Correspondence File*, 1938–59, Letter of June 13, 1949.
8 Ibid. Letter of November 15, 1951.
9 *The Times Literary Supplement*, August 18, 1961.
10 G. Lichtheim, *The Concept of Ideology and Other Essays*, Random House, New York 1967, p. 119, cited in: S. J. Whitfield, *Into the Dark: Hannah Arendt and Totalitarianism*, Temple University Press, Philadelphia 1980, p. 53.

11 In part, this imbalance could be attributed to both the unavailability of extensive literature on the Soviet Union in the 1940s and Arendt's more intimate grasp and attachment to circumstances and events within Germany. In her preface to Part Three of the third edition (1966), Arendt remarks that new, if still insufficient, materials prove her earlier statements to be correct. See OT, pp. xxiii–xl.

12 R. Aron, "The Essence of Totalitarianism according to Hannah Arendt," *Partisan Review*, vol. 60, no. 3 (1993), translated by M. Le Pain, D. Mahoney, pp. 366–76 (text initially published in 1954).

13 Indeed, this assertion has proven to be a major point of contention in *The Origins of Totalitarianisms* lasting reception, and remains an unresolved dispute among historians and political scientists. The most dramatic evidence of the inconclusiveness of historical debates resurfaced during the *Historikerstreit* ("historians' dispute"), which erupted in Germany in the 1980s and continues to this day. The historical specificity of totalitarianism was highlighted by various thinkers prior to Arendt. In *Escape from Freedom* (1941), Erich Fromm argued that modern capitalism played a uniquely important role in ensuring the rise of fascism. Franz Neumann similarly pointed to the uniqueness of Nazism in *Behemoth* (1942), emphasizing the significant roles played by big business and bureaucracy. On the other hand, Arendt herself never claimed that the scale of the terror and total ideology of totalitarianism was unprecedented in history; she only maintained that there was a qualitative difference between previous regimes and modern totalitarianism, particularly with respect to the genocides committed in their names. The American political scientist, Hans Morgenthau, shared these convictions. H. Morgenthau, "Hannah Arendt on Totalitarianism and Democracy," *Social Research*, vol. 44, no. 1 (1977), pp. 127–31. In subsequent reflections upon the issue, John L. Stanley followed Arendt in arguing that King Shaka, who united the Zulu tribes at the beginning of the nineteenth century, also ruled in a totalitarian fashion. See J. L. Stanley, "Is Totalitarianism a New Phenomenon? Reflections on Hannah Arendt's *Origins of Totalitarianism*," *Review of Politics*, vol. 49, no. 2 (1987), pp. 177–207.

14 Ibid., p. 280.

15 C. H. van Duzer, "Review of *The Origins of Totalitarianism*," *The American Historical Review*, vol. 57, no. 4 (1952), p. 934.

16 W. Baer, "Review of *The Origins of Totalitarianism*," *The American Economic Review*, vol. 42, no. 3 (1952), pp. 437–8.

17 See J. F. Brown, "Review of *The Origins of Totalitarianism*," *The Annals of the American Academy of Political and Social Science*, vol. 277 (1951), p. 272.

18 J. Parkes, "Present Discontents," *The Jewish Chronicle*, vol. 6 (November 1951).

19 T. I. Cook, "Review of *The Origins of Totalitarianism*," *Political Science Quarterly*, vol. 66, no. 2 (1951), p. 291.

20 van Duzer, op. cit., p. 934.
21 H. Kohn, "Where Terror Is the Essence," *Saturday Review*, no. 34 (1951), p. 10.
22 Arendt considered these possibilities in a draft of the book she was preparing for the Houghton & Mifflin Company publishing house. See attachment to the letter to Mary B. Underwood of September 24, 1946; HAP, *Speeches and Writing File*, 1923–75, n.d. (*Miscellany, Outlines and Research Memoranda* 1946, n.d., folder 1).
23 P. Brooks, a letter of October 23, 1949, in HAP, *Correspondence File*, 1938–76, n.d., Houghton & Mifflin 1946-9.
24 HAP, *Correspondence File*, 1938–76, n.d., Special Correspondence, Publishers, R. Giroux, letters of October 3, 1949, May 16, 1950, September 11, 1950, and September 18, 1950. The Polish edition's metaphorical title (translated by Daniel Grinberg and Mariola Szawiel)—*Korzenie totalitaryzmu*—which literally means *The Roots of Totalitarianism*, turns out to be surprisingly well chosen. Unlike origins, roots are hidden, dispersed and tangled, yet provide a basis for what is visible on the surface.
25 H. Arendt, *The Burden of Our Time*, Secker & Warburg, London 1951.
26 H. Arendt, *Elemente und Ursprünge Totaler Herrschaft*, Piper, München–Zürich 1991.
27 "Hannah Arendt, Elemente und Ursprünge Totaler Herrschaft," *Gewerkschaftliche Monatshefte*, Köln, December 1957, p. 761.
28 J. Pohlmann, "Elemente und Ursprünge Totaler Herrschaft," *Welt der Arbeit*, January 27, 1956.
29 R. Reich, "Vom Wesen totaler Herrschaft. Zur deutschen Ausgabe von Hannah Arendts *The Origins of Totalitarianism*," *Neue Zürcher Zeitung*, September 28, 1957.
30 W. Berkefeld, "Ideologie und Terror. Zu Hannah Arendt's Forschungen über Elemente und Ursprünge totaler Herrschaft," *Sonntagsblatt*, Hamburg, April 15, 1956.
31 W. Höpker, "Hitler oder Stalin—Kehrseiten der gleichen Medaille," *Die Welt*, November 19, 1955.
32 W. Höpker, "Röntgenbild totalitärer Herrschaft," *Christ und Welt*, April 5, 1956.
33 R. Haerdter, "Pathologie eines Zeitalters," *Literatur*, March 24, 1956.
34 K. Knorr, "Theories of Imperialism," *World Politics*, vol. 4, no. 3 (1952), p. 424.
35 In a conversation with Bernard Crick. See B. Crick, "Hannah Arendt and 'The Burden of Our Times,'" *Political Quarterly*, vol. 68, no. 1 (1997), p. 78.
36 E. Voegelin, "The Origins of Totalitarianism," *The Review of Politics*, vol. 15, no. 1 (1953), pp. 70 and 73.
37 Voegelin also claimed that instead of explaining human behavior through subjective and spiritual factors, Arendt turned to a kind of institutional determinism. This assessment of the role of the bureaucratic factor in Arendt's line of reasoning was largely overestimated.

38 D. Riesman, "Review of *The Origins of Totalitarianism*," *Commentary*, vol. 11 (1951), pp. 392, 398, and 393.
39 P. Rieff, "The Theology of Politics: Reflections on Totalitarianism as the Burden of Our Time," *Journal of Religion*, vol. 32, no. 2 (1952), p. 121.
40 K. Jaspers, Geleitwort, in H. Arendt, *Elemente und Ursprünge Totaler Herrschaft*, München–Zürich 1991, p. 10 (originally in German).
41 Max Bense, "Ein Buch und Meining," Süddeutscher Rundfunk, May 3, 1956.
42 Aron, op. cit., p. 367.
43 N. C. Moruzzi, "Re-Placing the Margin: (Non)Representations of Colonialism in Hannah Arendt's *The Origins of Totalitarianism*," *Tulsa Studies in Women's Literature*, vol. 10, no. 1 (1991), pp. 109–20.
44 OT, p. xi.
45 OT, p. xiii.
46 For the former, the illusion expressed their ideological thinking. For the latter, it confirmed their ideas of martyrdom, which served to underpin the communal unity; OT, pp. 7–8. In this sense, the idea of eternal anti-Semitism offered a convenient explanation that revoked the responsibility of both parties. It offered a historical alibi to the perpetrators and a pseudo-religious consolation to the victims.
47 Arendt, who had had a brief Zionist period in her life, began to examine anti-Semitism from a historical-theoretical point of view in the 1930s. In her extensive but unfinished essay "Anti-Semitism," written in German and published only posthumously, she analyzed the phenomenon in only two main historical appearances: classical—medieval and modern religious-based hatred of Jews, and novel—nineteenth-century, secular anti-Semitism. Numerous seeds of the distinctions developed in *The Origins of Totalitarianism* can be discerned within secular anti-Semitism alongside the formation of the abstract idea of Jewishness. See H. Arendt, "Antisemitism," in: *The Jewish Writings*, ed. J. Kohn, R. H. Feldman, Schocken Books, New York 2007, trans. John E. Woods, pp. 46–121.
48 OT, p. xv.
49 D. Goldhagen, *Hitler's Willing Executioners: Ordinary Germans and the Holocaust*, Alfred A. Knopf, New York, 1996.
50 OT, p. 10.
51 OT, p. 132.
52 OT, p. 156.
53 J. Schumpeter, *Imperialism and Social Classes*, trans. H. Norden, Meridian Books, Cleveland–New York 1951.
54 On the lack of economic explanations as well as Marxist inconsistencies in Arendt, see Whitfield, op. cit., pp. 80–9.
55 Knorr, op. cit., p. 425.

56 L. O'Boyle, "The Class Concept in History," *Journal of Modern History*, vol. 24, no. 4 (1952), pp. 391–7. O'Boyle focused on Arendt's explanation of the emergence of mass society through the disintegration of nineteenth-century class structure, but Arendt clearly had no intention of applying the concept of class in a precise explanatory manner.

57 OT, p. 183.

58 R. Masters, "Review of *Origins of Totalitarianism*," *Libertarian Review*, April 1975.

59 E. Varikas, "'The Burden of Our Time': Hannah Arendt and the Critique of Political Modernity," trans. D. Macey, *Radical Philosophy*, vol. 92 (1998), p. 19.

60 OT, pp. 4–5.

61 On this issue, see also EU, pp. 206–11. In the nation-state structure, Arendt argues, the state may become an instrument of a group (even if broadly construed as a nation) for achieving its own goals leading to a conflict with the rights of the citizen.

62 EU, p. 299.

63 Whitfield, op. cit., pp. 8–14.

64 Z. Norkus, "Why Hannah Arendt's Ideas on Totalitarianism are Heterodox?," *Topos*, vol. 2, no. 19 (2008), pp. 114–36.

65 For a concise account of Arendt's theory of totalitarianism see R. Boesche, "Arendt: Totalitarianism as a New Form of Government," in: idem, *Theories of Tyranny from Plato to Arendt*, Pennsylvania State University Press, University Park 1996, pp. 419–54.

66 M. Canovan, "Arendt's Theory of Totalitarianism: A Reassessment," in: *The Cambridge Companion to Hannah Arendt*, ed. D. R. Villa, Cambridge University Press, Cambridge 2000, p. 26.

67 See C. J. Friedrich, "The Unique Character of Totalitarian Society," in: *Totalitarianism*, ed. C. J. Friedrich, The Universal Library, Grosset & Dunlap, New York 1964, pp. 47–60.

68 C. J. Friedrich, Z. Brzezinski, *Totalitarian Dictatorship and Autocracy*, Harvard University Press, Harvard 1965 (1st ed.—1956), pp. 22–3.

69 D. Diner, "Hannah Arendt Reconsidered: On the Banal and the Evil in Her Holocaust Narrative," *New German Critique*, no. 71 (1997), pp. 187–8.

70 See *On the Nature of Totalitarianism: An Essay in Understanding* (EU, pp. 328–60) that elaborates the structure of the forms of governments much more thoroughly than *The Origins of Totalitarianism*; quotation p. 331.

71 Montesquieu, *The Spirit of the Laws*, Cambridge University Press, Cambridge 1989, pp. 21–30.

72 H. Arendt, "Montesquieu's Revision of the Tradition," in: *The Promise of Politics*, Schocken Books, New York 2005, pp. 63–9.

73 EU, p. 338.

74 See T. Mann, *Germany and the Germans*, Library of Congress, Washington, DC 1945.
75 Rieff, op. cit., pp. 119–26.
76 Whitfield, op. cit., pp. 95–8.
77 Canovan, op. cit., pp. 25–43.
78 EU, pp. 347–8.
79 Z. Bauman, *Modernity and the Holocaust*, Cornell University Press, Ithaca, NY 1989.
80 EU, pp. 106–20.
81 EU, pp. 297–306.
82 OT, p. 468.
83 D. Roberts, "Crowds and Power or the Natural History of Modernity: Horkheimer, Adorno, Canetti, Arendt," *Thesis Eleven*, no. 45 (1996), p. 60.
84 OT, p. 343.
85 M. R. Marrus, "Reflections on the Historiography of the Holocaust," *The Journal of Modern History*, vol. 66, no. 1 (1994), pp. 92–116.

Chapter 2

1 OT, pp. 447–55.
2 EU, p. 408.
3 OT, pp. 474–6.
4 Apart from isolation and loneliness, Arendt also distinguishes solitude, which is the experience of thinking. A thinker does not experience the world as the space of appearances, which emerges only through contact with others. A thinker, however, keeps herself company by maintaining an internal dialogue. When this dialogue is lost, solitude turns into loneliness.
5 OT, p. 477.
6 HC, p. 97.
7 HC, p. 98.
8 BPF, pp. 42–3.
9 HC, pp. 80–4. This book does not problematize this political topic, in particular Arendt's criticism of corporeality and the validity of her arguments for the strict distinction between the private and the public. See HC, § 4–10.
10 D. R. Villa, *Arendt and Heidegger: The Fate of the Political*, Princeton University Press, Princeton–New Jersey 1996, p. 27.
11 HC, p. 96.
12 HC, pp. 99–100.
13 HC, pp. 106–8.

14 BPF, pp. 205–7.
15 HC, p. 93.
16 Free time spent on consumption also belongs to labor. Life itself is still sustained and produced, even if the toil and effort traditionally associated with labor are abolished. On one occasion, Arendt distinguishes vacant time, which belongs to the biological cycle from left-over and leisure time, which can be filled with action, but she does not develop this distinction further. See BPF, p. 205.
17 HC, p. 94.
18 HC, p. 118.
19 BPF, pp. 87–9.
20 Although the section of *The Human Condition* on labor is critical of Marx, Arendt regards Marx as a great labor theoretician. She does not acknowledge the possibility of the liberation from labor, which she considers the greatest paradox of Marx's thinking. See HC, p. 104; P. Hansen, *Hannah Arendt: Politics, History and Citizenship*, Stanford University Press, Stanford 1993, p. 40. Arendt's critique of Marx is twofold. In treating man as a productive creature, Marx allegedly blurred the distinction between labor and work. The ultimate result of this was the introduction of labor's necessity within the historical process, imagined now as being both necessary and produced. Secondly, Marx supposedly did not take proper action into account. Arendt's deterministic interpretation thus disregards the revolutionary and communicative potential of Marxist thought—not unlike her own. See, for example, É. Balibar, *The Philosophy of Marx*, Verso, London 2014.
21 M. Canovan, *Hannah Arendt: A Reinterpretation of Her Political Thought*, Cambridge University Press, Cambridge 1992, p. 127. One might conclude that there are two types of labor. Remaining within Arendt's nomenclature, however, labor responds to both types of necessities. See, HC, pp. 33 and 61–7.
22 HC, p. 47.
23 HC, pp. 89 and 132–3.
24 J. Hartman, "Erotyczna czasoprzestrzeń rynku," *Marketing w Praktyce*, vol. 7, no. 101 (2006), pp. 68–9.
25 OR, p. 194.
26 HC, p. 171. Similar assertions were made in BPF, p. 269.
27 A further equivalent to labor are mental experiences associated with what Arendt terms the soul. Despite belonging to an individual, they are recurrent within the species. Moods and emotions are embodied in a very biological sense and thus correspond to the concept of bare life. It is therefore entirely feasible to interpret the life of the soul, as opposed to that of the mind, as an "internal equivalent" of the activity of labor. J. Taminiaux, *The Thracian Maid and the Professional Thinker: Arendt and Heidegger*, trans. M. Gendre, State University of New York Press, New York 1997, p. 201.

28 Note that in Arendt's view, the reduction of man to *animal laborans* takes place merely on the historical surface and does not concern the ahistorical potentiality of political action.
29 BPF, p. 26.
30 LOM I, pp. 211–2.
31 LOM I, pp. 212–13. Emphasis MM.
32 LOM I, p. 212.
33 LOM I, p. 12.
34 Arendt argues that together with the distinction between the sensible and the supersensible, the "age-old distinction between the many and the 'professional thinkers'" loses its plausibility. While the credibility of the previous outcomes of professional thinking is questioned, the capacity to think remains unaffected. LOM I, p. 13.
35 Arendt also presents the fact of loss as an opportunity in BPF, pp. 28–9, when she speaks of culture as the "field of ruins," and of the past as lacking any authority.
36 BPF, p. 3.
37 Some philosophers of history reserve the term non-classical historiography for scientific historiography (such as that of the Annales School) in order to distinguish it from the more traditional, nineteenth-century descriptive political history (see e.g. W. Wrzosek, *History, Culture, Metaphor: The Facets of Non-Classical Historiography*, Adam Mickiewicz University, Poznań 1997). In the case of Arendt's fragmented historical writing, by contrast, the term "non-classical" is used against classical scientism.
38 D. Luban, "Explaining Dark Times: Hannah Arendt's Theory of Theory," *Social Research*, vol. 50, no. 1 (1983), pp. 215–48.
39 LOM I, p. 216.
40 LOM I, p. 210.
41 BPF, pp. 1–14.
42 As suggested by the above quotation, among others. At times, however, Arendt presents an incongruent view. In *Thinking*, for instance, she suggests that the gap metaphor cannot be applied to "the historical or biographical time," and that it is only proper to the activity of thinking (LOM I, p. 210). And yet, just two pages later and in the very same context, she cites the concept of the break in the historical sense.
43 BPF, p. 7. These are Tocqueville's words from *Democracy in America*.
44 LOM II, p. 204.
45 LOM II, p. 205.
46 See R. Koselleck, "'Space of Experience' and 'Horizon of Expectation': Two Historical Categories," in: idem, *Futures Past*, op. cit., pp. 255–75.
47 OR, pp. 13–52.

Chapter 3

1. The distinction between the substantive and the analytical philosophy of history, the latter merely delineating the limits of historical knowledge, comes from Arthur Danto. See A. Danto, *Narration and Knowledge*, Columbia University Press, New York 2007, pp. 1–16.
2. R. H. King, *Endings and Beginnings: Politics in Arendt's Early Thought*, Political Theory, vol. 12, no. 2 (1984), p. 245.
3. A. Vowinckel, *Geschichtsbegriff und Historisches Denken bei Hannah Arendt*, Böhlau Verlag GmbH & Cie, Köln 2001, p. 212.
4. M. Jay, *Adorno*, Harvard University Press, Cambridge, MA 1984, pp. 104–10.
5. F. Ankersmit, "Six Theses on Narrativist Philosophy of History," in: idem, *History and Tropology: The Rise and Fall of Metaphor*, University of California Press, Berkeley–Los Angeles–Oxford 1994, p. 37 (thesis 4.2.2).
6. H. White, *Metahistory: The Historical Imagination in Nineteenth-Century Europe*, Johns Hopkins University Press, Baltimore–London 1973, p. 428.
7. J. Topolski, "Przestrzenie Ontologiczne," in: idem, *Rozumienie historii*, PIW, Warszawa 1978, pp. 35–56.
8. According to Wrzosek, microhistoriosophies materialize mostly in the metaphors of origins and development. They define various scientific modes of agency and change, and convey specific values. W. Wrzosek, "O trzech rodzajach stronniczości w historii," in: *Pamięć i polityka historyczna. Doświadczenia Polski i jej sąsiadów*, ed. S. M. Nowinowski, J. Pomorski, and R. Stobiecki, Instytut Pamięci Narodowej, Łódź 2008, pp. 77–90. See also idem, *History, Culture, Metaphor: The Facets of Non-Classical Historiography*, Adam Mickiewicz University Press, Poznań 1997. In the classical view of Topolski, the frequently unarticulated research premises "lead us to the evaluative basis of a general view on history represented by the one who asks a question" (J. Topolski, *Metodologia historii*, PWN, Warszawa 1984, p. 385).
9. Dray distinguished its three main types, based on linear, cyclical, and chaotic patterns. W. H. Dray, *Philosophy of History*, Prentice-Hall Inc., Englewood Cliffs, NJ 1964, pp. 61–2.
10. Dray distinguished three components of the speculative question of the meaning of history—regarding the pattern, the mechanism of historical change, and the purpose of the whole of history. See ibid., pp. 64–6.
11. K. R. Popper, *The Open Society and Its Enemies*, Routledge, London–New York 2002, p. 840.
12. The contemporary crisis of speculative philosophy of history is apparent inasmuch as the impossibility of systematization of history appears to constitute the very crux of historicity. Regardless of the forms that the contemporary critique of the Enlightenment project (in which History exists in the singular) assumes—the

neo-Kantian critique of historical cognition, hermeneutic reflection on historicity, or even the postmodern affirmation of plurality—one still find oneself in a redefined field of philosophy of history. See Emil Angehrn, *Geschichtsphilosophie*, Kohlhammer, Stuttgart-Berlin-Köln 1991.

13 The most intuitive understanding of the concept of speculative philosophy of history refers to history as a whole and such figures as Immanuel Kant, Georg Wilhelm Friedrich Hegel, and Karl Marx. In the Anglo-Saxon discourse, the philosophy of history also denotes epistemological reflection on history—in other words, the theory or methodology of history. Finally, the philosophy of history is inescapably present in the practice of historical writing, in the narratives about the past. Following Frank Ankersmit's distinction, this reading refers to the philosophy of history in the first sense as speculative, in the second sense as critical, and in the third sense as practical, simply historiography. See F. Ankersmit, "The Reality Effect in the Writing of History. The Dynamics of Historiographical Topology," in: idem, *History and Tropology: The Rise and Fall of Metaphor*, University of California Press, Berkeley-Los Angeles-Oxford 1994, pp. 125-6.

14 H. Jonas, "Acting, Knowing, Thinking: Gleanings from Hannah Arendt's Philosophical Work," *Social Research*, vol. 44, no. 1 (1977), p. 27.

15 M. Passerin D'Entrèves, *The Political Philosophy of Hannah Arendt*, Routledge, London-New York 1994, p. 34. It is important to add, however, that from Arendt's perspective, "recent phenomenological existentialism," similarly to the whole of modern philosophy, suffers from the affliction of subjectivism. See HC, 272. Arendt's theory of politics is supposed to avoid this.

16 Early Heidegger already detached himself from not only empirical but also philosophical anthropology, replacing it with his fundamental ontology. One should inquire into what is more original than man, and "more original than man is the finitude of the Dasein in him." M. Heidegger, *Kant and the Problem of Metaphysics*, trans. R. Taft, Indiana University Press, Bloomington-Indianapolis 1997, p. 160. See also idem, *Being and Time*, trans. J. Stambaugh, State University of New York Press, Albany 1996, pp. 45-6; idem, *Kant and the Problem of Metaphysics*, op. cit., pp. 144-52. Heidegger pointed to the vagueness of anthropology, the difficulty of grasping man as such, and its claims to the first philosophical discipline, a position which fundamental ontology of course also claims.

17 HC, p. 7. Note that from this perspective, both Marxism and existentialism are anthropological. Irrespective of whether we are speaking of a historically variable social practice or of the openness of human existence, we essentially determine what humans really are. See R. Schacht, "Philosophical Anthropology: What, Why and How," *Philosophy and Phenomenological Research*, vol. 50, Supplement (1990), pp. 155-76.

18 P. Ricoeur, *Memory, History, Forgetting*, trans. K. Blamey and D. Pellauer, University of Chicago Press, Chicago 2004, p. 283.
19 P. Ricoeur, "Action, Story and History: On Re-reading *The Human Condition*," *Salmagundi*, no. 60 (1983), p. 60.
20 For example, Jean Grondin includes Arendt within a broad understanding of postwar hermeneutics. See J. Grondin, *Introduction to Philosophical Hermeneutics*, trans. J. Weinsheimer, Yale University Press, New Haven, CT 1997, p. 9.
21 See Angehrn, *Geschichtsphilosophie*.
22 EU, p. 1. Also expressed in the famous Gaus interview, among other sources.
23 EU, p. 32.
24 In the words of Phillip Hansen, Arendt "offers an ontology, a conception of what it means to be distinctively human." P. Hansen, *Hannah Arendt: Politics, History and Citizenship*, Stanford University Press, Stanford 1993, p. 5. Sarah Sorial analogically claims that Arendt merely determines the ontological conditions for the possibility of politics. See S. Sorial, "Hannah Arendt's Concept of the Political," *Cadernos de Filosofia*, vol. 19, no. 20 (2006), pp. 373–90. As argued above, if this is a speculative philosophy of history, then it is only in the negative sense of an exposition of a structure underlying all historical happenings and is precluding of any deterministic scenarios. The only moral of *The Human Condition* is "to recognize more clearly the conditions of [human] existence, and to accept and be grateful." See M. Canovan, *Hannah Arendt: A Reinterpretation of Her Political Thought*, Cambridge University Press, Cambridge 1992, p. 154.
25 Existentials are essential determinations of the structure of Dasein, as opposed to categories as determinations of beings other than Dasein. See Heidegger, *Being and Time*, op. cit., §9.
26 Heidegger, *Kant and the Problem of Metaphysics*, op. cit., 85–8.
27 In *The Life of the Mind*, Arendt closely follows Kant's critical venture, thereby nominally entering the field of metaphysics in a general sense—*metaphysica generalis*—that is supposed to replace discredited traditional metaphysics, including Kant's. Arendt's "metaphysics" is revolutionary and one of praxis, and it is followed by radical historiographical postulates. The term "metaphysics" here does not denote a permanently established system but rather a "mode of thinking that is constantly validating and questioning itself" (H. Buczyńska-Garewicz, *Metafizyczne rozważania o czasie*, Universitas, Kraków 2003, p. 5. Cf. B. Skarga, "O źródle i źródłowości," in: idem, *Kwintet metafizyczny*, Universitas, Kraków 2005, pp. 7–23), and from a radical Heideggerian perspective, thinking alone is metaphysics taking place: "the understanding of Being, its projection and its rejection, *happens* in Dasein as such. 'Metaphysics' is the basic happening for the incursion into the being" (Heidegger, *Kant and the Problem of Metaphysics*, op. cit., p. 170). Arendt does not accord any final status to her "metaphysical"

insights. Not unlike *Thinking*, the book that is itself a presentation of the activity of thinking, *The Human Condition* is an attempt "to think what we are doing" (HC, p. 5). Bearing in mind the connections between thinking and acting, addressed in detail at the end of Chapters 5 and 6, Arendt's "metaphysics" should be ultimately viewed as a proposal, an opinion, that is to say, a revelatory political action. This "performative" interpretation, if one likes, precludes the reproach of falling into the aporia of self-reference, which is the chief Habermasian argument against total modern critiques of reason (J. Habermas, *The Philosophical Discourse of Modernity: Twelve Lectures*, trans. F. Lawrence, MIT Press, Cambridge, MA 1990). Arendt was an engaged thinker and she never claimed to speak from a position external to the categories of the practical and theoretical life that she proposed.

28 LOM I, p. 88.
29 LOM I, p. 174.
30 LOM I, pp. 74–5.
31 LOM I, p. 57.
32 LOM I, pp. 64–5.
33 LOM I, pp. 187 and 193.
34 LOM I, pp. 184–5. The thinking ego "actually exists only in duality" (LOM I, p. 187), Arendt claims, and the fact that in solitude, inert self-consciousness transforms into a dialogue testifies to the fundamental condition of human plurality. Difference is the domain of thinking—identity is the domain of action (LOM I, 184–5). The experience of the thinking ego brings about a false conviction on the existence of two worlds—that of things in themselves and that of phenomena (LOM I, pp. 40–5). In Arendt's history of philosophy, this dualistic and hierarchical view is characteristic of the Western tradition in general and Kant in particular. Arendt follows Heidegger in arguing that the dualistic view is incorrect, as it assumes the constant presence of the *subiectum*. The thinking ego does not appear to itself in the inner intuition; only thoughts (*cogiationes*—Kant's representations) exist but not the *res cogitans* (Kantian transcendental consciousness), upon the certainty of which the outer reality could be based (LOM I, pp. 48–9). As Heidegger noted, "the I think is not something represented, but the formal structure of representing as such, and this formal structure alone makes it possible for anything to be represented" (Heidegger, *Being and Time*, op. cit., § 64, pp. 294–5). Instead of saying, "I think, therefore I am," implying that thinking emerges from subjectivity, one should rather say, "I think, therefore I think," implying that thinking emerges from itself. Arendt expresses this fact characteristically by a metaphor—the mind is "bottomless" (LOM I, pp. 30–4).
35 **Self-presentation** as an expression of the mind mediated through speech differs from **self-display** as the unmediated expression of the psyche. For example, the unreflective feeling of anger is psychic, whereas its reflective self-presentation

is individualized and presents one's self, unlike a scream in reaction to pain, for example. LOM I, p. 35. The concept of self-presentation shall be examined more closely in the chapter on action.
36   LOM, p. 77.
37   The meaningful essences are by no means ideal in Arendt. What distinguishes thinking from traditional contemplation, whose modern incarnation is mathematics, is that Arendtian thinking is not an act of direct beholding. Contemplation (Gr. *theoria*, from *theorein*) takes place by the way of *noein*, an act of intuition, and entails an inner beholding of what is eternally present (HC, pp. 20–1). Intuition is the highest form of truth, while thinking, unlike contemplation and cognition, does not lead to truth.
38   LOM I, p. 14. Arendt separates knowledge from meaning by exploring Kant's classic distinction between reason (*Vernunft*) and understanding (*Verstand*), and maintains that Kant, unwittingly, as it were, freed thinking from being limited by truth. Arendt presents the confusion of these notions as another "metaphysical fallacy," the latest example of which is Heidegger's *Being and Time*—a meditation on the meaning of being, and not truth concerning being (LOM I, p. 15). Thinking in Arendt's view does not reach reality, and its identification with being leads to the fallacy of regarding mental reality as the only reality. See LOM I, p. 198.
39   LOM, p. 186.
40   LOM I, p. 121.
41   LOM I, pp. 111–2.
42   LOM I, p. 99.
43   This should not imply that the purposelessness of life and the purposiveness in itself of thinking are of the same kind. Any similarity to the concept of life as presented in *The Human Condition*, which Jacques Taminiaux uses in his argument on their resemblance, is merely metaphorical (See J. Taminiaux, *The Thracian Maid and the Professional Thinker*, op. cit., Appendix.). For Arendt, indeed, the question of the purpose of thinking is as absurd as the question of the purpose of life (LOM I, p. 197) but their underlying temporalities—the timelessness of life and the authentic temporality of thinking—are strictly distinct.
44   LOM I, p. 123.
45   LOM I, p. 62.
46   LOM I, p. 15.
47   LOM I, pp. 178–9.
48   LOM I, p. 87.
49   LOM I, p. 78.
50   LOM I, p. 100.
51   Taminiaux, *The Thracian Maid and the Professional Thinker*, op. cit., p. 199.
52   LOM I, p. 201.

53 LOM I, p. 20.
54 LOM I, p. 201.
55 A similar view is expressed in: J. Yarbrough, P. Stern, "*Vita Activa* and *Vita Contemplativa*: Reflections on Hannah Arendt's Political Thought in *The Life of the Mind*," *The Review of Politics*, vol. 43, no. 3 (1981), p. 327.
56 R. Fine, "Judgment and the Reification of the Faculties. A Reconstructive Reading of Arendt's *Life of the Mind*," *Philosophy and Social Criticism*, vol. 34, nos. 1–2 (2008), p. 171.
57 LOM I, p. 213.
58 LOM I, p. 76.
59 E. Young-Bruehl, "Reflections on Hannah Arendt's *The Life of the Mind*," *Political Theory*, vol. 10, no. 2 (1982), p. 281.
60 Arendt posits that the deeper ground of particular faculties for is imagination, namely, the "exceptional gift" that Kant considered to be the "common root" of sensibility and intellect. "Every mental act rests on the mind's faculty of having to present to itself what is absent from the senses" (LOM I, pp. 75–6). The operation of de-sensing "precedes all thought processes. ... Even the simple *telling* of what has happened ... is *preceded* by the de-sensing operation. ... All thought arises out of experience, but no experience yields any meaning or even coherence without undergoing the operations of imagining and thinking" (LOM I, p. 87). Arendt's thesis that both the "not-yet" and the "no-longer" depend on imagination is likely to have been inspired by Heidegger's reading of the relationship between time and imagination from his *Kant and the Problem of Metaphysics*. Heidegger argued that for Kant, time as an inner sense does not exist next or in opposition to pure apperception but only within it. The I is temporal to an extent that it is itself time. "The 'fixed' I is so called because as 'I think', i.e., as 'I place before', it brings before itself [something] like standing and enduring"; Heidegger, *Kant and the Problem of Metaphysics*, op. cit., pp. 135. Cf. the section *The Interpretative Function of Free Imagination* in Chapter 8.
61 In the analytic tradition of reflection on time, these incompatible views are commonly referred to as "A-series" and "B-series" of time. For a discussion of this problem, see e.g. P. Turetzky, "McTaggart's problem," in: idem, *Time*, Routledge, London–New York 1998, pp. 121–55.
62 See P. Ricoeur, *Time and Narrative*, vol. 3, trans. K. Blamey, D. Pellauer, University of Chicago Press, Chicago–London 1988.
63 For a more detailed yet accessible discussion of this problem see J. J. A. Mooij, "In Search of Authentic Time. Bergson and the Phenomenologists," in: idem, *Time and Mind: The History of a Philosophical Problem*, trans. P. Mason, Brill, Leiden–Boston 2005, pp. 190–215; and K. Michalski, *Logic and Time. An Essay on Husserl's Theory of Meaning*, trans. A. Czerniawski, J. Dodd, Kluwer Academic Publishers, Dordrecht–Boston–London 1997.

64 See E. Husserl, *On the Phenomenology of the Consciousness of Internal Time (1893–1917)*, trans. John Barnett Brough, Kluwer Academic Publishers, Dordrecht–Boston–London 1991.
65 The most famous and earliest anticipation of the phenomenological thinking about time is St. Augustine's idea of *distentio animi*—a "distension in the mind" (Saint Augustine, *Confessions*, trans. H. Chadwick, Oxford University Press, Oxford 1998, p. 241). The later predecessors of Husserl include Franz Brentano, Henri Bergson, and William James. The latter, in *The Principles of Psychology*, already argued that the temporal structure of consciousness provides it with internal unity and continuity. James spoke of the present as "specious" as it always contains no-longer and not-yet.
66 Heidegger, *Being and Time*, op. cit., § 65.
67 Heidegger, *Being and Time*, op. cit., § 76, p. 358. For Heidegger, this means that "historiographical disclosure temporalizes itself out of the future," ibid., pp. 360–1; for Arendt, on the other hand, it temporalizes itself out of the gap in time.
68 LOM I, p. 202. For a detailed description of the parables see Chapter 20 of *Thinking*.
69 HC, p. 97.
70 LOM I, p. 203.
71 LOM I, p. 205.
72 LOM I, p. 207.
73 LOM I, p. 209.
74 LOM I, pp. 85–6.
75 LOM I, p. 206.
76 LOM I, pp. 199–200.
77 LOM I, p. 206.

Chapter 4

1 EU, p. 355.
2 OT, pp. 470–1; EU, p. 349.
3 OT, p. 469.
4 OT, p. 470.
5 OT, p. 463.
6 Leszek Nowak argued that this unity is based on the methodological universality of the procedure of idealization. L. Nowak, "On the Hidden Unity of Social and Natural Sciences," *Poznan Studies in the Philosophy of the Sciences and the Humanities*, vol. 100, no. 1 (2012), pp. 15–50.
7 C. G. Hempel, "The Function of General Laws in History," *The Journal of Philosophy*, vol. 39, no. 2 (1942), p. 38.

8   In the explanations of human action, in which the *explanans* is conscious, the general law is only indirectly present. Following Topolski's naturalized model of structural explanation, the deductive-nomological procedure of explanation requires the system of general norms of conduct of a specific group to be viewed as an *explanandum*, and this is further explained by referring to some objective factors (See J. Topolski, *Rozumienie historii*, op. cit., pp. 173 and 180–2). In Arendt's view, historical reality does not conform to either type of explanation as it is essentially constituted by actions that in Topolski's nomenclature would be called "autonomous factors," which elude the procedures of rational explanation, such as talent, discovery, and creative experience.
9   OT, p. 472.
10 EU, p. 317.
11 Topolski, *Metodologia historii*, op. cit., p. 206.
12 As rightly pointed out by Phillip Hansen, *Hannah Arendt: Politics, History and Citizenship*, Stanford University Press, Stanford 1993, p. 116.
13 K. R. Popper, *The Poverty of Historicism*, Routledge, London–New York 2004, pp. 96–109. Popper's differentiation between laws and trends and the suggestion that these are often confused is one of his main arguments against so-called historicism. Even though Popper believes in conditional scientific prognoses (as opposed to unscientific and unconditional prophecies), he regards trends as being historically particular and incapable of forming predictions.
14 OT, p. viii.
15 HC, § 20, pp. 144–53.
16 HC, pp. 140–1. In Arendt's reading of Plato, his doctrine of ideas comes from the experience of fabrication, and similarly the notion of idea comes directly from visible forms, and not from invisible, geometric sources. See HC, pp. 142–3.
17 HC, § 18, pp. 136–9. P. Ricoeur, "Action, Story and History: On Re-reading *The Human Condition*," *Salmagundi*, no. 60 (1983), pp. 64–5.
18 It is worth noting that Arendt's notion of work goes beyond the early Heidegger's concept of ready-to-handness (*Zuhandenheit*). Comparably to ready-to-handness, work corresponds to worldliness (*Weltlichkeit*), but in addition to being based on the means-ends structure, it leads to the durability of its products—their positively valued presence. See H. Jonas, "Acting, Knowing, Thinking: Leanings from Hannah Arendt's Philosophical Work," *Social Research*, vol. 44, no. 1 (1977), pp. 32–3.
19 M. Canovan, *Hannah Arendt: A Reinterpretation of Her Political Thought*, Cambridge University Press, Cambridge 1992, pp. 106–7.
20 HC, p. 143.
21 HC, p. 154.
22 HC, § 21, pp. 153–9.

23 Arendt does not specify where the boundary between proper instrumentalism and its degraded version lies. However, it seems that the breaking of the chain of means is the merit of *zoon politikon* and his category of meaning (as different from utility). With regard to *homo faber* considered autonomously, instrumentalism would always be infinite.

24 Symbolic actions that leave no durable products behind, such as any linguistic message, also achieve something, e.g., passing information. Symbolic actions do not transform the material world and, unlike production, are culturally relative (whether the message reaches its recipient depends on the common framework of understanding, unlike, for example, the production of tables). Nevertheless, as long as the structure of means and ends remains intact, they are still actions of the structure of making. For example, a legislative activity or voting would not be a proper political action for Arendt because it results in a specific "product" (See HC, p. 195).

25 For Arendt, behaviors belong to the social sphere, and their content is mainly economic issues. They are predictable and thus subject to scientific research.

26 HC, pp. 258–60. Arendt makes use of Alexandre Koyré's book *From the Closed World to the Infinite Universe*, and of Werner Heisenberg's philosophy, among others. As for the progressing subjectivization of modernity, her analysis clearly owes most to Heidegger.

27 HC, p. 264.

28 HC, p. 274.

29 HC, p. 287.

30 HC, p. 284.

31 HC, p. 278.

32 LOM I, p. 93.

33 HC, p. 303.

34 HC, p. 304. Arendt's view is that both contemplation and production require durability and presence. In Plato's philosophical system, the purpose of action is contemplation, while from the point of view of contemplation, the highest form of activity is work. In Aristotle's *Metaphysics*, similarly, work and contemplation do not oppose each other, but "have an inner affinity" (HC, p. 301).

35 H.G. Gadamer, "Praise of Theory" (A speech given in Bonn, June 3, 1980), in: idem, *Praise of Theory*, trans. C. Dawson, Yale University Press, New Haven, CT 1998, p. 19.

36 Ibid., p. 27.

37 HC, p. 290.

38 Still, "the highest, ultimate form of cognitive truth is indeed intuition," LOM I, 121. It is also the outcome of this purposive process.

39 HC, pp. 170–1.

40 LOM I, p. 62.
41 LOM I, p. 56.
42 LOM I, p. 57. In this context, Arendt uses the concept of "common sense" as well as "common sense reasoning," as opposed to *sensus communis*. Cf. the section "*Sensus Communis—A Historical Sense*" in Chapter 8.
43 OT, pp. 159-60. In *The Origins of Totalitarianism*, Arendt only states that science results from ideology in the sense that research usually follows a specific doctrine, and not the other way round.
44 Koselleck, "On the Disposability of History," in: idem, *Futures Past. On the Semantics of Historical Time*, op. cit., pp. 192-204. Koselleck showed how the mid-eighteenth-century notions of history as a subject were later justified in speculative-scientific terms. Supposedly, objective history created an alibi for its own fabrication. Acting individuals could now identify with the laws of history, and at the same time, could strive to accelerate the events that they in any case regarded as objectively necessary, thus ridding themselves of the responsibility for their actions.
45 OT, p. 346. The quotation comes from Voegelin's article "The Origins of Scientism," *Social Research*, vol. 15 no. 4 (1948), pp. 462-94.
46 The linear structure of fabrication, the existential basis of which is in the actual process of making, can represent both subjective and objective explanation. In the latter case, the acting subjects are anthropomorphized. In Arendt's words, they become "authors" or "personified concepts" (such as nations or states that act purposefully as if they were individuals).
47 OT, p. 471.
48 Popper, *The Poverty of Historicism*, op. cit., p. 11.
49 Ibid., p. 12. One can understand the Oedipus effect—the impact of knowledge about the future on the shape of this future—both positively, as enabling prediction, and negatively, as the prevention of what has been foreseen (Topolski, *Metodologia historii*, op. cit., pp. 548-52).
50 OT, p. 349.
51 OT, p. 353.
52 OT, p. 350.
53 OT, p. 477.
54 OT, p. 458.
55 OT, pp. 457-8.
56 EU, p. 356.
57 OT, p. 472.
58 OT, pp. 352-3.
59 BPF, p. 279.
60 D. R. Villa, *Arendt and Heidegger: The Fate of the Political*, Princeton University Press, Princeton–New Jersey 1996, pp. 199-201.

61 W. Benjamin, "Theses on the Philosophy of History," in: *Illuminations*, ed. H. Arendt, trans. H. Zohn, Brace & World, Harcourt 1968, p. 262.
62 OT, p. viii.
63 EU, p. 403. Emphasis MM.
64 HAP, *Speeches and Writings File*, 1923–75, n.d. (Miscellany, Outlines and Research Memoranda 1946, n.d., folder 1), *Outline, The Elements of Shame*, p. 1.
65 Ibid. (folder 2).
66 EU, p. 325. Arendt's remark that the totalitarian rule that broke the continuity of history was "non-deliberate" does not contradict the presence of the factor of freedom. It only implies that it was not purposively designed. See BPF, pp. 26–7.
67 H. Arendt, *Elemente und Ursprünge Totaler Herrschaft*, Piper, München–Zürich 1991, p. 14.
68 EU, p. 326.
69 A. Heller, "An Imaginary Preface to the 1984 Edition of Hannah Arendt's *The Origins of Totalitarianism*," in: *Eastern Left, Western Left. Totalitarianism, Freedom and Democracy*, ed. F. Feher, A. Heller, Polity Press, Cambridge 1987, p. 256.
70 Heller also notes that from Arendt's point of view, totalitarianism could not have appeared earlier, although this does not imply that it was historically necessary.
71 EU, p. 324. Also in the introduction to the third edition of the book, Arendt expresses the conviction that elements of imperialism also exist in the postwar world. See OT, pp. xvii–xxii.
72 R. J. Bernstein, *Why Read Hannah Arendt Now?*, Polity Press, Cambridge 2018, p. 34.
73 EU, p. 402.
74 E. Young-Bruehl, "Hannah Arendt's Storytelling," *Social Research*, vol. 44, no. 1 (1997), pp. 183–90.
75 I. Nordmann, "How to Write About Totalitarianism? Entwicklung eines Konzepts, das Fragen offenlegt," in: *Über den Totalitarismus, Berichte und Studien*, Nr. 17, Hannah-Arendt-Institut für Totalitarismusforschung e. V. an der Technischen Universität Dresden, Dresden 1998, p. 60.
76 R. Masters, "Review of *Origins of Totalitarianism*," in: *Libertarian Review*, April 1975.
77 EU, pp. 374–9. See also P. Baehr, "Identifying the Unprecedented: Hannah Arendt, Totalitarianism, and the Critique of Sociology," *American Sociological Review*, vol. 67, no. 6 (2002), pp. 804–31. However, Baehr rightly notes the procedural difficulties of identifying the unprecedented character of the phenomenon as such, which would necessitate proving its dissimilarity from everything that had happened.
78 Baehr, op. cit., p. 826. Baehr also rightly notices that Arendt's vision of historical sociology was close to a caricature, and that she failed to realize her own

functionalism. Nonetheless, we may add that Arendt's use of incompatible methods and theories of different provenance prevented the domination of functionalism in her oeuvre as a whole.

79 From this point of view, she notes, it might turn out that both Jesus and Hitler represent the same type of charismatic leader. In such situations, argues Arendt, the functional similarity conceals the phenomenal difference. EU, p. 378.
80 R. J. Bernstein, "The Origins of Totalitarianism: Not History, but Politics," *Social Research*, vol. 69, no. 2 (2002), pp. 381–401.
81 "Only the final crystallizing catastrophe brought these subterranean trends into the open." See OT, p. xv. Arendt expresses the same idea somewhat differently in: ibid., p. 9.
82 EU, p. 319.
83 Crick, op. cit., pp. 121–2.
84 EU, p. 402.
85 H. Arendt, "Totalitarianism," *Meridian*, vol. 2, no. 2 (1958), quoted in Bernstein, op. cit., p. 399.
86 Topolski, *Metodologia historii*, op. cit., pp. 207–8. This is because even individual agency is put in doubt by the discontinuity between intentions and their immediate outcomes; see Chapter 5.
87 H. Paul, *The Masks of Meaning: Existentialist Humanism in Hayden White's Philosophy of History*, University of Groningen, Groningen 2006, pp. 189–92. See also H. Paul, *Hayden White. The Historical Imagination*, Polity Press, Cambridge 2011.
88 E. J. Hobsbawm, "Hannah Arendt on Revolution," in: idem, *Revolutionaries. Contemporary Essays*, Weidenfeld and Nicolson, London 1973, pp. 201–8.
89 EU, p. 326.
90 B. Crick, "On Rereading *The Origins of Totalitarianism*," *Social Research*, vol. 44, no. 1 (1977), pp. 106–26. Crick argued that Arendt aimed at understanding (but not explaining) not so much the functioning of totalitarian regimes as the very possibility of ideological thinking.
91 See the comments in the essay "Social Science Techniques and the Study of Concentration Camps" in: EU, pp. 232–47.
92 OT, p. 459; EU, p. 241.
93 Formal rationality does not evaluate the efficacy of means and ends but refers solely to the formal structure of action. A rational action is one aimed at purposefully designed ends and using means that are considered to be adequate to reach these ends by the agents (where "adequate" means only considered appropriate within the knowledge concerning the conditions of action and the socially acceptable norms of conduct). Topolski, *Rozumienie historii*, op. cit., pp. 161–2.
94 HC, p. 154.

95 EU, pp. 311–2. Arendt emphasizes that comprehending the new experience of totalitarianism through previous categories does not yet constitute proper understanding.
96 M. Canovan, "Arendt's Theory of Totalitarianism: A Reassessment," in: *The Cambridge Companion to Hannah Arendt*, ed. D. R. Villa, Cambridge University Press, Cambridge 2000, p. 29.
97 EU, p. 402.
98 EU, p. 407.
99 EU, p. 407.
100 HAP, *Speeches and Writings File*, 1923–75, n.d. (Miscellany, Outlines and Research Memoranda 1946, n.d., folder 1), *Outline, The Elements of Shame*, p. 1.
101 EU, pp. 403–4.
102 K. R. Popper, *The Open Society and Its Enemies*, Routledge, Abingdon 2011, p. 484.

Chapter 5

1 LOM I, p. 187.
2 HC, pp. 25–6.
3 HC, p. 178.
4 Arendt maintains that an action conceived as a means to an end is "mere talk" that can easily be replaced with "sign language" (HC, p. 180). Such action would have the structure of making, the sense of which, analogically to a fabricated product, would lie in its end. Meanwhile, a verbal reaction to external stimuli (such as a scream in reaction to pain) is solely an unmediated expression of the "soul" that fits the behavior category. What sets the language of action apart from the language of behaviors and actions of the structure of making is that it does not pronounce on reality but on its subject. Furthermore, the disclosure of the "who" is supposed to take place through assertions concerning phenomena and objects (HC, p. 182). Arendt claims, for example, that "finding the right words at the right moment, quite apart from the information or communication they may convey, is action" (HC, p. 26). She also calls it "inevitable" that the self is disclosed through descriptive language. The revealing aspect of action thus also accompanies actions of the structure of making, irrespective of whether they fulfill the intended informational function (HC, p. 183).
5 Taminiaux, *The Thracian Maid and the Professional Thinker*, op. cit., pp. 56 and 87.
6 Heidegger, *Being and Time*, op. cit., § 27, pp. 118–19.
7 Ibid., § 26, pp. 110–17.
8 Ibid., § 64, p. 297.
9 See Taminiaux, *The Thracian Maid and the Professional Thinker*, op. cit., pp. 56–79.

10 Ibid., p. 77.
11 HC, p. 176.
12 HC, p. 179.
13 HC, p. 95.
14 HC, pp. 197–8.
15 HC, p. 181.
16 HC, pp. 179–80.
17 Julia Kristeva rightly observes that Arendt's conception of action is critical toward ontology focused on searching for the essence of man. J. Kristeva, *Hannah Arendt: Life Is a Narrative*, trans. F. Collins, University of Toronto Press, Toronto–Buffalo–London 2001, pp. 55–70. Since there are no foundations behind phenomena, individual actions do not express any lasting essence of a person, an essence that would exceed her actions.
18 HC, p. 179.
19 HC, p. 188.
20 HC, p. 192.
21 Only acts into nature (BPF, pp. 60–1), which Arendt considers in the context of modern natural science, share most of the characteristics of action except for the communication aspect.
22 HC, p. 205.
23 Taminiaux, *The Thracian Maid and the Professional Thinker*, op. cit., p. 97.
24 According to Arendt, Aristotle saw the highest activity of *energeia* in contemplation, and not, like her, in language.
25 HC, p. 207.
26 Greatness has much in common with the republican concept of virtue or excellence (*arete. virtus*), involving standing out among equal citizens (HC, p. 49). It invokes the Greek spirit of *agon* that denotes a strive toward exceptionality in the face of social conformity (HC, pp. 42–3). Although identical as species, humans are differently endowed with natural abilities. There are also innumerable social and economic aspects of inequality. In Arendt's view, a political community equalizes its citizens by giving them equal rights, but it does to enable them to set themselves apart from the crowd of equals (HC, p. 41). Freedom and equality are not mutually exclusive since political equality is a precondition of freedom.
27 EU, p. 191.
28 In the second part of *The Life of the Mind*, Arendt proceeds both phenomenologically and historically. She deconstructs the history of willing in defiance of hostile "philosophers" in order to extract its true image from the alleged mass of metaphysical fallacies. Arendt regards sheer inner experience as the phenomenological proof of the existence of willing (LOM I, p. 214; LOM II, p. 3), which is no different from the philosophical certainty associated with the

experience of thinking. Also, knowledge that one could not have done something that one did is for Arendt a sufficient proof of the existence of willing (LOM II, p. 26). Arendt's willing is neither a biological desire or instinct nor a psychological motive. The word "life" in *The Life of the Mind* is merely a metaphor: "The will transforms the desire into an intention," and establishes a new, contingent beginning that could not have otherwise occurred (LOM I, p. 76).

29 P. Bowen-Moore, *Hannah Arendt's Philosophy of Natality*, Macmillan Press, Houndmills–London 1989, p. 87. Only action is equivalent to "freedom to call something into being which did not exist before, which was not given, not even as an object of cognition or imagination" (BPF, p. 151).

30 J. Yarbrough, P. Stern, "Vita Activa and Vita Contemplativa: Reflections on Hannah Arendt's Political Thought in *The Life of the Mind*," *The Review of Politics*, vol. 43, no. 3 (1981), op. cit.

31 B. Honig, "Arendt, Identity, and Difference," *Political Theory*, vol. 16, no. 1 (1988), pp. 77–98.

32 P. Hansen, *Hannah Arendt, Politics, History and Citizenship*, Stanford University Press, Stanford 1993, pp. 54–7. For example, when in the early essay Arendt quotes Augustine and his concept of *initium*, she does not link it to willing as in *The Life of the Mind*, but to man as a beginning.

33 Sovereignty and autonomy belong to the category of *homo faber*. While the projects of willing resemble making, the willed future is rarely achieved. Willing is sovereign only in the sense of being independent from others, but not in terms of the sovereign power of making. In *Willing*, Arendt certainly does not place politics in the interior as she still distinguishes unlimited philosophical from limited political freedom—"I will" from "I can" (LOM II, p. 200). Willing is entirely free only until it transforms into action, which annihilates it.

34 BPF, p. 160. Arendt argues that Christian linking of mental and political freedom leads to the identification of power with ruling, and sometimes with the oppression of the ruled (BPF, p. 162). The resulting escape from unpredictability leaves two possibilities: either, as with Jean-Jacques Rousseau, particular wills create a conglomerate of *volonté Générale* or one individual or a group of people rule everybody else. Power becomes the opposite of freedom, which in turn begins to mean "inner freedom" from politics (BPF, pp. 146–7). This is a liberal consequence, Arendt claims, since it separates freedom from politics, understanding the latter solely as managing the necessities of life (BPF, p. 155).

35 BPF, p. 153. As Bowen-Moore puts it, "The will fails to emerge as the political faculty of the mind. For although its interests do indeed lie with the experience of action, its context is entirely interior and belongs, as it were, to the mind's private realm" (Bowen-Moore, op. cit., p. 90).

36 LOM II, p. 89.

37 LOM II, pp. 108–9.
38 Arendt quotes this on a number of occasions, including: LOM II, pp. 108 and 217; OT, p. 479; BPF, p. 167; HC p. 177.
39 LOM II, pp. 130–1. On Duns Scotus see LOM II, pp. 125–46.
40 LOM II, p. 141.
41 LOM II, p. 29.
42 I. Kant, *Critique of Pure Reason*, trans. P. Guyer, A. W. Wood, Cambridge University Press, Cambridge–New York 1998, A 450, B 478.
43 LOM II, pp. 63 and 149. Arendt considers Kant's practical philosophy as moral philosophy only and not a political philosophy.
44 MDT, p. 27.
45 D. R. Villa, *Arendt and Heidegger: The Fate of the Political*, Princeton University Press, Princeton–New Jersey 1996, p. 74.
46 Kant, *Critique of Pure Reason*, op. cit., A 532–3, B 560–1.
47 Ibid., p. 396.
48 LOM II, p. 30.
49 LOM II, p. 32.
50 LOM II, pp. 109–10.
51 LOM II, pp. 207–8.
52 HC, pp. 176–7.
53 CR, pp. 132–3.
54 HC, p. 300.
55 BPF, p. 169.
56 HC, p. 246. The historical context of these breaks is of a secondary role for Arendt. It is relevant only as far as that what exists must be "removed or destroyed" (CR, p. 5).
57 EU, p. 183.
58 K. F. Curtis, "Aesthetic Foundations of Democratic Politics in the Work of Hannah Arendt," in: *Hannah Arendt and the Meaning of Politics*, ed. C. Calhoun, J. McGowan, University of Minnesota Press, Minneapolis–London 1997, pp. 27–52; idem, *Our Sense of the Real: Aesthetic Experience and Arendtian Politics*, Cornell University Press, Ithaca–London 1999, pp. 1–22.
59 Kristeva, op. cit., p. 43.
60 Jay initially argued that Arendt's politics is essentially elitist, autonomous, and even class-bound (M. Jay, "Hannah Arendt: Opposing Views," *Partisan Review*, vol. 45, no. 3 [1978], pp. 348–68), but later, following *The Lectures on Kant's Political Philosophy*, he changed his mind ("The Aesthetic Ideology as Ideology: Or What Does It Mean to Aestheticize Politics," in: idem, *Force Fields, between Intellectual History and Cultural Critique*, Routledge, New York–London 1993, pp. 82–3; idem, *Songs of Experience: Modern American and European Variations on a Universal*

61 R. Wolin, *Heidegger's Children: Hannah Arendt, Karl Löwith, Hans Jonas, and Herbert Marcuse*, Princeton University Press, Princeton–Oxford 2003, pp. 31–69.
62 BPF, p. 153.
63 BPF, p. 153.
64 Arendt's inattention to the beauty of nature, which after all is the main subject of the *Critique of the Power of Judgment* is striking. She might herself have clarified the issue further in the intended third volume of *The Life of the Mind*, of which her *Lectures on Kant's Political Philosophy* serve as a substitute.
65 CPJ, § 46, p. 186.
66 CPJ, § 43, p. 182.
67 Kant distinguishes art from science and handicraft. The former is a theoretical faculty, and the latter is not necessarily pleasant and is performed only for the sake of its effect (such as wages). These distinctions are of minor importance even to Kant.
68 CPJ, § 44, p. 184.
69 As far as mechanical art is concerned, judgment or taste does not correspond to the pleasure derived from reflection; it depends solely on the accordance of a product with its concept and on whether its purpose has been adequately achieved. The mechanical element is also present in fine arts: "For some purpose must be conceived; otherwise we could not ascribe its product to any art at all; it would be a mere product of chance" (CPJ, § 47, pp. 189). Hence, fine arts also contain purposeful action, if understood in a slightly different sense.
70 CPJ, § 45, p. 185.
71 CPJ, § 46, pp. 186–7.
72 CPJ, § 49, 195.
73 The term "presentation" is used hereafter to render the German *Darstellung*.
74 CPJ, § 46, 187.
75 Elsewhere, Arendt disagrees explicitly with this characteristic of Kant's definition: "genius is, rather, the disposition through which Mankind [and not nature] gives the rule to Art" (EU, p. 79). It is this fourth characteristic that is of preeminent importance to Kant, for it at least indirectly allows for the preservation of the idea of the supremacy of the beauty of nature over the beauty of man-made products.
76 The disparity between fine and mechanical arts mirrors the difference between action and making. Kant says that art consists of doing (*facere*) and results in a piece of work (*opus*). In the case of nature, there is acting or producing (*agere*) and its resultant effect (*effectus*) (CPJ, § 43, p. 182). Arendt derives the notion of *homo faber* from the Latin word *facere*, in its meaning of making something (HC, p. 136, footnote 1), whereas *agere* (proper action) is an equivalent of the Greek word

archein, which originally meant "to set something into motion" (HC, pp. 177 and 189). From this perspective, and taking into account the purposiveness without a purpose of nature, it seems as if action should be interpreted as a counterpart to Kantian nature. This is correct, but only as long as speaking of the fine arts bearing resemblance to nature rather than nature itself.

77 HC, p. 187.
78 HC, p. 206.
79 BPF, pp. 153–4. In *The Human Condition*, seemingly contrary to what has been argued here, Arendt associates the notion of genius with *homo faber* rather than *zoon politikon*. This results from her conviction of the tangibility of his product. As she observes, however, this product differs from that of a craftsman in that it is greater than the creator himself. Viewed in this way, it "appears to have absorbed those elements of distinctness and uniqueness which find their immediate expression only in action and speech … the artist transcends his skill and workmanship in a way similar to the way each person's uniqueness transcends the sum total of his qualities," HC, p. 210.
80 CPJ, § 49, p. 192.
81 CPJ, § 49, p. 192. An aesthetic idea is the opposite of a rational idea, which is a concept with no corresponding intuition.
82 The creative capacity of imagination lies in the fact that it "aesthetically enlarges the concept itself in an unbounded way" (CPJ, § 49, p. 193). The representation is "associated with a given concept," but "no expression designating a determinate concept can be found for it" (CPJ, § 49, p. 194). When creating aesthetic ideas, imagination is free and independent of intellect, and expands our comprehension. Genius symbolically and metaphorically presents what cannot be unambiguously named.
83 CPJ, § 49, p. 193.
84 This primacy results from the fact that it links the presentation of a concept with "a fullness of thought to which no linguistic expression is fully adequate" (CPJ, § 53, p. 204).
85 LOM I, p. 21.
86 LOM I, p. 27. Arendt distinguishes inauthentic appearances (associated with the internal construction of organisms) from the authentic appearances (that characterize their external construction). Inauthentic appearances are repetitive, the similarity of the internal construction frequently transgressing differences in species. Authentic appearances present diversity even within particular species. It therefore seems as if natural life processes served appearances in a comparable manner to naked life serving politics (HC, pp. 36–7).
87 LOM I, pp. 36–7.
88 LOM I, p. 115. Not to forget that for Gadamer the modern aesthetic consciousness, whose historical beginning is marked by Kant, distorts the proper ontology of art.

89 Ibid., p. 109.
90 H.-G. Gadamer, *Truth and Method*, trans. Joel Weinsheimer, Donald G. Marshall, Continuum, London 2004, p. 108.
91 Ibid., pp. 134–5.
92 Ibid., p. 142.
93 This conclusion will come into play in the epistemological analysis of the autobiographical story in Chapter 10.
94 Heidegger, op. cit., § 27, p. 119; MDT, p. 9.
95 EU, p. 433.
96 J. A. Barash, "The Political Dimension of the Public World: On Hannah Arendt's Interpretation of Martin Heidegger," in: *Hannah Arendt: Twenty Years Later*, ed. L. May, J. Kohn, MIT Press, Cambridge, MA 1996, pp. 251–68.
97 Arendt views subjectivism as alienating from the common world (S. Dossa, *The Public Realm and the Public Self: The Political Theory of Hannah Arendt*, Wilfrid Laurier University Press, Waterloo 1989, pp. 73–113). She juxtaposes it with preferred perspectivism, according to which the same world can appear in an infinite number of ways (HC, pp. 57–8). Subjectivism characterizes mass society in which everybody thinks the same. Tyranny is similarly subjective since it renders communication between individuals impossible.
98 LOM I, pp. 23–6.
99 Opinion differs from truth in being formulated through *sensus communis*, whereas truth is "despotic" in nature. See BPF, pp. 227–64.
100 LOM I, p. 19.
101 LKPP, p. 63.
102 J. Habermas, "On the German-Jewish Heritage," *Telos*, no. 44 (1980), pp. 127–31. The difference between Habermas's and Arendt's understanding of the public sphere is fundamental. For Habermas, *Öffentlichkeit* is the space created by modern mass media, whereas for Arendt, it is a space of local and direct interaction. Arendt is no Habermasian—politics is not striving for agreement and communicative consensus.
103 Villa, *Arendt and Heidegger*, pp. 59–72.
104 HC, p. 199.
105 S. Benhabib, *The Reluctant Modernism of Hannah Arendt*, Sage Publications, Thousand Oaks–London–New Delhi 1996, pp. 127–30.
106 Benhabib, op. cit., s. 198.
107 CR, p. 143. Arendt's distinctions are very clear in this respect. Strength as well as instrumental violence can at most belong to an individual. Nature and quasi-natural social phenomena are characterized by force. See CR, pp. 143–5.
108 HC, pp. 200–2. Public space also sustains public institutions that are ultimately founded upon the agreement and opinions of people: "all political institutions are manifestations and materializations of power." CR, p. 140. The colloquial meaning

of power—top-down control of society—is much closer to what Arendt understands by violence. The mutual relationship of power and violence basically corresponds to the dichotomy of action and work. As Arendt notes in *On Violence*, although power and violence usually occur together, they are essentially mutually exclusive. Power is the more primordial of the two phenomena. As an end in itself, it preconditions the secondary use of means and ends. Only the complete elimination of the human factor could lead to a final replacement of power with violence (CR, pp. 148–9). Even mute violence imposing obedience is based on preceding communication, and even if it is able to destroy power, it cannot sustain itself without it (HC, p. 203).

109 LOM I, p. 1.
110 LOM I, p. 71. Arendt also suggest, quoting Cato, that thinking is the purest and possibly the "highest" of all activities. See HC, pp. 5 and 325.
111 The interdependence of action and thinking is even closer than work and cognition. In *The Human Condition* Arendt states that "validity and meaningfulness [of action] are destroyed the moment thought and action part company;" this is clearly not true for fabrication and knowledge (HC, p. 225).
112 LKPP VI, p. 37.
113 BPF, p. 14.
114 On this subject see LKPP VII.
115 LKPP, p. 43.
116 It is hard to plot the exact boundary between such understanding of critical thinking (involving imagined interlocutors), and the activity of judgment.
117 I. Kant, "Was heisst: Sich im Denken orientieren?," in: idem, *Gesammelte Werke*, Hrsg. von der Königlich-Preussischen Akademie der Wissenschaften zu Berlin, Bd. 8, Berlin 1912, p. 144. Translation by Hannah Arendt.
118 LKPP VI, p. 40.
119 LKPP VI, p. 38.
120 LKPP VI, p. 40. Arendt attempts a similar interpretation of Kant's moral philosophy. She argues that since the maxims of action must be made public, openness is the ultimate criterion of the moral action.
121 LOM I, p. 99.
122 See H. Jonas, "Acting, Knowing, Thinking: Gleanings from Hannah Arendt's Philosophical Work," *Social Research*, vol. 44, no. 1 (1977), pp. 41–3.
123 L. Weissberg, "In Search of the Mother Tongue: Hannah Arendt's German-Jewish Literature," in: *Hannah Arendt in Jerusalem*, ed. S. E. Aschheim, University of California Press, Berkeley–Los Angeles–London 2001, pp. 153–4.
124 One could argue further that in the acute and radical situations known from totalitarian systems, thinking that is destructive toward the currently binding social rules of conduct can prevent one from following the voice of the crowd and become "a kind of action" (LOM I, p. 192). Silence may then appear as an act of greatest

courage, and refraining from action (say, refusal to follow an order) discloses one's identity better than any words.

125 D. R. Villa, "The Development of Arendt's Political Thought," op. cit., pp. 18–19.
126 R. J. Bernstein, "Arendt on Thinking," op. cit., p. 291.

Chapter 6

1 LOM II, pp. 34–8.
2 The psychological moods (taking place not within the mind but in what Arendt referred to as a soul) reflect the tension between thinking and willing. The moods of "serenity" and "quietness" associated with thinking clash with the "tenseness" and "disquiet" characteristic of willing (LOM II, p. 38).
3 LOM I, p. 97.
4 LOM I, p. 78.
5 J. Taminiaux, *The Thracian Maid and the Professional Thinker*, op. cit., Appendix, pp. 199–217.
6 Ibid., p. 216.
7 Arendt's power of judgment unites the present (from which it stems) and the past, but it excludes the future. Whether Taminiaux's thesis is correct with regard to Kant is another matter and is not adjudicated upon here. The chapter on judgment argues in favor of a view that the past seen from the perspective of judgment is not necessary (as from the perspective of thinking) but purposive without a purpose.
8 The connection between judgment and the temporal in-betweenness has been pointed out by Ronald Beiner. See Beiner, "Interpretive Essay," in: LKPP, pp. 144–56 as well as by Peg Birmingham, "Hannah Arendt: The spectator's vision," in: *The Judge and the Spectator. Hannah Arendt's Political Philosophy*, ed. Joke J. Hermsen, Dana R. Villa, Peeters, Leuven 1999, p. 39.
9 LOM I, p. 175.
10 LOM I, p. 192. The destruction of generally accepted rules may prove to be constructive. Thinking gains a political significance in critical situations, when there are no pre-given values to hold on to. As Arendt notes, "critical thought is in principle antiauthoritarian" (LKPP VI, p. 38).
11 Arendt's story of German philosophical modernity follows the plot of willing gaining advantage over thinking. Ultimately, however, the future is harnessed to the movement of necessity. When particular wills work together for the sake of the progress of the whole, willing subordinates to thinking. In Schiller, Schelling and Schopenhauer, and culminating in Hegel, willing acquires a status of reason (see LOM II, p. 20). Nietzsche and Heidegger's rejection of willing marks the end of modernity for Arendt.

12 LOM II, pp. 23–8.
13 LOM II, pp. 139–40.
14 LOM II, p. 138.
15 LOM II, p. 139.
16 LOM II, pp. 36 and 105.
17 LOM II, p. 36.
18 E. Levinas, *Time and the Other*, trans. R. A. Cohen, Duquesne University Press, Pittsburgh 1987, pp. 76–7.
19 LOM II, p. 15.
20 J. Yarbrough, P. Stern, "*Vita Activa* and *Vita Contemplativa*," op. cit., p. 346. From the point of view of willing, continuity between present and future is maintained, but not between past and future.
21 LOM I, pp. 214–15.
22 Among those to underline the essential discontinuity between the willing of disclosing oneself in a specific way and what is finally disclosed is Bonnie Honig. See B. Honig, "Arendt, Identity, and Difference," *Political Theory*, vol. 16, no. 1 (1988), pp. 97–8.
23 LOM II, pp. 195–6.
24 HC, p. 300. Emphasis MM.
25 LOM I, p. 216.
26 LOM I, p. 216.
27 LKPP, p. ii; Lucan, *Civil War*, trans. S. Braund, Oxford University Press, Oxford 1999.
28 E. Young-Bruehl, "Reflections on Hannah Arendt's *The Life of the Mind*," *Political Theory*, vol. 10, no. 2 (1982), pp. 293.
29 HAP, Series Addition III, Writings—Notes and excerpts, 033029. Emphasis MM.
30 Beiner, LKPP, pp. 91–3, 109, and 138–9. According to Beiner, in the later work of Arendt (around the late 1960s and early 70s), judgment as an activity of political actors "is implicitly denied" (LKPP, p. 138). Indeed, several remarks by Arendt published in the essays *The Crisis in Culture* and *Truth and Politics* point to the idea of the enlarged thought in regard to the political world. Among those to promote the two theories of judgment were Richard Bernstein, Martin Jay, Majid Yar, and Maurizio Passerin D'Entrèves. See R. Bernstein, "Judging—The Actor and the Spectator," in: idem, *Philosophical Profiles: Essays in Pragmatic Mode*, University of Pennsylvania Press, Philadelphia 1986, pp. 221–37; M. Jay, "Reflective Judgments by a Spectator on a Conference that Is Now History," in: *Hannah Arendt and the Meaning of Politics*, ed. C. Calhoun, J. McGowan, University of Minnesota Press, Minneapolis–London 1997, pp. 338–50; M. Yar, "From Actor to Spectator. Hannah Arendt's 'Two Theories' of Political Judgment," *Philosophy & Social Criticism*, vol. 26, no. 2 (2000), pp. 1–27; M. Passerin D'Entrèves, *The Political Philosophy of Hannah Arendt*, Routledge, London–New York 1994, pp. 101–38; idem, "Arendt's Theory of Judgment," in: *The Cambridge Companion to Hannah Arendt*, op. cit., pp. 245–60;

D'Entrèves presents the opposition of the two theories less strongly than the others—both powers are supposed to supplement each other as past-directed and future-directed capacities. Meanwhile, Annelies Degryse maintains that a seemingly unpolitical judgment is rooted in *sensus communis* and is in fact already political (A. Degryse, "Arendt's Theory of Judgment and *Sensus communis*," Cadernos de Filosofia, vol. 19, no. 20 [2006], pp. 91–106). Leora Bilsky also argues convincingly in favor of the continuity between the two theories: L. Y. Bilsky, "When Actor and Spectator Meet in the Courtroom, Reflections on Hannah Arendt's Concept of Judgment," *History and Memory*, vol. 8, no. 2 (1996), pp. 137–75.

31 Beiner, op. cit., p. 131.
32 See HC, p. 192.
33 LKPP X, p. 63.
34 In her later texts, Arendt does not reject judgment in the narrower sense. She writes, for example, that everything that appears, the whole of the phenomenal world, is an object that either pleases or displeases. See HAP, *Subject File, 1949–1975, Kant's Critique of Judgment Seminar*, University of Chicago, Chicago 1964, 1970, 032417.
35 Ricoeur well recognized this broad, historical conception judgment. Although Ricoeur considered those qualities of the Kantian judgment that would allow transforming aesthetic into political judgment, the latter is wide-ranging and refers to the past. P. Ricoeur, "Aesthetic Judgment and Political Judgment according to Hannah Arendt," in: idem, *The Just*, trans. D. Pellauer, University of Chicago Press, Chicago–London 2000, pp. 94–108.
36 In a political judgment, one deals with the unintended consequences of an action only in the sense that action exceeds the actor's intention. The proper unintended consequences are later, and include free actions unthinkable without their precedents (their reciprocal relationship will be interpreted as the one between two works of beautiful art—see the paragraph "Purposiveness without a purpose" in Chapter 8). A procedure of "de-sensing" also takes place in political judgment that is likely to be a reflective activity of the mind.
37 LKPP XII, pp. 68–9.
38 LKPP X, p. 58.
39 LKPP X, p. 62.
40 Beiner also argued that in the later work of Arendt, judgment did not have a practical significance; it was not supposed to tell one how to act. See Beiner, op. cit., p. 169.
41 BPF, pp. 221–4. This is despite the fact that the maxim of general communicability is a principle of both judgment and action, of "theory" and practice (the term theory comes from the Greek concept of spectators (*theatai*), and originally means watching something from the outside); see LOM I, p. 93.
42 LKPP XIII, p. 75.
43 See LOM I, pp. 69–70 and 213.
44 HC, pp. 90 and 170.

45 HC, p. 173.
46 This conclusion is drawn at least in part by Taminiaux. See Taminiaux, *The Thracian Maid and the Professional Thinker*, op. cit., p. 207. Arendt suggests it, among other places, in: HC, p. 171 and LOM I, p. 197.
47 HC, p. 171.
48 HC, p. 170.
49 BPF, p. 168.
50 LOM II, p. 205.
51 See K. Braun, "Biopolitics and Temporality in Arendt and Foucault," *Time & Society*, vol. 16, no. 1 (2007), p. 20.
52 B. Skarga, *Kwintet metafizyczny*, Universitas, Kraków 2005, pp. 82–3.
53 See G. Haeffner, *The Human Situation. A Philosophical Anthropology*, trans. E. Watkins, University of Notre Dame Press, Notre Dame, IN 1989. As Gadamer put it, the pure scheme of consecutiveness cannot be applied to interpretation. Speech is "there-now" and presents the whole of the linguistic content, not its individual fragments; Gadamer H-G (2007) Text and interpretation. Edited and translated by Palmer RE. The Gadamer Reader. A Bouquet of the Later Writings. Evanston, IL: Northwestern University Press, pp. 156–191.
54 J. Kohn, "Freedom: The Priority of the Political," in: *The Cambridge Companion to Hannah Arendt*, p. 113. Sheldon Wolin also stresses that Arendtian authentic politics denotes presence—albeit, of course, not in the sense of duration. S. Wolin, "Hannah Arendt and the Ordinance of Time," *Social Research*, vol. 44, issue 1 (1977), pp. 91–105.
55 Arendt excludes the possibility of shared thinking. A dialogue with a close friend can be compared with the internal dialogue of thinking despite not being identical to it. Friendship is worldly, whereas thinking is worldless, invisible, inaudible and intangible. S. Gray, "Hannah Arendt and the Solitariness of Thinking," *Philosophy Today*, vol. 25, no. 2 (1981), pp. 121–30.
56 Among those to note that, for Arendt, logos unites theory and practice is Julian Honkasalo, see "Praxis, Logos and Theoria—The Threefold Structure of the Human Condition," *Topos*, vol. 2, no. 19 (2008), pp. 169–80. Theory here means thinking understood as the conversation of the soul with itself, and practice means action understood as dialogue. Both take place through finite and non-predicative language and both are unending and incapable of an ultimate expression of meaning. See also J. Grondin, *Introduction to Philosophical Hermeneutics*, op. cit., pp. xiii–xiv, 32–8, 117–23, and 140–4.

Chapter 7

1 HC, p. 185.
2 On the distinction between real and vulgar history, see A. Vowinckel, "Hannah Arendt and Martin Heidegger: History and Metahistory," in: *Hannah Arendt*

in Jerusalem, ed. S. E. Aschheim, University of California Press, Berkeley–Los Angeles–London 2001, pp. 338–46. Richard King identified two analogous kinds of history—conventional, subordinate to necessity and subject to explanation, and the history of freedom. See R. H. King, "Endings and Beginnings: Politics in Arendt's Early Thought," *Political Theory*, vol. 12, no. 2(1984), p. 247.

3   HC, p. 183.
4   HC, p. 184.
5   HC, p. 184.
6   HC, p. 19.
7   HC, p. 186.
8   The difference between an actor and an author as well as between a real and a fictional history is analyzed in greater depth in Chapter 9.
9   These phrases used by Arendt come from Johann Wolfgang Goethe. See BPF, pp. 82 and 242.
10 LOM II, p. 133. Arendt also cites Henri Bergson, and says that, like Duns Scotus, he saw necessity as an illusion of consciousness, and freedom (exemplified by art) as reality that loses its contingent character only in retrospection. See LOM II, pp. 30–1.
11 LOM II, p. 137.
12 LOM II, p. 146.
13 *Within Four Walls. The Correspondence between Hannah Arendt and Heinrich Blücher 1936–1968*, ed. L. Kohler, trans. P. Constantine, Harcourt Inc., New York–San Diego–London 2000, p. 188.
14 LOM II, pp. 173 and 178.
15 LOM II, pp. 188–94.
16 HC, p. 220.
17 HC, p. 178.
18 CR, p. 109.
19 HC, pp. 191–2.
20 HC, p. 190.
21 G. W. F. Hegel, *Reason in History*, trans. R. S. Hartman, Bobbs-Merrill, Indianapolis 1953, p. 35.
22 HC, p. 233.
23 EU, p. 325.
24 HC, p. 190. The concept of reaction should not be understood in a behavioral sense but as an action constituting a contingent response.
25 A. Vowinckel, *Geschichtsbegriff und Historisches Denken bei Hannah Arendt*, op. cit., p. 7.
26 W. H. Auden also asserted that for *homo faber*, time is not linear and does not assume change but duration. See W. H. Auden, "Thinking What We Are Doing," *Encounter*, June 1959, p. 73.
27 Taminiaux, *The Thracian Maid and the Professional Thinker*, op. cit., p. 216.

28 Work involves reifying an idea, and duration means both the lasting of this idea and the lasting of its fabricated version, where the latter usually exceeds the duration of an individual life.

29 Arendt contrasts the concepts of process and thing via the difference between what and how, the distinguishing criterion being durability (BPF, p. 51). An element within a process is a function of the whole while all processes are destructive for their parts. Arendt speaks of three types of processes (BPF, pp. 41–90): 1) a purposeless process of life with no beginning or end; 2) a process of fabrication that has both a beginning and an end that are external to the process; 3) a process initiated by action with an external beginning but without an end (BPF, p. 168). This implies that unlike labor, the processes of work and action do not fully overlap with these activities. Neither predictable products of making nor actions setting off unpredictable consequences are processes. In addition, Arendt distinguishes singular processes (a characteristic feature of modern philosophies of history) from the incommensurable processes in the plural that follow the break in tradition (BPF, p. 89).

30 HC, pp. 296–7, 301, and 304. Arendt refers to this phenomenon as "the introduction of the concept of process into making." She describes the change as a shift from "what and why?" to "how?" This, supposedly, takes place first in the natural and then in historical sciences. The objects of both disciplines are no longer conceived as durable and become processes instead. Both nature and history become processes with no author or purpose.

31 LOM I, pp. 54–5.

32 LOM II, pp. 151–2.

33 K. Löwith, *Meaning in History*, University of Chicago Press, Chicago–London 1949, p. 18.

34 LOM II, p. 50.

35 LOM II, p. 44.

36 OT, p. 145.

37 LOM II, pp. 18 and 220.

38 HC, p. 312.

39 CR, p. 128.

40 CR, pp. 130 and 132. Arendt criticizes this image also because it contains implications of violence: "If we look on history in terms of a continuous chronological process, whose progress, moreover, is inevitable, violence in the shape of war and revolution may appear to constitute the only possible interruption."

41 HC, p. 306. The first is the reversal to fabrication.

42 HC, pp. 105–6.

43 HC, p. 312.

44 HC, pp. 105 and 116.

Chapter 8

1. R. Beiner, "Rereading Hannah Arendt's Kant Lectures," in: *Judgment, Imagination, and Politics. Themes from Kant and Arendt*, ed. R. Beiner, J. Nedelsky, Rowman & Littlefield Publishers Inc., Lanham–Boulder–New York–Oxford 2001, p. 93.
2. LKPP I.
3. LKPP IV.
4. R. J. Dostal, "Judging Human Action: Arendt's Appropriation of Kant," *Review of Metaphysics*, vol. 37, no. 4 (1984), p. 740.
5. A. Norris, "Arendt, Kant, and the Politics of Common Sense," *Polity*, vol. XXIX, no. 2 (1996), p. 190.
6. CPJ, pp. 47–50.
7. See CPJ, § 42, p. 181. This complicated issue is intentionally not dealt with here.
8. CPJ, Introduction IV, p. 13. In Kant's *Critique of Pure Reason*, judgment proceeds from the universal to the particular, subsuming a given empirical fact under a specific rule of the intellect. This judgment is determinant and has an objective validity with regard to appearances, but not to the thing in itself. In Kant's third *Critique*, judgment runs the other way round, from the particular to the universal. This time it is reflective, and does not say anything about its object.
9. CPJ, § 14, p. 108.
10. CPJ, § 15, p. 113.
11. LKPP II, p. 15; She repeats the same claim in: LKPP XI, p. 67; LKPP XIII, p. 72; and in LOM I, p. 193.
12. LKPP II, p. 14.
13. R. A. Makkreel, *Imagination and Interpretation in Kant, The Hermeneutical Import of the Critique of Judgment*, University of Chicago Press, Chicago–London 1990, pp. 166–71. Ricoeur showed how the teleological judgment is always primarily aesthetic (Ricoeur, op. cit., pp. 95–6). Bernstein, on the other hand, pointed out how aesthetic judgments disturb the narrow epistemic dichotomy of truth and morality, and suggested the primacy of reflective judgment to the application of categories of intellect. See J. M. Bernstein, "Memorial Aesthetics: Kant's Critique of Judgment," in: idem, *The Fate of Art: Aesthetic Alienation from Kant to Derrida and Adorno*, Pennsylvania State University Press, University Park 1992, pp. 17–65.
14. LOM I, p. 69.
15. As Gadamer contends, "such a sense is obviously needed where we are concerned with the whole, which is however not given or thought of by the concept of purposiveness: in this way taste is not at all restricted to the beauty of nature and art"; Gadamer, *Truth and Method*, op. cit., p. 35.
16. LKPP II, p. 14; Immediately after stating that the particular as an object of judgment is what links aesthetics and teleology, Arendt notes that this latter

part of Kantian philosophy does not interest her because "it does not deal with judgment of the particular, strictly speaking, and its topic is nature." What Arendt manifestly means by this is that history is seen here as a part of nature and judged teleologically.

17 CPJ, "Analytic of the Beautiful," § 1–22.
18 What pleases through the senses cannot be communicated universally, whereas pleasure in the good is universal, albeit based upon reason and its concepts. Meanwhile, taking pleasure in the beautiful is neither one nor the other since it can be communicated universally without the mediation of concepts—it is a pleasure of reflection consisting in the free play of the imagination and the intellect.
19 CPJ, § 5, p. 95.
20 BPF, pp. 49–52.
21 LKPP XIII, p. 73.
22 Saying "roses in general are beautiful" would be a logical judgment based on aesthetic judgment concerning a particular rose. Cf. CPJ, § 8, p. 100.
23 CPJ, § 9, p. 102.
24 CPJ, § 35, p. 167.
25 Beiner, "Interpretive Essay," op. cit., note 155. The German word *allgemein* corresponds both to the Latin *generalis* and *universalis*; in the case of judgments of taste, however, it is their universality that is in question, not their generality. Guyer and Matthews say that "The term allgemein can be translated as either 'general' or 'universal;' we will generally use the former where there is a contrast with 'particular,' and the latter when a claim to the assent of all is contrasted to an idiosyncratic or private judgment." CPJ, p. 8.
26 Beiner, "Rereading Hannah Arendt's Kant Lectures," op. cit., p. 96.
27 CPJ, § 10, p. 105.
28 CPJ, § 10, p. 105.
29 Kant distinguishes free beauty (*freie Schönheit*) from dependent beauty (*anhängende Schönheit*): the former does not presuppose any concept of the object, any internal purposiveness, while the latter views the object as falling under a particular concept of purpose. At the basis of judgment is an internal purposiveness of an object, which, if it is real, can be seen as a perfect object. See CPJ, § 16.
30 LKPP XIII, p. 76.
31 The term *Gemeinsinn*, in contrast to the terms *gemeiner Verstand* and *gesunder Verstand* (literally, common and healthy intellect), could be translated as *sensus communis*. In the Guyer/Matthews translation, the term "common sense" is used for both. Since in § 40 Kant introduces the Latin concept of *sensus communis*, the term "community sense" is favored here. On the shifts on meaning involved in these terms, see the later paragraph "*Sensus Communis*—A Historical Sense."
32 CPJ, § 20, p. 122.
33 LKPP IX, p. 52.

34 LOM I, pp. 92–6.
35 LOM I, p. 94.
36 LKPP IV, p. 26.
37 LKPP V, p. 31.
38 Arendt claims that "The very idea of progress ... contradicts Kant's notion of man's dignity. It is against human dignity to believe in progress," LKPP XIII, 77.
39 LKPP VIII.
40 I. Kant, "Idea for a Universal History with a Cosmopolitan Intent," trans. L. W. Beck, in: idem, *On History*, Bobbs-Merrill, Indianapolis 1963, p. IX.
41 LKPP IV.
42 LKPP IX.
43 Only occasionally does Arendt refer to the "hope" for progress in Kant. Essentially, she interprets it dogmatically, as an objective phenomenon.
44 LKPP XIII, p. 77.
45 LKPP VIII, p. 48.
46 LOM I, p. 96.
47 LKPP IX, p. 56.
48 R. A. Makkreel, *Imagination and Interpretation*, p. 150. Arendt criticizes the possibility of judging history in advance in Kant, and for her own purposes, she interprets this judgment as an aesthetic decision.
49 Makkreel, *Imagination and Interpretation*, pp. 63 and 65.
50 Makkreel, *Imagination and Interpretation*, p. 64.
51 This withdrawal concerns all three activities of the mind as it is first a move away from the sensible world toward "thought-things" de-sensed through the imagination. See LOM I, pp. 75–7.
52 LKPP V.
53 LOM I, p. 96.
54 LKPP X, p. 59.
55 LKPP XII, p. 68.
56 LKPP, 80.
57 EU, pp. 322–3. Arendt makes the same claim in her *Reply to Eric Voegelin* from 1953, where, in the context of historical understanding, she states: "I am convinced that understanding is closely related to that faculty of imagination which Kant called *Einbildungskraft* and which has nothing in common with fictional ability," EU, p. 404.
58 LOM I, pp. 75–6. Imagination also conditions thinking, the most primal of the activities of the mind. See LOM I, p. 85.
59 HAP, *Speeches and Writings File, Kant, Immanuel*, 032138.
60 In *The Critique of Pure Reason*, imagination provides the schemata for concepts and is dependent upon intellect, whereas in *The Critique of Judgment* it provides the examples for judgments and acts independently. H. Arendt, "Imagination, Seminar

on Kant's *Critique of Judgment*, given at the New School for Social Research, Fall 1970," in: LKPP, 84.
61 Makkreel, *Imagination and Interpretation*, pp. 45–66.
62 A scheme is a model related to a certain whole constituted by the concept. It is not so much an image as a schematic image. Conceptual imagining is schematic by necessity.
63 Kant, *Critique of Pure Reason*, pp. 271–8.
64 H. Arendt, "Imagination," p. 82.
65 In *Thinking*, imagination also appears as reproductive, secondary to perception but primary to thinking. See LOM I, pp. 86–7. Arendt also refers to the problem of schematism as a condition of any ordinary experience, See LOM I, pp. 100–1.
66 M. Heidegger, *Kant and the Problem of Metaphysics*, op. cit., p. 56. In Heidegger's terminology, imagination is ontologically creative. It does not produce objects but allows them to be revealed. "The productive, i.e., here the pure power of imagination, is purely reproductive in that it makes possible reproduction in general" (ibid., p. 127).
67 Ibid., p. 91.
68 Ibid., p. 107. For Heidegger imagination is the original basis of sensibility and intellect—the unity of pure intuition and pure concepts.
69 CPJ, § 22, p. 124.
70 CPJ, § 35, p. 167.
71 LOM I, p. 215.
72 HAP, *Speeches and Writing File*, *Thinking*, § 21 first draft, p. 148.
73 LKPP, *Imagination*, pp. 84–5.
74 R. A. Makkreel, "Reflection, Reflective Judgment, and Aesthetic Exemplarity," in: *Aesthetics and Cognition in Kant's Critical Philosophy*, ed. R. Kukla, Cambridge University Press, Cambridge 2006, p. 239.
75 LKPP XIII, pp. 76–7.
76 LKPP, *Imagination*, p. 85.
77 LOM I, p. 144.
78 In Kant's teleological judgment concerning the French Revolution, imagination played an additional role that it would not play in Arendt's system. It recognized the purpose thereby serving the anticipation of progress (see R. A. Makkreel, *Imagination and Interpretation*, p. 153). The imagination of genius is also projecting but it projects freely and in an indeterminate way, unlike a specific teleological judgment.
79 L. P. Thiele, "Judging Hannah Arendt," *Political Theory*, vol. 33, no. 5 (2005), p. 707.
80 H.-G. Gadamer, *Truth and Method*, op. cit., pp. 17–26.
81 CPJ, § 20, p. 122. "Common sense" is used for both in the Guyer/Matthews translation.

82 CPJ, § 40, p. 213, note.
83 CPJ, § 20, p. 122. *Sensus communis* here is a certain postulate: "it does not say that everyone will agree with my judgment, but that he ought." It is a subjective principle, which "is nevertheless assumed to be subjectively universal ... [and] could demand universal assent just like an objective one." CPJ, § 22, p. 124.
84 H.-G. Gadamer, op. cit., p. 23. If one follows a Polish logician of the Lvov-Warsaw School, Leon Chwistek, and distinguishes between healthy intellect (zdrowy rozsądek) and common worldview (as synonymous with common sense), the former will also be merely logical and consisting of the law of noncontradiction. See L. Chwistek, "Granice zdrowego rozsądku," in: idem, *Pisma filozoficzne i logiczne*, vol. II. PWN, Warszawa 1963, pp. 1–26.
85 H.-G. Gadamer, *Truth and Method*, op. cit., p. 30.
86 CPJ, § 40, pp. 172–3.
87 LKPP XI, p. 67.
88 CPJ, § 40, pp. 173.
89 LKPP XI, p. 67. In *Thinking*, Arendt appeals to the definition of *sensus communis* by Thomas Aquinas, which is different from the one discussed in *Lectures*. Here, she calls it a "sixth sense" that provides a sense of reality as exceeding the content of particular sensations. Such *sensus communis* also brings communicability but only within the senses of an individual. It assures that they are sensing the same object.
90 LKPP XII, pp. 70–1.
91 LKPP X, p. 64.
92 I. Kant, *Anthropology from a Pragmatic Point of View*, trans. M. J. Gregor, Martinus Nijhoff, The Hague 1974, § 53, 88.
93 R. A. Makkreel, *Imagination and Interpretation*, p. 164. Makkreel argues that it expresses the "transcendental condition of traditional common sense," and thus concrete normative beliefs of a given community (ibid., p. 158).
94 Arendt's translation of the German *allgemeiner Standpunkt*. See I. Kant, "Kritik der Urteilskraft," in: idem, *Gesammelte Werke*, Hrsg. von der Königlich-Preussischen Akademie der Wissenschaften zu Berlin, Bd. 5, Berlin 1908, p. 295.
95 LKPP VII, p. 44.
96 R. A. Makkreel, *Imagination and Interpretation*, p. 160.
97 HAP, *Speeches and Writing File, Judgment*, 032171. On this subject see also BPF, pp. 241–2.
98 Where cultivation means being elevated to a level of generality (See H-G. Gadamer, *Truth and Method*, op. cit., pp. 15–16).
99 CPJ, § 41, p. 177; Kant indirectly expresses the same thought in § 2.
100 R. A. Makkreel, *Imagination and Interpretation*, p. 162.
101 CPJ, § 41, p. 176.

102 CPJ, § 60, p. 229.
103 I. Kant, "Conjectural Beginning of Human History," in: *On History*, ed. Beck, op. cit., p. 54.
104 LKPP IV, p. 26.
105 LKPP XIII, pp. 73-4.
106 Makkreel, *Reflection, Reflective Judgment, and Aesthetic Exemplarity*, p. 234. Rudolf Makkreel interprets the Kantian *gemeinschaftlicher Sinn* not so much as the basis of judgment but rather as its "orientational principle."
107 CPJ, § 19, p. 121.
108 LKPP XIII, p. 74. Emphasis Hannah Arendt.
109 L. M. G. Zerilli, "We Feel Our Freedom. Imagination and Judgment the Thought of Hannah Arendt," *Political Theory*, vol. 33, no. 2 (2005), p. 182.
110 J. Josefson, *Hannah Arendt's Aesthetic Politics: Freedom and the Beautiful*, Springer, Cham 2019.
111 BPF, p. 226.
112 M. T. Cicero, *Tusculan Disputations*, pp. 1 and 39-40.
113 See P. Bourdieu, *Distinction. A Social Critique of the Judgment of Taste*, trans. R. Nice, Routledge, London 1989.
114 CPJ, § 45, p. 185.
115 LKPP X, pp. 64-5.
116 Every scientific community—whether large or small—is already a political organization in Arendt's broad meaning: "An organization … is always a political institution. … No scientific teamwork is pure science," HC, p. 271.
117 LKPP X, p. 64.
118 LKPP XII, p. 69.
119 LKPP XII, p. 69.
120 J. Nedelsky, "Judgment, Diversity, and Relational Autonomy," in: *Judgment, Imagination, and Politics. Themes from Kant and Arendt*, op. cit., p. 118.
121 BPF, p. 151.
122 CPJ, § 45, p. 185.
123 An important caveat is that this argument only applies to what Arendt understands by a proper political action analogous to the operation of an artist endowed with genius. It does not concern history as a collection of behaviors, in the case of which the continuity between the particular events assumes a different guise.
124 CPJ, § 47, p. 188. Art, unlike science, cannot be communicated in the form of certain rules of conduct, because an artist is unable to demonstrate the way in which he produced his work, Kant claims.
125 CPJ, § 49, pp. 195-6.
126 CPJ, § 48, p. 190.
127 CPJ, § 49, p. 195.

128 Ricoeur points to this temporal aspect by noting Arendt's transformation of the distinction between genius and taste into the relationship between historical actors and spectators but does develop the analogy further. Ricoeur, op. cit., p. 100.
129 For example, Kant writes that "the satisfaction in the beautiful must depend upon reflection on an object that leads to some sort of concept (it is indeterminate which)." CPJ, § 4, p. 93.
130 This is a quotation from the *Critique of Pure Reason,* B 104.
131 Makkreel, *Reflection, Reflective Judgment, and Aesthetic Exemplarity,* p. 243. Makkreel claims that these concepts may be inadequate or just "representational," but they are not determinant.
132 CPJ, § 49, p. 194.
133 LKPP XIII, p. 72.
134 Makkreel expresses this view in *Imagination and Interpretation,* pp. 51–8.
135 BPF, p. 241.
136 Beiner agrees: see "Interpretive Essay," op. cit., p. 137.
137 The critics of philosophical modernity insist that it is impossible to do so. Gadamer, for example, blames Kant for restricting the traditional reflection on taste to the sphere of aesthetics. This, in turn, led to establishing a new framework for the self-interpretation of the humanities according to natural-scientific standards. H-G. Gadamer, *Truth and Method,* op. cit., pp. 3–101.
138 Makkreel, among others, discerns the same potential, arguing directly against Gadamer and his view of the dichotomy of epistemology and aesthetics in Kant. See R. Makkreel, *Imagination and Interpretation,* pp. 157–8 and 168–9.
139 CPJ, § 50, p. 197. Emphasis MM.
140 R. Beiner, "Rereading Hannah Arendt's Kant Lectures," op. cit., pp. 98 and 100.
141 Cf. F. Ankersmit, *Sublime Historical Experience,* Stanford University Press, Stanford 2005, pp. 193–239.
142 There is also objective formal purposiveness (without a purpose), which Kant finds in geometrical figures (purposive only for solving mathematical problems) and subjective material purposiveness (associated with what is merely pleasant to the senses).
143 CPJ, § 61, pp. 233–4.
144 With regard to the intellect, a certain whole may be considered only as a mechanical product of its parts—such a whole is then not a purpose but merely an effect (CPJ, § 77, pp. 274–9). In the Kantian system, one does not find purposive connections in nature, yet one must take them into consideration in reflection, in which the parts are dependent upon the whole. This leads to the concept of a primordial intellect as the ultimate cause of the world, the idea of nature as a system, and ultimately, to the concept of the ultimate purpose (*letzter Zweck*) of nature, which is culture. Indirectly, meanwhile, it leads to the concept of the final purpose (*Endzweck*),

which lies outside of nature but for the sake of which, nature exists. The reflective teleological judgment thus provides the regulative coherence to the whole.

145 LKPP X, p. 62.
146 CPJ, § 86, pp. 308–9.
147 CPJ, General Remark on the Teleology, p. 340.
148 Makkreel, *Reflection, Reflective Judgment, and Aesthetic Exemplarity*, p. 243; idem, *Imagination and Interpretation*, pp. 137–8, 147, and 151. Kant claims that the transition from the purposes of nature to the purpose of freedom (from physical teleology to moral teleology) is not smooth and just takes place unnoticed. Physical teleology discerns purposes in nature, but only moral teleology is able to design the final purpose, which exists not in nature but in the mind.
149 HAP, Subject File, 1949–1975, *Kant's Critique of Judgment Seminar*, University of Chicago, Chicago 1964, 1970, 032438.
150 R. A. Makkreel, "Differentiating Dogmatic, Regulative, and Reflective Approaches to History in Kant," in: *Proceedings of the Eighth International Kant Congress, Memphis 1995*, vol. 1, Part 1, Sections 1–2, ed. H. Robinson, Marquette University Press, Milwaukee 1995, p. 123.
151 Idem, *Imagination and Interpretation*, pp. 130–41.
152 A similar view is expressed by Edi Pucci, who argues that any reference to teleology "would seriously risk a rebirth of a speculative philosophy of history." See E. Pucci, "History and the Question of Identity: Kant, Arendt, Ricoeur," *Philosophy and Social Criticism*, vol. 21, no. 5–6 (1995), p. 127.
153 HAP, *Kant's Critique of Judgment Seminar*, 032437.
154 P. Ricoeur, "Aesthetic Judgment," op. cit., p. 103.
155 Ibid., p. 109.
156 Makkreel, *Reflection, Reflective Judgment, and Aesthetic Exemplarity*, p. 233.
157 Among those to address the problem of the temporal orientation of the power of judgment were Jean Yarbrough and Peter Stern ("*Vita Activa* and *Vita Contemplativa*," op. cit., pp. 343–4), but they did not suggest an explicit solution.
158 G. Kateb, "The Judgment of Arendt," in: *Judgment, Imagination, and Politics. Themes from Kant and Arendt*, ed. R. Beiner, J. Nedelsky, Rowman & Littlefield Publishers Inc., Lanham–Boulder–New York–Oxford 2001, p. 121.
159 CPJ, § 15, pp. 111–13.
160 CPJ, § 22, p. 126.

Chapter 9

1 HC, p. 173.
2 HC, p. 168.
3 HC, pp. 167–8.

4 HC, p. 187. Emphasis MM.
5 HC, p. 95.
6 HC, p. 95.
7 HC, p. 169.
8 HC, p. 184. Emphasis MM.
9 HC, pp. 181–2.
10 HC, p. 186.
11 HC, p. 185.
12 HC, p. 228.
13 HC, p. 228.
14 This metaphor appears in the introduction to *Men in Dark Times*, where it relates to action. Meanwhile, commemoration as reification corresponds to work. See A. Herzog, "Illuminating Inheritance: Benjamin's Influence on Arendt's Political Storytelling," *Philosophy & Social Criticism*, vol. 26, no. 5 (2000), pp. 1–27.
15 HC, § 31. This argumentation is possibly inspired by Heidegger's *Seinsvergessenheit*—the criticism of the representational character of post-Cartesian philosophy and the transformation of metaphysics into technology. If the affinity of philosophy and work engenders violence, then scientific history, with which Arendt takes issue, also contains an element of cognitive violence.
16 EU, p. 350.
17 HC, p. 220.
18 LOM I, p. 25.
19 HC, p. 312.
20 HC, pp. 184–5.
21 HC, p. 256.
22 HC, p. 214.
23 LOM II, pp. 156–7.
24 J.-F. Lyotard, "Missive on Universal History," in: *The Postmodern Explained*, trans. and ed. J. Pefanis and M. Thomas, University of Minnesota Press, Minneapolis–London 1997, p. 25. It is no different with the grand narrative of decadence, of which Arendt was a kind. Lyotard says that it "was already in place at the beginning of Western thought … It follows the narrative of emancipation like a shadow." Ibid., p. 29.
25 The metaphor of genesis is present both in the classical (event-based and individualistic) and non-classical (anti-event-based and processual) historiography. However, it assumes epistemologically incommensurable forms. Cf. W. Wrzosek, *History, Culture, Metaphor: The Facets of Non-Classical Historiography*, op. cit. The principle of causality as originally derived from the experience of *homo faber* has an event-based and individualistic structure.
26 CR, p. 172.

27 The main problem of behavioral theories "is not that they are wrong but that they could become true." HC, p. 322. Making history is possible with the use of violence, as totalitarianism proved; history can also be reduced to the level of naked life.
28 LOM II, pp. 203–16.
29 LOM II, p. 207.
30 LOM II, p. 215.
31 The Western phenomenon of renaissances or re-births illustrates the fact that to liberate itself from religion and alleviate the uncertainty of a beginning, the secular tradition sought to justify itself by reference to precedents, which turned out to point to ever deeper continuities. Arendt's pivotal conclusion in *Willing* is that the continuities prevailed. Even the beginning of the West, the foundation of Rome, was a repetition—the regeneration of Troy.
32 LOM II, p. 216.
33 LOM II, p. 217.
34 BPF, p. 85.
35 BPF, p. 262.
36 HC, p. 175. It also appears in the same form in the essay "Truth and Politics," in: BPF, p. 262.
37 MDT, p. 104.
38 MDT, p. 109.
39 MDT, p. 106.
40 MDT, p. 96.
41 In her choice of words, Arendt is not consistent in distinguishing life story from story. She often uses these words interchangeably and meaning either life itself or the story about it. This inconsistency too leads to the fundamental aporia.
42 RV, p. xvi.
43 MDT, p. 109.
44 MDT, p. 104.
45 MDT, p. 104.
46 HC, p. 193.
47 MDT, p. 97.
48 MDT, p. 105.
49 G. Kateb, "Ideology and Storytelling," *Social Research*, vol. 69, no. 2 (2002), p. 352.
50 The term redemption in the context of narrative comes from Seyla Benhabib, who argues that it is a function of Arendt's storytelling as long as it refers to the fragments of the past. See S. Benhabib, "Hannah Arendt and the Redemptive Power of Narrative," *Social Research*, vol. 57, no. 1 (1990), pp. 167–97. The opposition between the two kinds of redemption is not explicit in Arendt's thought, but it is underlined slightly and explored precisely as an opposition in order to reveal the underlying aporia in question.

51 The term oppression is used here as a synonym for the violence of narrative representation that manifests primarily through unnatural closure. See O. Guaraldo, *Storylines: Politics, History and Narrative from an Arendtian Perspective*, University of Jyvaskyla, SoPhi 2001.
52 Benhabib, op. cit., pp. 182, 186, and 191.
53 M. Redhead, "Making the Past Useful for a Pluralistic Present: Taylor, Arendt, and a Problem for Historical Reasoning," *American Journal of Political Science*, vol. 46, no. 4 (2002), p. 811.
54 A. Vowinckel, "Hannah Arendt and Martin Heidegger: History and Metahistory," in: *Hannah Arendt in Jerusalem*, op. cit., pp. 338–46.
55 Beiner, "Interpretive essay," in: LKPP, p. 118.
56 In his work *Introduction à la Philosophie de l'histoire* (1937), p. 183. As cited in: P. Ricoeur, *Memory, History, Forgetting*, op. cit., p. 382.
57 LOM I, p. 216. The maxim also appeared as the motto of the volume on judgment.
58 In *On Revolution*, Arendt presents the semantic change of the term revolution as a consequence of the spectators' storytelling and as largely responsible for the defeat of the revolutionary movement. This thesis is no less than the critical core of the entire book. Arendt argues there that the spectators' point of view leads to the interpretation of history as a means of revealing the truth. Revolutionaries were "fooled" by history insofar as they failed to look on it from the actors' perspective (OR, pp. 34–52). Given that elsewhere Arendt argues that the meaning of historical developments cannot be revealed until they are retrospectively considered, this is another symptom of Arendt's basic aporia.
59 In the words of Hayden White, "narrative discourse serves the purpose of moralizing judgments" (H. White, "The Value of Narrativity in the Representation of Reality," in: idem, *The Content of the Form, Narrative Discourse and Historical Representation*, Johns Hopkins University Press, Baltimore–London 1987, p. 24). White's late experiments with Benjamin's dialectical images and novel forms of historical representation aimed at limiting the consequences of narrative ideologies narrowing the future are somewhat comparable to Arendt's principal concerns. See H. Paul, *The Masks of Meaning, Existentialist Humanism in Hayden White's Philosophy of History*, Rijksuniversiteit, Groningen 2006, pp. 169–200.
60 HC, p. 206.
61 HC, p. 205. Another point supporting this view is that action and power are synonymous precisely because power for Arendt needs no justification in terms of an appeal to its future consequences but requires legitimacy in terms of an appeal to the consent that supports it (see CR, pp. 150–1).
62 HC, p. 192.
63 HC, p. 233.

64 LOM I, p. 96.
65 LOM I, p. 96.
66 HC, pp. 181 and 193.
67 LKPP I, p. 9.
68 CR, p. 128.
69 I. Kant, "The End of All Things," in: idem, *Religion and Rational Theology*, trans. and ed. A. W. Wood, G. di Giovanni, Cambridge University Press, Cambridge 2001, pp. 227–8.
70 LOM II, p. 171. Cf M. Moskalewicz, "Melancholy of Progress: The Image of Modernity and the Time-Related Structure of the Mind in Arendt's Late Work," *Topos*, vol. 2, no. 19(2008), pp. 181–93.
71 J. Kristeva, *Black Sun, Depression and Melancholia*, trans. L. S. Roudiez, Columbia University Press, New York 1989, p. 60.
72 LKPP I, p. 8.
73 LKPP IV, p. 24. See BPF, pp. 82, 85, and 242; LKPP, p. 24; LOM II, p. 154; MDT, p. 91.
74 LKPP IV, p. 25. As in the case of the melancholy of progress, the notion of contingent melancholy does not appear explicitly in Kant. Instead, the German word *trostlos* is used. *Trostlos* means bleak or miserable, so it reflects a mood, which may be associated with melancholy.
75 LKPP IX.
76 BPF, p. 85.
77 LKPP XIII, p. 37.
78 LKPP IX, p. 56.
79 LOM I, p. 164.
80 EU, p. 321.
81 EU, p. 309.
82 LOM II, p. 108.
83 LOM II, p. 108.
84 LOM II, p. 154.
85 HC, p. 188.
86 M. Kreiswirth, "Merely Telling Stories? Narrative and Knowledge in the Human Sciences," *Poetics Today*, vol. 21, no. 2 (2000), pp. 293–318.
87 LOM II, p. 155; L. O. Mink, "History and Fiction as Modes of Comprehension," in: idem, *Historical Understanding*, Cornell University Press, Ithaca–London 1987, p. 61.
88 Cf. Ankersmit's arguments in F. Ankersmit, "Six Theses on Narrativist Philosophy of History," in: idem, *History and Tropology: The Rise and Fall of Metaphor*, University of California Press, Berkeley–Los Angeles–Oxford 1994, pp. 36 and 43 (theses 3.1.4 and 6.1.1). Cf. Carr's arguments against Mink and White and in favor

of the continuity between narrative and experience; D. Carr, "Narrative and the Real World: An Argument for Continuity," *History and Theory*, vol. 25 (1986), pp. 117–31.

89 H. White, "The Fictions of Factual Representation," in: idem, *Tropics of Discourse. Essays in Cultural Criticism*, Johns Hopkins University Press, Baltimore–London 1978, pp. 121–34. There are various "poetic" ways of associating facts, resulting in multiple styles of historical writing. Crucially, White claims, there is no value-neutral mode of emplotment.

90 Cf. the distinguishing features of White's existential humanism according to Herman Paul. See Paul, op. cit., p. 18.

91 White, "The Value of Narrativity," op. cit., pp. 1–25.

92 Vowinckel, *Geschichtsbegriff und Historisches Denken bei Hannah Arendt*, op. cit., p. 326.

93 BPF, pp. 238, 239, 242, and 257. Arendt's use of literature as a historical source might be controversial from the perspective of more conservative historical writing. Despite being a narrativist, Arendt does not mix the orders of historical "truth telling" and literature—a charge sometimes leveled at narrativism. For example, her views on social anti-Semitism in France presented in *The Origins of Totalitarianism* are largely based upon the literary world created by Marcel Proust (J. Kristeva, *Hannah Arendt: Life Is a Narrative*, trans. F. Collins, University of Toronto Press, Toronto–Buffalo–London 2001, pp. 33–48). Arendt regards Proust's internal life, translated into literary language, as "a mirror in whose reflection truth might appear" (OT, p. 80). Further on, Conrad's *Heart of Darkness* is an important source illustrating the experience of racism. The idea of pseudo-mystic aspects of bureaucracy, meanwhile, stems mostly from the works of Franz Kafka. As Brian Danoff noted, in Kafka's works one can even find a threefold destruction of the human person, which Arendt used to describe concentration camps (B. Danoff, "Arendt, Kafka, and the Nature of Totalitarianism," *Perspectives on Political Science*, vol. 29, no. 4 (2000), pp. 211–18). *The Trial* exemplifies the faith of modern man in historical necessity. *The Castle*, meanwhile, represents the futility of the refusal to be subordinated to the functionalist machine. Arendt herself uses *The Castle* as articulating the predicament of Jewish assimilation (L. Weissberg, "In Search of the Mother Tongue: Hannah Arendt's German-Jewish Literature," in: *Hannah Arendt in Jerusalem*, op. cit., pp. 153–4). Furthermore, when discussing the example of what she considers the authentic racism of the Boer settlers in southern Africa, Arendt uses arguments taken mainly from the literary work of Joseph Conrad and Rudyard Kipling.

94 BPF, p. 249.

95 BPF, pp. 261–2.

96 BPF, p. 262.

97 L. J. Disch, *Hannah Arendt and the Limits of Philosophy*, Cornell University Press, Ithaca–London 1994, pp. 1–19. Disch argues that Arendt's notion of understanding situates itself in between traditional Western dichotomies: tradition and revolution, liberalism and communitarianism, abstract rationalism and particularity, empathy and rationalization, humanism and post-structuralism, and the assimilation of the parvenu and the alienation of the pariah. Piotr Nowak, meanwhile, locates it between continuity and discontinuity (P. Nowak, "Two Approaches to the Tradition in Hannah Arendt's Works," *Topos*, vol. 2, no. 19 (2008), pp. 42–7). This book argues, essentially in line with the above, that understating through storytelling stems from the basic aporia of meaning.

98 MDT, p. 20.

99 MDT, p. 21. Emphasis MM.

100 MDT, p. 22.

101 Configurational understanding is different from theoretical and categorial. See Mink, op. cit., pp. 56–7.

102 H. Arendt, *Denktagebuch. 1950 bis 1973*. Erste Band, ed. U. Ludz and I. Nordmann, Piper, München–Zürich 2002, pp. 352–3 (April 1953).

103 A. C. Danto, *Narration and Knowledge*, Columbia University Press, New York 2007, pp. 143–81.

104 LOM II, p. 208.

105 H. White, "Introduction: Tropology, Discourse, and the Modes of Human Consciousness," in: *Tropics of Discourse*, op. cit., pp. 1–25.

106 F. Ankersmit, "Danto's Philosophy of History in Retrospective," in: *Narration and Knowledge*, op. cit., pp. 389–93.

107 Kateb, "The Judgment of Arendt," op. cit., p. 129.

108 Thiele, "Judging Hannah Arendt," op. cit., p. 707.

109 D. Hammer, J. Bleiman, K. Park, "Between Positivism and Postmodernism: Hannah Arendt on the Formation of Policy Judgments," *Policy Studies Review*, vol. 16, no. 1 (1999), p. 158.

110 Leora Bilsky raises this issue and regards a story as a form of action whose function is judgment. See L. Y. Bilsky, "When Actor and Spectator Meet in the Courtroom: Reflections on Hannah Arendt's Concept of Judgment," *History and Memory*, vol. 8, no. 2 (1996), pp. 137–75; idem, "Between Justice and Politics: The Competition of Storytellers in the Eichmann Trial," in: *Hannah Arendt in Jerusalem*, op. cit., pp. 232–52.

111 D. Bell, "Anything Is Possible and Everything Is Permitted: Psychoanalytic Reflections on Hannah Arendt's Elements of Totalitarianism," *Cadernos de Filosofia*, vol. 19–20 (2006), pp. 43–57.

112 OT, p. ix.

113 EU, p. 405.

114 At first sight, this succession looks like Kant's external purposiveness, which is a regulative principle of teleological judgments. The advantage of formal purposiveness, however, is that it is given on the basis of reflective wholes, so that the connections between successive events can be imagined in many different ways.

115 A. Megill, *Historical Knowledge, Historical Error. A Contemporary Guide to Practice*, University of Chicago Press, Chicago–London 2007, pp. 89–92. Allan Megill argues that the fallacy does not belong to narrative as such, but to its improper use, when, for example, a historian presents causal-effective relations without justification.

116 CPJ, § 76, p. 274.

Chapter 10

1. "Philosophy and Sociology," in: EU, pp. 28–43.
2. Arendt's concept of ideology is closer to Mannheim's notion of utopia as it is aimed at the transformation of reality. Cf: K. Mannheim, *Ideology and Utopia. An Introduction to the Sociology of Knowledge*, trans. L. Wirth, E. Shils, Harcourt, Brace, New York 2015 (1936), pp. 55–108 and 229.
3. J. Topolski, *Jak się pisze i rozumie historię*, Oficyna Wydawnicza Rytm, Warszawa 1996, p. 366.
4. H. White, *Metahistory: The Historical Imagination in Nineteenth-Century Europe*, Johns Hopkins University Press, Baltimore–London 1973, pp. 22–9.
5. The tropes of metaphor, metonymy, synecdoche, and irony correspond respectively to (1) plots: romance, tragedy, comedy, satire, (2) arguments: formism, mechanicism, organicism, contextualism, (3) ideological implications: anarchism, radicalism, conservatism, liberalism.
6. White, *Metahistory*, p. 19.
7. Ibid., p. 28. The method employed by Burckhardt in *The Civilization of the Renaissance in Italy* is assumed to be anti-scientific and based to a larger extent on synchronic than on diachronic analysis. See J. Burckhardt, *The Civilization of the Renaissance in Italy*, trans. S. G. C. Middlemore, Dover Publications, Mineola, NY 2010.
8. White, *Metahistory*, p. 38. Such positive political action in Arendt's terms would mean fabricating a preferred social state and thus belong to the category of *homo faber* and not *zoon politikon*.
9. Topolski, *Jak się pisze i rozumie historię?*, op. cit., p. 369.
10. OT, p. viii.
11. OT, p. viii.
12. HC, p. 187.

13 Cf. S. Bahn, "Historian as Taxidermist," in: idem, *The Clothing of Clio*, Cambridge University Press, Cambridge 1984, p. 15.
14 For Collingwood, the history of thoughts is literally reenacted for these thoughts are not simply similar, but are the same thoughts, although now thought by a different subject. R. G. Collingwood, *The Idea of History*, ed. J. van der Dussen, Clarendon Press, Oxford 1993, pp. 282–302.
15 W. Benjamin, *The Arcades Project*, trans. H. Eiland, K. McLaughlin, Harvard University Press, Cambridge, MA–London 2002. Cf. I. Honohan, "Arendt and Benjamin on the Promise of History: A Network of Possibilities or One Apocalyptic Moment?," *Clio*, vol. 19, no. 4 (1990), pp. 311–30.
16 E. H. Skoller, *The In-Between of Writing. Experience and Experiment in Drabble, Duras, and Arendt*, The University of Michigan Press, Ann Arbor 1993, p. 117.
17 RV, p. xv. Emphasis MM.
18 RV, p. xviii.
19 At that stage, not unlike Benjamin, in order to grasp the openness of the historical moment and avoid the superior perspective of the future consequences of events, Arendt used a vast number of quotations from Rahel's extensive correspondence, thus permitting her to speak for herself.
20 RV, p. xvii.
21 S. Benhabib, "The Pariah and Her Shadow: Hannah Arendt's Biography of Rahel Varnhagen," in: *Feminist Interpretations of Hannah Arendt*, ed. B. Honig, The Pennsylvania State University Press, University Park, PA 1995, p. 87.
22 A. Herzog, "The Poetic Nature of Political Disclosure: Hannah Arendt's Storytelling," *Clio*, vol. 30, no. 2 (2001), pp. 169–94.
23 Ibid., p. 187. This is conveyed by the concept of "reflection," which alludes to the metaphor of a mirror. While the actions of people in the past "reflected" the light of the public space, "political stories … are the reflection of this reflection through writing. This is why they are illuminations" (p. 190). Herzog argues that in *Men in Dark Times* Arendt shows "real" stories or public revelations of people from the past. She maintains that Arendt's exposure of Eichmann served the same purpose of illuminating the public sphere of the present since his exposure "illuminated the world, in spite of the darkening activities of the story's character" (p. 191).
24 Elsewhere, Herzog makes a similar claim, contending that stories are a "phenomenal disclosure" that "reflect" the existence and experiences of people from the past—something akin to a second revelation. See A. Herzog, "Illuminating Inheritance," op. cit., pp. 9–10.
25 Skoller, *The In-Between of Writing*, op. cit. p. 101.
26 K. Evers, "The Holes of Oblivion: Arendt and Benjamin on Storytelling in the Age of Totalitarian Destruction," *Telos*, vol. 132 (2005), pp. 115 and 119.
27 R. Beiner, "Walter Benjamin's Philosophy of History," *Political Theory*, vol. 12, no. 3 (1984), pp. 423–34.

28 Cf. M. Pensky, "Method and Time: Benjamin's Dialectical Images," in: *The Cambridge Companion to Walter Benjamin*, ed. David S. Ferris, Cambridge University Press, Cambridge 2004, pp. 177–98.
29 Cf. Vowinckel, *Geschichtsbegriff und Historisches Denken bei Hannah Arendt*, op. cit., pp. 202–15; E. de Valk, "The Pearl Divers. Hannah Arendt, Walter Benjamin and the Demands of History" (unpublished MA thesis, Universiteit Maastricht 2006).
30 EU, p. 319.
31 H. Arendt, "Introduction. Walter Benjamin: 1892–1940," in: W. Benjamin, *Illuminations*, trans. H. Zohn, ed. and trans. H. Arendt, Schocken Books, New York 1969. Elsewhere, Arendt uses the same passage to convey the gift of "poetical thinking," writing that "this thinking delves into the depths of the past—but not in order to resuscitate it the way it was … [but is guided by the conviction] that although the living is subject to the ruin of time, the process of decay is at the same time **a process of crystallization**." See MDT, pp. 205–6. Emphasis MM. Arendt also directly described her own method as *Perlenfischerei* in a letter to Kurt Blumenfeld. See E. Young-Bruehl, *Hannah Arendt: For Love of the World*, Yale University Press, New Haven–London 1982, p. 95.
32 MDT, p. 201.
33 MDT, p. 193.
34 MDT, p. 10.
35 R. Koselleck, "Representation, Event and Structure," in: idem, *Futures Past*, p. 114.
36 D. Luban, "Explaining Dark Times: Hannah Arendt's Theory of Theory," *Social Research*, vol. 50, no. 1 (1983), p. 246.
37 Ibid., p. 239.
38 U. Hanau, "Geschichtsschreibung großen Stils. Elemente und Ursprünge totaler Herrschaft," in: *Vorwärts*, Köln, September 7, 1956, p. 7 (originally in German).
39 Á. Heller, "Hannah Arendt on Tradition and New Beginnings," in: *Hannah Arendt in Jerusalem*, op. cit., p. 21.
40 Benhabib, op. cit., p. 188.
41 Kristeva, op. cit., pp. 7–8; idem, *Hannah Arendt or Refoundation as Survival*, December 15–16, 2006, Bremen.
42 G. Kateb, "Ideology and Storytelling," *Social Research*, vol. 69, no. 2 (2002), p. 330.
43 Guaraldo, op. cit., p. 147.
44 Ibid., p. 66.
45 F. Ankersmit, "Danto's Philosophy of History in Retrospective," in: *Narration and Knowledge*, op. cit., p. 428.
46 Guaraldo, op. cit., p. 214.
47 Ibid., p. 215.

48 H. Arendt, *Thinking without A Bannister*, ed. J. Kohn, Schocken Books, New York 2018, p. 201.
49 Cf. Paul Ricoeur's reflections on the concept of *Darstellung*. See P. Ricoeur, *Memory, History, Forgetting*, op. cit., pp. 565–7.
50 E. H. Gombrich, "Meditations on a Hobby Horse or the Roots of Artistic Form," in: idem, *Meditations on a Hobby Horse and Other Essays on the Theory of Art*, Phaidon, London–New York 1971, pp. 1–11.
51 F. Ankersmit, "Danto on Representation, Identity and Indiscernibles," in: idem, *Historical Representation*, Stanford University Press, Stanford 2001, pp. 218–48. The concept of representation, derived from art history and theory of Ernst Gombrich and Nelson Goodman, was developed by Danto, among others, and applied to historiography by Ankersmit.
52 Idem, "Reply to Professor Zagorin," *History and Theory*, vol. 29, no. 3 (1990), pp. 275–96.
53 Ankersmit, "Historical Representation," in: idem, *History and Tropology*, pp. 97–124. In Ankersmit's narrative logic, narrative substances are analytically true. They are composed of narrative sentences, which on the one hand, describe the past, and on the other, individualize given narrative substances. Narrative substances are thus hidden behind their properties, which are individual sentences describing historical facts. Narrative substances can also be expressed by concepts (such as World War I) representing historical wholes comprising intentional actions and their unintended outcomes.
54 Idem, "Six Theses on Narrativist Philosophy of History," in: ibid., p. 38 (thesis 4.3).
55 Ibid., p. 37 (thesis 4.2.1).
56 P. Ricoeur, *Time and Narrative*, vol. 3, trans. K. Blamey, D. Pellauer, University of Chicago Press, Chicago–London 1988, pp. 246 and 320–1.
57 HC, pp. 186–7.
58 Cf. M. Moskalewicz, "Politics as a Substance of History: On Hannah Arendt's Critique of Narrative Ideology," *Cadernos de Filosofia*, no. 19–20 (2006), pp. 267–88.
59 J. N. Shklar, "Rethinking the Past," *Social Research*, vol. 44, no. 1 (1977), pp. 80–90.
60 M. Amaral, "Political Shipwreck—Authority and the End of Revolution," *Cadernos de Filosofia*, vol. 19–20 (2006), pp. 27–42.
61 OR, p. 225.
62 Cf. Heller's argument in "Hannah Arendt on Tradition and New Beginnings," in: *Hannah Arendt in Jerusalem*, op. cit., pp. 19–32.
63 Cf. the perspective of narrative psychology: H. Hermans, "Conceptions of Self and Identity: Toward a Dialogical View," *International Journal of Education and Religion*, vol. 2, no. 1 (2001), pp. 43–62.

64 BPF, p. 45.
65 LOM I, p. 132.
66 LOM I, p. 133.
67 BPF, p. 45.
68 A. Cavarero, *Relating Narratives, Storytelling and Selfhood*, trans. P. A. Kottman, Routledge, London–New York 2000. For Cavarero, Arendt is a valuable source of inspirations for her own concept of "narratable self." See ibid., pp. 33–4.
69 Ibid., p. 24.
70 Homer, *The Odyssey*, trans. I. Johnston, Richer Resources Publications, Arlington, VA 2006, p. 102.
71 Ibid.
72 Ibid., p. 144.
73 Ibid., p. 161.
74 Ibid., p. 320.
75 Ibid., p. 164.
76 Ibid., p. 162.
77 Ibid., p. 235.
78 Ankersmit, *Danto on Representation, Identity and Indiscernibles*, pp. 236–7.
79 BPF, p. 45.
80 Homer, *The Odyssey*, pp. 276ff. and 376ff.
81 Ibid., p. 389.
82 Ibid., p. 461.
83 Becoming someone else through representation is crucial, for example, in the process of recovery from addiction; Cf. M. Moskalewicz, "Three Modes of Distorted Temporal Experience in Addiction: Daily Life, Drug Ecstasy and Recovery—A Phenomenological Perspective," *Archive of the History of Philosophy and Social Thought. Special Issue: Phenomenology and Social Sciences*, vol. 61 (2016), pp. 197–211.

Conclusion

1 OT, p. vii.
2 Jaspers, *Von den Wahrheit*, R. Piper, München 1947, p. 25.
3 Arendt Personal Library, Bard College, The Hannah Arendt Collection, Marginalia, BD171. J317.
4 K. Löwith, *Meaning in History*, University of Chicago Press, Chicago–London 1949, p. 6.
5 CPJ, § 58, pp. 221–5.

6   Cf. F. Ankersmit, "Historiography and Postmodernism," *History and Theory*, vol. 28, no. 2 (1989), pp. 137–53.
7   The expression "disturbed narrative" comes from Kalle Pihlainen. See K. Pihlainen, "On History as Communication and Constraint," *Ideas in History*, vol. 4, no. 2 (2009), pp. 63–89. In Pihlainen's interpretation, it is the past itself, as opposed to coherent literary fiction, that creates gaps and disruptions in its narrative representation.
8   HC, pp. 104–5.
9   L. Kołakowski, "In Praise of Inconsistency," *Dissent*, vol. 11, no. 2, pp. 201–9.
10 G. Kateb, "Ideology and Storytelling," *Social Research*, vol. 69, no. 2 (2002), p. 335.
11 R. J. Bernstein, *Hannah Arendt and the Jewish Question*, MIT Press, Cambridge, MA 1996, p. 184.
12 P. J. Steinberger, "Hannah Arendt on Judgment," *American Journal of Political Science*, vol. 34, no. 3 (1990), p. 819.
13 G. Kateb, "The Judgment of Arendt," in: *Judgment, Imagination, and Politics. Themes from Kant and Arendt*, ed. R. Beiner, J. Nedelsky, Rowman & Littlefield Publishers Inc., Lanham–Boulder–New York–Oxford 2001, p. 126.
14 Cf. T. Parvikko, "Hannah Arendt and the Arrogance of Judgment," *Alternatives*, vol. 28 (2003), pp. 199–213.
15 Cf. M.-I. Brudny, *Hannah Arendt. Essai de biographie intellectuelle*, Grasset & Fasquelle, Paris 2006.
16 This comparison does not apply to an autobiographical story. As Arendt emphasizes, no one can forgive themself. See HC, § 33.
17 Disch, op. cit., p. 101.
18 Kristeva, op. cit., p. 77.
19 HC, p. 241.

Bibliography

Works by Hannah Arendt

Between Past and Future, Eight Exercises in Political Thought, The Viking Press, New York 1968.
Crises of the Republic, Harcourt Brace Jovanovich, Inc., New York 1972.
Denktagebuch. 1950 bis 1933. Erste Band, ed. U. Ludz and I. Nordmann, Piper, München–Zürich 2002.
Elemente und Ursprünge Totaler Herrschaft, Piper, München–Zürich 1991.
Essays in Understanding 1930–1954: Formation, Exile and Totalitarianism, ed. J. Kohn, Schocken Books, New York 1994.
Hannah Arendt Papers, Manuscript Division, Library of Congress, Washington, D.C.: "Kant's Critique of Judgment Seminar, University of Chicago,1964, 1970," in: *Subject File*, 1949–1975; "Outline: The Elements of Shame; Kant, Immanuel; Judgment; Thinking, first draft," in: *Speeches and Writings File*, 1923–1975; "Series Addition 3, Writings—Notes and excerpts; Special Correspondence, Publishers," in: *Correspondence File*, 1938–1976.
"Labor, Work, Action," in: *Amor Mundi: Explorations in the Faith and Thought of Hannah Arendt*, ed. J. W. Bernauer, S. J., Martinus Nijhoff Publishers, Boston–Dordrecht–Lancaster 1987, pp. 29–42.
Lectures on Kant's Political Philosophy, ed. R. Beiner, University of Chicago Press, Chicago 1982.
Love and Saint Augustine, ed. J. Vecchiarelli Scott and J. Chelius Stark, University of Chicago Press, Chicago–London 1996.
Men in Dark Times, Harcourt Brace & World, Inc., New York 1968.
"On Hannah Arendt," in: *Hannah Arendt: The Recovery of the Public World*, ed. M. A. Hill, St. Martin's Press, New York 1979.
On Revolution, Viking Press, New York 1963.
Rahel Varnhagen, The Life of a Jewish Woman, trans. R. and C. Winston, Harcourt Brace Jovanovich, San Diego–New York–London 1957.
The Human Condition, University of Chicago Press, Chicago–London 1958.
The Jewish Writings, ed. J. Kohn and R. H. Feldman, Schocken Books, New York 2007.
The Life of the Mind, Vol. 1: *Thinking*, Vol. 2: *Willing*, Harcourt Brace & Company, San Diego–New York–London 1978.
The Origins of Totalitarianism, Harcourt Brace & Company, New York 1967.
The Promise of Politics, Schocken Books, New York 2005.
Thinking without a Bannister, ed. J. Kohn, Schocken Books, New York 2018.

Within Four Walls. The Correspondence between Hannah Arendt and Heinrich Blücher 1936–1968, ed. L. Kohler, trans. P. Constantine, Harcourt Inc., New York–San Diego–London 2000.

Other works

Alvarez, A., "Art and Isolation," *The Listener*, January 3, 1957.
Amaral, M., "Political Shipwreck—Authority and the End of Revolution," *Cadernos de Filosofia*, vol. 19–20 (2006), pp. 27–42.
Angehrn, E., *Geschichtsphilosophie*, Kohlhammer, Stuttgart–Berlin–Köln 1991.
Ankersmit, F., "Danto's Philosophy of History in Retrospective," in: *Narration and Knowledge*, ed. A. Danto, Columbia University Press, New York 2007, pp. 364–93.
Ankersmit, F., *Historical Representation*, Stanford University Press, Stanford 2001.
Ankersmit, F., "Historiography and Postmodernism," *History and Theory*, vol. 28, issue 2 (1989), pp. 137–53.
Ankersmit, F., *History and Tropology: The Rise and Fall of Metaphor*, University of California Press, Berkeley–Los Angeles–Oxford 1994.
Ankersmit, F., "Reply to Professor Zagorin," *History and Theory*, vol. 29, issue 3 (1990), pp. 275–96.
Ankersmit, F., *Sublime Historical Experience*, Stanford University Press, Stanford 2005.
Ankersmit, F., "Trust and Representation," in: *Trust: Cement of Democracy?*, ed. F. Ankersmit and H. TeVelde, Peeters, Leuven–Paris–Dudley, MA 2004, pp. 29–48.
Aron, R., "The Essence of Totalitarianism according to Hannah Arendt," *Partisan Review*, vol. 60, issue 3 (1993), trans. M. Le Pain and D. Mahoney, pp. 366–76.
Auden, W. H., "Thinking What We Are Doing," *Encounter*, June 1959, pp. 72–6.
Baehr, P., "Identifying the Unprecedented: Hannah Arendt, Totalitarianism, and the Critique of Sociology," *American Sociological Review*, vol. 67, issue 6 (2002), pp. 804–31.
Baer, W., "Review of *The Origins of Totalitarianism*," *The American Economic Review*, vol. 42, issue 3 (1952), pp. 437–8.
Bahn, S., *The Clothing of Clio*, Cambridge University Press, Cambridge 1984.
Balibar, É., *The Philosophy of Marx*, trans. C. Turner, Verso, London–New York 2014.
Barash, J. A., "The Political Dimension of the Public World: On Hannah Arendt's Interpretation of Martin Heidegger," in: *Hannah Arendt: Twenty Years Later*, ed. L. May and J. Kohn, MIT Press, Cambridge, MA 1996, pp. 251–68.
Bauman, Z., *Modernity and the Holocaust*, Cornell University Press, Ithaca, NY 1989.
Be, "Hannah Arendt, Elemente und Ursprünge Totaler Herrschaft," in: *Gewerkschaftliche Monatshefte*, Köln, December 1957, p. 761.
Beiner, R., "Interpretive Essay," in: LKPP, pp. 89–156.

Beiner, R., "Love and Worldliness: Hannah Arendt's Reading of Saint Augustine," in: *Hannah Arendt: Twenty Years Later*, ed. L. May and J. Kohn, MIT Press, Cambridge, MA 1996, pp. 269–84.

Beiner, R., "Rereading Hannah Arendt's Kant Lectures," in: *Judgment, Imagination, and Politics. Themes from Kant and Arendt*, ed. R. Beiner and J. Nedelsky, Rowman & Littlefield Publishers Inc., Lanham–Boulder–New York–Oxford 2001, pp. 91–101.

Beiner, W., "Walter Benjamin's Philosophy of History," *Political Theory*, vol. 12, issue 3 (1984), pp. 423–34.

Bell, D., "Anything Is Possible and Everything Is Permitted: Psychoanalytic Reflection on Hannah Arendt's Elements of Totalitarianism," *Cadernos de Filosofia*, vol. 19–20 (2006), pp. 43–57.

Benhabib, S., "Hannah Arendt and the Redemptive Power of Narrative," *Social Research*, vol. 57, issue 1 (1990), pp. 167–97.

Benhabib, S., "The Pariah and Her Shadow: Hannah Arendt's Biography of Rahel Varnhagen," in: *Feminist Interpretations of Hannah Arendt*, ed. B. Honig, The Pennsylvania State University Press, University Park, PA 1995, pp. 83–104.

Benhabib, S., *The Reluctant Modernism of Hannah Arendt*, Sage Publications, Thousand Oaks–London–New Delhi 1996.

Benjamin, W., *Illuminations*, ed. H. Arendt, trans. H. Zohn, Harcourt, Brace & World, New York 1968.

Benjamin, W., *The Arcades Project*, trans. H. Eiland and K. McLaughlin, Harvard University Press, Cambridge, MA–London 2002.

Bense, M., "Ein Buch und eine Meinung," *Süddeutscher Rundfunk*, May 3, 1956.

Berkefeld, W., "Ideologie und Terror. Zu Hannah Arendt's Forschungen über Elemente und Ursprünge totaler Herrschaft," *Sonntagsblatt*, Hamburg, April 15, 1956.

Bernstein, R. J., "Arendt on Thinking," in: *The Cambridge Companion to Hannah Arendt*, ed. D. R. Villa, Cambridge University Press, Cambridge 2000, pp. 277–92.

Bernstein, R. J., *Hannah Arendt and the Jewish Question*, MIT Press, Cambridge, MA 1996.

Bernstein, R. J., "Judging—The Actor and the Spectator," in: idem, *Philosophical Profiles: Essays in Pragmatic Mode*, University of Pennsylvania Press, Philadelphia 1986, pp. 221–37.

Bernstein, J. M., "Memorial Aesthetics: Kant's Critique of Judgment," in: idem, *The Fate of Art: Aesthetic Alienation from Kant to Derrida and Adorno*, Pennsylvania State University Press, University Park 1992, pp. 17–65.

Bernstein, R. J., "The Origins of Totalitarianism: Not History, But Politics," *Social Research*, vol. 69, issue 2 (2002), pp. 381–401.

Bernstein, R. J., *Why Read Hannah Arendt Now?*, Polity Press, Cambridge 2018.

Bilsky, L. Y., "Between Justice and Politics: The Competition of Storytellers in the Eichmann Trial," in: *Hannah Arendt in Jerusalem*, ed. S. E. Aschheim, University of California Press, Berkeley–Los Angeles–London 2001, pp. 232–52.

Bilsky, L. Y., "When Actor and Spectator Meet in the Courtroom: Reflections on Hannah Arendt's Concept of Judgment," *History and Memory*, vol. 8, issue 2 (1996), pp. 137–75.

Birmingham, P., "Hannah Arendt: The spectator's vision," in: *The Judge and the Spectator. Hannah Arendt's Political Philosophy*, ed. Joke J. Hermsen and Dana R. Villa, Peeters, Leuven 1999, pp. 29–41.

Boesche, R., *Theories of Tyranny from Plato to Arendt*, Pennsylvania State University Press, University Park 1996.

Bourdieu, P., *Distinction. A Social Critique of the Judgment of Taste*, trans. R. Nice, Routledge, London 1989.

Bowen-Moore, P., *Hannah Arendt's Philosophy of Natality*, Macmillan Press, Houndmills–London 1989.

Bradshaw, L., *Acting and Thinking: The Political Thought of Hannah Arendt*, University of Toronto Press, Toronto–Buffalo–London 1989.

Braun, K., "Biopolitics and Temporality in Arendt and Foucault," *Time & Society*, vol. 16, issue 1 (2007), pp. 5–23.

Brown, J. F., "Review of *The Origins of Totalitarianism*," *The Annals of the American Academy of Political and Social Science*, vol. 277 (1951), pp. 272–3.

Brudny, M.-I., *Hannah Arendt. Essai de biographie intellectuelle*, Grasset & Fasquelle, Paris 2006.

Brzezinski, Z. and Friedrich, C. J., *Totalitarian Dictatorship and Autocracy*, Harvard University Press, Harvard 1965.

Buczyńska-Garewicz, H., *Metafizyczne rozważania o czasie*, Universitas, Kraków 2003.

Burckhardt, J., *The Civilization of the Renaissance in Italy*, trans. S. G. C. Middlemore, Dover Publications, Mineola, NY 2010.

Burrowes, R., "Totalitarianism: The Revised Standard Version," *World Politics*, vol. 21, issue 2 (1969), pp. 272–94.

Canovan, M., "Arendt's Theory of Totalitarianism: A Reassessment," in: *The Cambridge Companion to Hannah Arendt*, ed. D. R. Villa, Cambridge University Press, Cambridge 2000, pp. 25–43.

Canovan, M., *Hannah Arendt: A Reinterpretation of Her Political Thought*, Cambridge University Press, Cambridge 1992.

Carr, D., "Narrative and the Real World: An Argument for Continuity," *History and Theory*, vol. 25 (1986), pp. 117–31.

Cavarero, A., *Relating Narratives, Storytelling and Selfhood*, trans. P. A. Kottman, Routledge, London–New York 2000.

Chwistek, L., *Pisma filozoficzne i logiczne*, vol. 2, PWN, Warszawa 1963.

Collingwood, R. G., *The Idea of History*, ed. J. van der Dussen, Clarendon Press, Oxford 1993.

Cook, T. I., "Review of *The Origins of Totalitarianism*," *Political Science Quarterly*, vol. 66, issue 2 (1951), pp. 290–3.

Crick, B., "Hannah Arendt and 'The Burden of Our Times," *Political Quarterly*, vol. 68, issue 1 (1997), pp. 77–84.

Crick, B., "On Rereading *The Origins of Totalitarianism*," *Social Research*, vol. 44, issue 1 (1977), pp. 106–26.

Curtis, K. F., "Aesthetic Foundations of Democratic Politics in the Work of Hannah Arendt," in: *Hannah Arendt and the Meaning of Politics*, ed. C. Calhoun and J. McGowan, University of Minnesota Press, Minneapolis–London 1997, pp. 27–52.

Curtis, K. F., *Our Sense of the Real: Aesthetic Experience and Arendtian Politics*, Cornell University Press, Ithaca–London 1999.

Danoff, B., "Arendt, Kafka, and the Nature of Totalitarianism," *Perspectives on Political Science*, vol. 29, issue 4 (2000), pp. 211–18.

Danto, A., *Narration and Knowledge*, Columbia University Press, New York 2007.

Darack, A., "A Plunge into Hell," *The Cincinnati Enquirer*, May 13, 1966.

de Valk, E., *The Pearl Divers: Hannah Arendt, Walter Benjamin and the Demands of History* (unpublished MA thesis, Universiteit Maastricht 2006).

Degryse, A., "Arendt's Theory of Judgment and *Sensus Communis*," *Cadernos de Filosofia*, vol. 19, issue 20 (2006), pp. 91–106.

Diner, D., "Hannah Arendt Reconsidered: On the Banal and the Evil in Her Holocaust Narrative," *New German Critique*, issue 71, Spring–Summer (1997), pp. 177–90.

Disch, L. J., *Hannah Arendt and the Limits of Philosophy*, Cornell University Press, Ithaca–London 1994.

Donoghue, D., "Hannah Arendt's *The Life of the Mind*," *Hudson Review*, vol. 32, issue 2 (1979), pp. 281–8.

Dossa, S., *The Public Realm and the Public Self: The Political Theory of Hannah Arendt*, Wilfrid Laurier University Press, Waterloo 1989.

Dostal, R. J., "Judging Human Action: Arendt's Appropriation of Kant," *Review of Metaphysics*, vol. 37, issue 4 (1984), pp. 725–55.

Dray, W. H., *Philosophy of History*, Prentice-Hall Inc., Englewood Cliffs, NJ 1964.

Duzer, C. H. van, "Review of *The Origins of Totalitarianism*," *The American Historical Review*, vol. 57, issue 4 (1952), pp. 933–5.

Evers, K., "The Holes of Oblivion: Arendt and Benjamin on Storytelling in the Age of Totalitarian Destruction," *Telos*, vol. 132 (2005), pp. 109–20.

Ferrara, A., "Judgment, Identity and Authenticity. A Reconstruction of Hannah Arendt's Interpretation of Kant," *Philosophy & Social Criticism*, vol. 24, issue 2/3 (1998), pp. 113–36.

Fine, R., "Judgment and the Reification of the Faculties. A Reconstructive Reading of Arendt's *Life of the Mind*," *Philosophy and Social Criticism*, vol. 34, issue 1–2 (2008), p. 171.

Friedrich, C. J., "The Unique Character of Totalitarian Society," in: idem, *Totalitarianism*, The Universal Library, Grosset & Dunlap, New York 1964, pp. 47–60.

Gadamer, H.-G., "Praise of Theory" (A speech given in Bonn, June 3, 1980), in: idem, *Praise of Theory*, trans. C. Dawson, Yale University Press, New Haven, CT 1998, pp. 16–36.

Gadamer H-G (2007) Text and interpretation. Edited and translated by Palmer RE. The Gadamer Reader. A Bouquet of the Later Writings. Evanston, IL: Northwestern University Press, pp. 156–191.

Gadamer, H.-G., *Truth and Method*, trans. J. Weinsheimer and D. G. Marshall, Continuum, London 2004.

Gandesha, M., "Writing and Judging: Adorno, Arendt and the Chiasmus of Natural History," *Philosophy & Social Criticism*, vol. 30, issue 4 (2004), pp. 445–75.

Goldhagen, D., *Hitler's Willing Executioners: Ordinary Germans and the Holocaust*, Alfred A. Knopf, New York 1996.

Gombrich, E. H., *Meditations on a Hobby Horse and Other Essays on the Theory of Art*, Phaidon, London–New York 1971.

Gray, S., "Hannah Arendt and the Solitariness of Thinking," *Philosophy Today*, vol. 25, issue 2 (1981), pp. 121–30.

Grondin, J., *Introduction to Philosophical Hermeneutics*, trans. J. Weinsheimer, Yale University Press, New Haven, CT 1997.

Guaraldo, O., *Storylines: Politics, History and Narrative from an Arendtian Perspective*, University of Jyvaskyla, SoPhi 2001.

Habermas, J., "Hannah Arendt's Communications Concept of Power," *Social Research*, vol. 44, issue 1 (1977), pp. 3–24.

Habermas, J., "On the German-Jewish Heritage," *Telos*, issue 44 (1980), pp. 127–31.

Habermas, J., *The Philosophical Discourse of Modernity: Twelve Lectures*, trans. F. Lawrence, MIT Press, Cambridge, MA 1990.

Haeffner, G., *The Human Situation. A Philosophical Anthropology*, trans. E. Watkins, University of Notre Dame Press, Notre Dame, IN 1989.

Haerdter, R., "Pathologie eines Zeitalters," *Literatur*, March 24, 1956.

Hammer, D., Bleiman, J., and Park, K., "Between Positivism and Postmodernism: Hannah Arendt on the Formation of Policy Judgments," *Policy Studies Review*, vol. 16, issue 1 (1999), p. 158.

Hanau, U., "Geschichtsschreibung großen Stils. Elemente und Ursprünge totaler Herrschaft," in: *Vorwärts*, Köln, September 7, 1956, p. 7.

Hansen, P., *Hannah Arendt: Politics, History and Citizenship*, Stanford University Press, Stanford 1993.

Hartman, J., "Erotyczna czasoprzestrzeń rynku," *Marketing w Praktyce*, vol. 7, issue 101 (2006), pp. 68–9.

Hegel, G. W. F., *Reason in History*, trans. R. S. Hartman, Bobbs-Merrill, Indianapolis 1953.

Heidegger, M., *Being and Time*, trans. J. Stambaugh, State University of New York Press, Albany 1996.

Heidegger, M., *Kant and the Problem of Metaphysics*, trans. R. Taft, Indiana University Press, Bloomington–Indianapolis 1997.
Heller, Á., "An Imaginary Preface to the 1984 Edition of Hannah Arendt's *The Origins of Totalitarianism*," in: *Eastern Left, Western Left. Totalitarianism, Freedom and Democracy*, ed. F. Feher and Á. Heller, Polity Press, Cambridge 1987, pp. 243–59.
Heller, Á., "Hannah Arendt on Tradition and New Beginnings," in: *Hannah Arendt in Jerusalem*, ed. S. E. Aschheim, University of California Press, Berkeley–Los Angeles–London 2001, pp. 19–32.
Hempel, C. G., "The Function of General Laws in History," *The Journal of Philosophy*, vol. 39, issue 2 (1942), pp. 35–48.
Hermans, H., "Conceptions of Self and Identity: Toward a Dialogical View," *International Journal of Education and Religion*, vol. 2, issue 1 (2001), pp. 43–62.
Herzog, A., "Illuminating Inheritance: Benjamin's Influence on Arendt's Political Storytelling," *Philosophy & Social Criticism*, vol. 26, issue 5 (2000), pp. 1–27.
Herzog, P., "The Poetic Nature of Political Disclosure: Hannah Arendt's Storytelling," *Clio*, vol. 30, issue 2 (2001), pp. 169–94.
Hobsbawm, E. J., "Hannah Arendt on Revolution," in: idem, *Revolutionaries. Contemporary Essays*, Weidenfeld and Nicolson, London 1973, pp. 201–8.
Homer, *The Odyssey*, trans. I. Johnston, Richer Resources Publications, Arlington, VA 2006.
Honig, B., "Arendt, Identity, and Difference," *Political Theory*, vol. 16, issue 1 (1988), pp. 77–98.
Honig, B., "Toward an Agonistic Feminism: Hannah Arendt and the Politics of Identity," in: *Feminist Interpretations of Hannah Arendt*, ed. B. Honig, The Pennsylvania State University Press, University Park, PA 1995, pp. 135–66.
Honkasalo, J., "Praxis, Logos and Theoria—The Threefold Structure of the Human Condition," *Topos*, vol. 2, issue 19 (2008), pp. 169–80.
Honohan, I., "Arendt and Benjamin on the Promise of History: A Network of Possibilities or One Apocalyptic Moment?," *Clio*, vol. 19, issue 4 (1990), pp. 311–30.
Höpker, W., "Hitler oder Stalin—Kehrseiten der gleichen Medaille," *Die Welt*, November 19, 1955.
Höpker, W., "Röntgenbild totalitärer Herrschaft," *Christ und Welt*, April 5, 1956.
Horowitz, I. L., "Open Societies and Free Minds: The Last Testament of Hannah Arendt," *Contemporary Sociology*, vol. 8, issue 1 (1979), pp. 15–19.
Jackson, S. W., *Melancholia and Depression, From Hippocratic Times to Modern Times*, Yale University Press, New Haven–London, 1986.
Jay, M., *Adorno*, Harvard University Press, Cambridge, MA 1984.
Jay, M., "Hannah Arendt: Opposing Views," *Partisan Review*, vol. 45, issue 3 (1978), pp. 348–68.
Jay, M., "Reflective Judgments by a Spectator on a Conference That Is Now History," in: *Hannah Arendt and the Meaning of Politics*, ed. C. Calhoun and J. McGowan, University of Minnesota Press, Minneapolis–London 1997, pp. 338–50.

Jay, M., *Songs of Experience: Modern American and European Variations on a Universal Theme*, University of California Press, Berkeley–Los Angeles–London 2005.
Jay, M., "The Aesthetic Ideology as Ideology: Or What Does It Mean to Aestheticize Politics," in: idem, *Force Fields, between Intellectual History and Cultural Critique*, Routledge, New York–London 1993.
Jonas, H., "Acting, Knowing, Thinking: Gleanings from Hannah Arendt's Philosophical Work," *Social Research*, vol. 44, issue 1 (1977), pp. 32–3.
Josefson, J., *Hannah Arendt's Aesthetic Politics: Freedom and the Beautiful*, Springer, Cham 2019.
Kant, I., *Anthropology from a Pragmatic Point of View*, trans. M. J. Gregor, Martinus Nijhoff, The Hague 1974.
Kant, I., *Critique of Judgment*, trans. J. H. Bernard, Hafner Publishing Co., New York 1951.
Kant, I., *Critique of Pure Reason*, trans. P. Guyer and A. W. Wood, Cambridge University Press, Cambridge–New York 1998.
Kant, I., *Critique of the Power of Judgment*, trans. J. H. Bernard, Hafner, New York 1951.
Kant, I., *Kritik der Urteilskraft*, in: idem, *Gesammelte Werke*, Hrsg. von der Königlich-Preussischen Akademie der Wissenschaften zu Berlin, Bd. 5, Berlin 1908.
Kant, I., *Krytyka władzy sądzenia*, trans. J. Gałecki, PWN, Warszawa 2004.
Kant, I., "Was heisst: Sich im Denken orientieren?," in: idem, *Gesammelte Werke*, Hrsg. von der Königlich-Preussischen Akademie der Wissenschaften zu Berlin, Bd. 8, Berlin 1912.
Kateb, G., "Ideology and Storytelling," *Social Research*, vol. 69, issue 2 (2002), pp. 331–57.
Kateb, G., "Political Action: Its Nature and Advantages," in: *The Cambridge Companion to Hannah Arendt*, ed. D. R. Villa, Cambridge University Press, Cambridge 2000, pp. 130–48.
Kateb, G., "The Judgment of Arendt," in: *Judgment, Imagination, and Politics. Themes from Kant and Arendt*, ed. R. Beiner and J. Nedelsky, Rowman & Littlefield Publishers Inc., Lanham–Boulder–New York–Oxford 2001, pp. 121–38.
King, R. H., "Endings and Beginnings: Politics in Arendt's Early Thought," *Political Theory*, vol. 12, issue 2 (1984), pp. 235–51.
Knorr, K., "Theories of Imperialism," *World Politics*, vol. 4, issue 3 (1952), pp. 402–31.
Kohn, H., "Where Terror Is the Essence," *Saturday Review*, vol. 34 (1951), pp. 10–1.
Kołakowski, L., "In Praise of Inconsistency," *Dissent*, vol. 11, issue 2 (1964), pp. 201–9.
Koselleck, R., "History, Histories and Formal Time Structures," in: idem, *Futures Past. On the Semantics of Historical Time*, trans. K. Tribe, Columbia University Press, New York 2004.
Koselleck, R., "Representation, Event and Structure," in: idem, *Futures Past*, trans. K. Tribe, Columbia University Press, New York 2004.
Kracauer, S., "Time and History," *History and Theory: History and the Concept of Time*, vol. 6 (1966), pp. 65–78.

Kreiswirth, M., "Merely Telling Stories? Narrative and Knowledge in the Human Sciences," *Poetics Today*, vol. 21, issue 2 (2000), pp. 293–318.
Kristeva, J., *Black Sun. Depression and Melancholia*, trans. L. S. Roudiez, Columbia University Press, New York 1989.
Kristeva, J., *Hannah Arendt: Life Is a Narrative*, trans. F. Collins, University of Toronto Press, Toronto–Buffalo–London 2001.
Kristeva, J., *Hannah Arendt or Refoundation as Survival*, Bremen December 15–16, 2006.
Levinas, E., *Time and the Other*, trans. R. A. Cohen, Duquesne University Press, Pittsburgh 1987.
Löwith, K., *Meaning in History*, University of Chicago Press, Chicago–London 1949.
Luban, D., "Explaining Dark Times: Hannah Arendt's Theory of Theory," *Social Research*, vol. 50, issue 1 (1983), pp. 215–48.
Lyotard, J.-F., *The Postmodern Explained: Correspondence, 1982–1985*, trans. and ed. J. Pefanis and M. Thomas, University of Minnesota Press, Minneapolis–London 1997.
MacDonald, D., "A New Theory of Totalitarianism," *New Leader*, vol. 34 (1951), pp. 17–19.
Maier, J., "Über Flüssigmachung des Menchen," *Aufbau*, Friday, March 30, 1951, p. 11.
Makkreel, R. A., "Differentiating Dogmatic, Regulative, and Reflective Approaches to History in Kant," in: *Proceedings of the Eighth International Kant Congress, Memphis 1995*, vol. 1, Part 1, Sections 1–2, ed. H. Robinson, Marquette University Press, Milwaukee 1995.
Makkreel, R. A., *Imagination and Interpretation in Kant. The Hermeneutical Import of the Critique of Judgment*, University of Chicago Press, Chicago–London 1990.
Makkreel, R. A., "Reflection, Reflective Judgment, and Aesthetic Exemplarity," in: *Aesthetics and Cognition in Kant's Critical Philosophy*, ed. R. Kukla, Cambridge University Press, Cambridge 2006.
Mann, T., *Germany and the Germans*, Library of Congress, Washington, DC 1945.
Mannheim, K., *Ideology and Utopia. An Introduction to the Sociology of Knowledge*, trans. L. Wirth and E. Shils, Harcourt, Brace, New York 2015 (1936).
Marrus, M. R., "Reflections on the Historiography of the Holocaust," *The Journal of Modern History*, vol. 66, issue 1 (1994), pp. 92–116.
Masters, R., "Review of *Origins of Totalitarianism*," *Libertarian Review*, April 1975.
McCormick, J. P., "Irrational Choice and Mortal Combat as Political Destiny: The Essential Carl Schmitt," *Annual Review of Political Science*, vol. 10, issue 3 (2007), pp. 315–39.
Megill, A., *Historical Knowledge, Historical Error. A Contemporary Guide to Practice*, University of Chicago Press, Chicago–London 2007.
Michalski, K., *Logic and Time. An Essay on Husserl's Theory of Meaning*, trans. A. Czerniawski and J. Dodd, Kluwer Academic Publishers, Dordrecht–Boston–London 1997.

Milgram, S., *Obedience to Authority: An Experimental View*, Harper & Row, New York 1974.
Mink, L. O., *Historical Understanding*, Cornell University Press, Ithaca–London 1987.
Montesquieu, *The Spirit of the Laws*, Cambridge University Press, Cambridge 1989.
Mooij, J. J. A., *Time and Mind: The History of a Philosophical Problem*, trans. P. Mason, Brill, Leiden–Boston 2005.
Morgenthau, H., "Hannah Arendt on Totalitarianism and Democracy," *Social Research*, vol. 44, issue 1 (1977), pp. 127–31.
Moruzzi, N. C., "Re-Placing the Margin: (Non)Representations of Colonialism in Hannah Arendt's *The Origins of Totalitarianism*," *Tulsa Studies in Women's Literature*, vol. 10, issue 1 (1991), pp. 109–20.
Moruzzi, N. C., *Speaking through the Mask: Hannah Arendt and the Politics of Social Identity*, Cornell University Press, Ithaca–London 2000.
Moskalewicz, M., "Melancholy of Progress: The Image of Modernity and the Time-Related Structure of the Mind in Arendt's Late Work," *Topos*, vol. 2, issue 19 (2008), pp. 181–93.
Moskalewicz, M., "Politics as a Substance of History: On Hannah Arendt's Critique of Narrative Ideology," *Cadernos de Filosofia*, vol. 19–20 (2006), pp. 267–88.
Moskalewicz, M., "Three Modes of Distorted Temporal Experience in Addiction: Daily Life, Drug Ecstasy and Recovery—A Phenomenological Perspective," *Archive of the History of Philosophy and Social Thought. Special Issue: Phenomenology and Social Sciences*, vol. 61 (2016), pp. 197–211.
Nedelsky, J., "Judgment, Diversity, and Relational Autonomy," in: *Judgment, Imagination, and Politics. Themes from Kant and Arendt*, ed. R. Beiner and J. Nedelsky, Rowman & Littlefield Publishers Inc., Lanham–Boulder–New York–Oxford, Oxford 2001, p. 103–20.
Nordmann, I. "How to Write about Totalitarianism? Entwicklung eines Konzepts, das Fragen offenlegt," in: *Über den Totalitarismus, Berichte und Studien*, Nr. 17, Hannah-Arendt-Institut für Totalitarismusforschung e. V. an der Technischen Universität Dresden, Dresden 1998, pp. 53–68.
Norkus, Z., "Why Hannah Arendt's Ideas on Totalitarianism Are Heterodox?," *Topos*, vol. 2, issue 19 (2008), pp. 114–36.
Norris, A., "Arendt, Kant, and the Politics of Common Sense," *Polity*, vol. XXIX, issue 2 (1996), pp. 165–11.
L. Nowak, *On the Hidden Unity of Social and Natural Sciences*, Poznan Studies in the Philosophy of the Sciences and the Humanities, vol. 100, no. 1 (2012), pp. 15–50.
Nowak, P., "Two Approaches to the Tradition in Hannah Arendt's Works," *Topos*, vol. 2, issue 19 (2008), pp. 42–7.
O'Boyle, L., "The Class Concept in History," *The Journal of Modern History*, vol. 24, issue 4 (1952), pp. 391–7.
O'Meara, T., "The Life of the Mind," *Theology Today*, vol. 36, issue 1 (1979), pp. 99–103.

Parekh, B., *Hannah Arendt and the Search for a New Political Philosophy*, Macmillan Press, London–Basingstoke 1981.

Parkes, J., "Present Discontents," *The Jewish Chronicle*, November 6, 1951.

Parvikko, T., "Hannah Arendt and the Arrogance of Judgment," *Alternatives*, vol. 28 (2003), pp. 199–213.

Passerin D'Entrèves, M., "Arendt's Theory of Judgment," in: *The Cambridge Companion to Hannah Arendt*, ed. D. R. Villa, Cambridge University Press, Cambridge 2000, pp. 245–60.

Passerin D'Entrèves, M., *The Political Philosophy of Hannah Arendt*, Routledge, London–New York 1994.

Paul, H., *Hayden White. The Historical Imagination*, Polity Press, Cambridge 2011.

Paul, H., *The Masks of Meaning: Existentialist Humanism in Hayden White's Philosophy of History*, Rijksuniversiteit Groningen, Groningen 2006.

Pensky, M., "Method and Time: Benjamin's Dialectical Images," in: *The Cambridge Companion to Walter Benjamin*, ed. David S. Ferris, Cambridge University Press, Cambridge 2004, pp. 177–98.

Pihlainen, K., "On History as Communication and Constraint," *Ideas in History*, vol. 4, issue 2 (2009), pp. 63–89.

Pohlmann, J., "Elemente und Ursprünge Totaler Herrschaft," *Welt der Arbeit*, January 27, 1956.

Popper, K. R., *The Open Society and Its Enemies*, Routledge, Abingdon 2011.

Popper, K. R., *The Poverty of Historicism*, Routledge, London–New York 2004.

Pucci, E., "History and the Question of Identity: Kant, Arendt, Ricoeur," *Philosophy and Social Criticism*, vol. 21, issue 5–6 (1995), pp. 125–36.

Radden, J., "From Melancholic States to Clinical Depression," in: *The Nature of Melancholy*, ed. J. Radden, Oxford University Press, New York 2000, pp. 3–51.

Redhead, M., "Making the Past Useful for a Pluralistic Present: Taylor, Arendt, and a Problem for Historical Reasoning," *American Journal of Political Science*, vol. 46, issue 4 (2002), p. 803–18.

Reich, R., "Vom Wesen totaler Herrschaft. Zur deutschen Ausgabe von Hannah Arendts *The Origins of Totalitarianism*," *Neue Zürcher Zeitung*, September 28, 1957.

Reinhold, H. A., "The State as Monster," *Commonweal*, June 8, 1951, pp. 217–18.

Ricoeur, P., "Action, Story and History: On Re-reading," *The Human Condition*, *Salmagundi*, vol. 60 (1983), pp. 60–72.

Ricoeur, P., "Aesthetic Judgment and Political Judgment according to Hannah Arendt," in: idem, *The Just*, trans. D. Pellauer, University of Chicago Press, Chicago–London 2000, pp. 94–108.

Ricoeur, P., *Memory, History, Forgetting*, trans. K. Blamey and D. Pellauer, University of Chicago Press, Chicago 2004.

Ricoeur, P., *Time and Narrative*, vol. 3, trans. K. Blamey and D. Pellauer, University of Chicago Press, Chicago–London 1988.

Rieff, P., "The Theology of Politics: Reflections on Totalitarianism as the Burden of Our Time," *Journal of Religion*, vol. 32, issue 2 (1952), pp. 119–26.
Riesman, D., "Review of *The Origins of Totalitarianism*," *Commentary*, vol. 11 (1951), pp. 392–8.
Ring, J., *The Political Consequences of Thinking: Gender and Judaism in the Work of Hannah Arendt*, State University of New York Press, New York 1998.
Roberts, D., "Crowds and Power or the Natural History of Modernity: Horkheimer, Adorno, Canetti, Arendt", *Thesis Eleven*, vol. 45 (1996), pp. 39–68.
Schacht, R., "Philosophical Anthropology: What, Why and How," *Philosophy and Phenomenological Research*, vol. 50, supplement (1990), pp. 155–76.
Schall, J. V., S. J., "The Life of the Mind," *Theological Studies*, vol. 40, issue 1 (1979), pp. 204–6.
Schumpeter, J., *Imperialism and Social Classes*, trans. H. Norden, Meridian Books, Cleveland–New York 1951.
Shier, D., "Why Kant Finds Nothing Ugly," *The British Journal of Aesthetics*, vol. 38 (1998), pp. 412–18.
Shklar, J. N., "Rethinking the Past," *Social Research*, vol. 44, issue 1 (1977), pp. 80–90.
Shorris, E., "In Praise of Sheer Nonsense," *Harper's Magazine*, vol. 257, issue 1539 (1978), pp. 84–6.
Skarga, B., *Kwintet metafizyczny*, Universitas, Kraków 2005.
Skoller, E. H., *The In-Between of Writing. Experience and Experiment in Drabble, Duras, and Arendt*, The University of Michigan Press, Ann Arbor 1993, p. 117.
Sorial, S., "Hannah Arendt's Concept of the Political," *Cadernos de Filosofia*, vol. 19–20 (2006), pp. 373–90.
Stanley, J. L., "Is Totalitarianism a New Phenomenon? Reflections on Hannah Arendt's," *The Origins of Totalitarianism*, *Review of Politics*, vol. 49, issue 2 (1987), pp. 177–207.
Starr, C. G., "Historical and Philosophical Time," *History and Theory: History and the Concept of Time*, vol. 6 (1966), pp. 24–35.
Steinberger, P. J., "Hannah Arendt on Judgment," *American Journal of Political Science*, vol. 34, issue 3 (1990), pp. 803–21.
Stern, P. and Yarbrough, J., "*Vita Activa* and *Vita Contemplativa*: Reflections on Hannah Arendt's Political Thought in *The Life of the Mind*," *The Review of Politics*, vol. 43, issue 3 (1981), pp. 323–54.
Taminiaux, J., *The Thracian Maid and the Professional Thinker: Arendt and Heidegger*, trans. M. Gendre, State University of New York Press, New York 1997.
Thiele, L. P., "Judging Hannah Arendt," *Political Theory*, vol. 33, issue 5 (2005), pp. 706–14.
Topolski, J., *Jak się pisze i rozumie historię*, Oficyna Wydawnicza Rytm, Warszawa 1996.
Topolski, J., *Metodologia historii*, PWN, Warszawa 1984.
Topolski, J., *Rozumienie historii*, PIW, Warszawa 1978.
Turetzky, P., *Time*, Routledge, London–New York 1998.

Varikas, E., "'The Burden of Our Time': Hannah Arendt and the Critique of Political Modernity," trans. D. Macey, *Radical Philosophy*, vol. 92 (1998), pp. 17–24.

Villa, D. R., *Arendt and Heidegger: The Fate of the Political*, Princeton University Press, Princeton–New Jersey 1996.

Villa, D. R., "The Development of Arendt's Political Thought," in: *The Cambridge Companion to Hannah Arendt*, ed. D. R. Villa, Cambridge University Press, Cambridge 2000, pp. 1–21.

Voegelin, E., "The Origins of Totalitarianism," *The Review of Politics*, vol. 15, issue 1 (1953), pp. 68–76 and 84–5.

Vowinckel, A., *Geschichtsbegriff und Historisches Denken bei Hannah Arendt*, Böhlau Verlag GmbH & Cie, Köln 2001.

Vowinckel, A., "Hannah Arendt and Martin Heidegger: History and Metahistory," in: *Hannah Arendt in Jerusalem*, ed. S. E. Aschheim, University of California Press, Berkeley–Los Angeles–London 2001, pp. 338–46.

Weissberg, L., "In Search of the Mother Tongue: Hannah Arendt's German-Jewish Literature," in: *Hannah Arendt in Jerusalem*, ed. S. E. Aschheim, University of California Press, Berkeley–Los Angeles–London 2001, pp. 149–64.

White, H., *Metahistory: The Historical Imagination in Nineteenth-Century Europe*, Johns Hopkins University Press, Baltimore–London 1973.

White, H., *The Content of the Form, Narrative Discourse and Historical Representation*, Johns Hopkins University Press, Baltimore–London 1987.

White, H., *Tropics of Discourse. Essays in Cultural Criticism*, Johns Hopkins University Press, Baltimore–London 1978.

Whitfield, S. J., *Into the Dark: Hannah Arendt and Totalitarianism*, Temple University Press, Philadelphia 1980.

Wolin, R., *Heidegger's Children: Hannah Arendt, Karl Löwith, Hans Jonas, and Herbert Marcuse*, Princeton University Press, Princeton–Oxford 2003.

Wolin, S., "Hannah Arendt and the Ordinance of Time," *Social Research*, vol. 44, issue 1 (1977), pp. 91–105.

Wrzosek, W., *History, Culture, Metaphor: The Facets of Non-classical Historiography*, Wydawnictwo Naukowe Uniwersytetu im. Adama Mickiewicza, Poznań 1997.

Wrzosek, W., "In Search of Historical Time. An Essay on Time, Culture, and History," in: *Narration and Explanation*, ed. J. Topolski, Rodopi, Amsterdam–Atlanta, GA 1990, pp. 119–29.

Wrzosek, W., "O trzech rodzajach stronniczości w historii," in: *Pamięć i polityka historyczna. Doświadczenia Polski i jej sąsiadów*, ed. S. M. Nowinowski, J. Pomorski, and R. Stobiecki, Instytut Pamięci Narodowej, Łódź 2008, pp. 77–90.

Yar, M., "From Actor to Spectator. Hannah Arendt's 'Two Theories' of Political Judgment," *Philosophy & Social Criticism*, vol. 26, issue 2 (2000), pp. 1–27

Young-Bruehl, E., *Hannah Arendt: For Love of the World*, Yale University Press, New Haven–London 1982.

Young-Bruehl, E., "Hannah Arendt's Storytelling," *Social Research*, vol. 44, issue 1 (1997), pp. 183–90.
Young-Bruehl, E., "Reflections on Hannah Arendt's *The Life of the Mind*," *Political Theory*, vol. 10, issue 2 (1982), pp. 277–305.
Zaner, R. M., "An Approach to a Philosophical Anthropology," *Philosophy and Phenomenological Research*, vol. 27, issue 1 (1966), pp. 55–68.
Zerilli, L. M. G., "We Feel Our Freedom. Imagination and Judgment the Thought of Hannah Arendt," *Political Theory*, vol. 33, issue 2 (2005), pp. 158–88.

Index

A
absolute beginning 9, 72–4, 142
Achilles (mythological character) 118
action (concept) 55, 69–71, 92, 135, 185n (13), 211n (76)
  and history 97–101, 126, 130, 155
  and meaning 147–8, 151, 166–8, 174
  as narrative 167–8
  as new beginning 74, 141
  as performative work of art 75–7, 79–81
  political 125–6
  as reenactment 161–3, 173
  and storytelling 170–2, 182
  temporality of 93–5, 105
  and thinking 81–3, 93–5, 214n (124)
  and willing 72–3, 89
  and work 136–9, 203n (24), 207n (4)
actor and spectator 76, 80, 91–3, 112–16, 117, 127, 130–1, 147–8, 150, 176
Adorno, Theodor 39
Aeneas (mythological character) 141
Alcinous (mythological character) 174–5
Alvarez, Al 14
animal laborans (*see*: labor)
Ankersmit, Frank
  on narrative 155–6, 175
  on philosophy of history 39–40
  on representation 169, 238n (53)
anthropology 41–2, 196n (16–17)
anti-Semitism 19–25, 190n (47)
Argus (mythological character) 175–6
Aristotle 69, 71, 89, 152, 203n (34)
Aron, Raymond 15, 17, 146
Augustine (St.) 72–4, 142, 151

B
Baehr, Peter 62
Baer, Werner 15
Bauman, Zygmunt 28
Beiner, Ronald 111, 130
  on two conceptions of judgment 91–2, 146, 216n (30)
Being and Time (Heidegger) 25, 47, 69–70, 79–80, 198n (34)
Bell, David 156
Benhabib, Seyla 1, 80, 163
  on narrative and storytelling 145–6, 166, 230n (50)
Benjamin, Walter 5, 60, 63, 146
  on historical method 162–5, 231n (59), 236n (19)
Bense, Max 18
Bentham, Jeremy 65
Berkefeld, Wolfgang 17
Berlin, Isaiah 17, 30, 181
Bernard, John Henry 111
Bernstein, Jay M.
  on aesthetic judgment 221n (13)
Bernstein, Richard 61, 63, 83, 181–2
  on early and late Arendt 2, 184n (6), 216n (30)
Blixen, Karen 142–5, 153, 163
Bloch, Marc 64
Blücher, Heinrich 13, 27
Bonaparte, Napoleon 118
Boulainvilliers, Henri de (Count) 23
Bradshaw, Leah 2
Braun, Kathrin 94
break in tradition (*see*: time – gap in)
Brooks, Paul 16
Brzeziński, Zbigniew 26–7
Buffett, Warren 103
Burckhardt, Jacob 160, 235n (7)
Burrowes, Robert 15, 62

C
Calypso (mythological character) 174–5
Canovan, Margaret
  on *The Human Condition* 197n (24)
  on totalitarianism 28, 66
Cato (the Younger) 146

Cavarero, Adriana 173
Char, René 35
Cicero 87–8, 124
Circe (mythological character) 175
cognition 43–4, 55–6, 102, 131
Collingwood, Robin 162–3, 236n (14)
common sense (*see*: sensus communis)
consciousness 32, 43–4, 46, 198n (34)
contingency (*see*: history – contingency)
Cook, Thomas 16
Crick, Bernard
    on Arendt's historical method 63, 65, 205n (78)
Critique of the Power of Judgment (Kant) (*see*: Kant)
Critique of Practical Reason (Kant) 73, 107, 109
Critique of Pure Reason (Kant) 73–4, 107, 109, 116, 118, 221n (8), 223n (60)

D
Danto, Arthur 154
Darack, Arthur 14
Demodocus (mythological character) 172–6
Descartes, René 55–6
Disch, Lisa 182, 234n (97)
Disraeli, Benjamin 21
Dostal, Robert 107
Dray, William
    philosophy of history 40, 195n (9)
Duns Scotus, John 72–3, 98

E
Eichmann in Jerusalem (Arendt) 86, 163
Eumaeus (mythological character) 175
Eurycleia (mythological character) 176
Evers, Kai 163

F
Fine, Robert 45
Francis of Assisi (St.) 118
Frankfurt School 28
freedom 37, 71–4, 87, 141–2
    and power 80–2, 209n (34)
Friedrich, Carl J. 14, 26–7
future (*see*: time – future)

G
Gadamer, Hans-Georg 120, 129–30
    judgment 109

representation 78–9
theory and practice 56
genius (*see*: Kant – genius)
Gentile, Giovanni 25
Ginzburg, Carlo 21
Giroux, Robert 16
Gobineau, Arthur de 23
Goldhagen, Daniel 19
Gombrich, Ernst
    on representation 168–9, 238n (51)
Guaraldo, Olivia
    on narrative and representation 146, 166–7, 231n (51)

H
Habermas, Jürgen 1
    on public sphere 80, 213n (102)
Haerdter, Robert 17
Hanau, Ursel 166
Hayek, Friedrich von 25
Hegel, Georg Wilhelm Friedrich 115, 153, 196n (13), 215n (11)
    on history 90, 100, 104, 113–14, 150
    on time 103
Heidegger, Martin 4, 9, 25, 37, 41, 81, 83, 89, 160, 169, 197n (27)
    on existentials 42, 70
    on imagination 116–18
    on self 69–70, 79–80, 196n (16), 198n (34)
    on time 46–7, 200n (60)
    on turn 99
Heller, Ágnes 166, 172
    on totalitarianism 61, 205n (70)
Hempel, Carl 52, 67
hermeneutics 41–2
Herzog, Annabel 162–3, 236n (23–4)
historical event 61, 91, 94, 99, 114–15, 153
    as crystallization 29, 60–1, 63–4, 180
historical writing (*see*: historiography)
historicism (*see* Popper)
historiography (*see also*: story) 39–41, 67, 135–8, 154, 169, 196n (13)
    fragmented 35, 37, 135, 165, 168, 171–2, 181–3
    and ideology 159–61
    and literary fiction 137, 152, 233n (93)
    postmodern 181
    scientific 67, 98, 194n (37)
history 39–40, 97–101

contingency of 98, 137–8, 145, 151–3,
157, 167–8, 171–2
decline of 105
end of 34, 101, 113–15, 154
as fabrication 139–40
monumental 171
necessity of 87, 145–6, 151, 193n (20)
progress of 102–4, 113–14, 132, 148–9
unpredictability of 99–101
Hobbes, Thomas 25
Hobsbawm, Eric 64
homo faber (*see*: work)
Honig, Bonnie 1, 72
Honkasalo, Julian 218n (56)
Höpker, Wolfgang 17
Husserl, Edmund 46

I
ideology 23, 27, 51–4, 57–9, 65–6
narrative 159–61
imagination 82, 116–19, 123–4, 128–9,
200n (60), 212n (82)
imperialism 21–5

J
Jaspers, Karl 18, 179
Jay, Martin 39, 75, 210n (60)
Jonas, Hans 41, 82
Josefson, Jim 124
judgment 86, 217, 221n (8, 13)
aesthetic 107–12, 119, 128–9
as forgiveness 182
historical 90–3, 113–15, 118–19,
127–30, 133–4
and narrative 143, 155–7, 180–1
and *sensus communis* 121–5
teleological 131–2

K
Kafka, Franz 47
literature as historical source 233n (93)
Kant, Immanuel
on absolute beginning 73–4
on aesthetic judgment 107–12, 119,
128–9
on common sense and *sensus
communis* 120–4, 222n (31)
on genius 9–10, 75–8, 125–9, 211n
(75), 212n (79)
on history 90, 107, 112–15, 132–3
on imagination 116–18, 223n (60)

on presentation 77–8
on progress 148–9, 224n (78)
on public use of reason 81–2
on purposiveness 125–6, 130–2, 157,
180, 222n (29), 227n (142, 144),
235n (114)
on sociability 122–4
Kant and the Problem of Metaphysics
(Heidegger) 117–18, 197n (27),
200n (60)
Kateb, George 133, 145, 155, 166, 181
Kierkegaard, Søren 2
King, Richard 39
Knorr, Klaus 17, 22
Kohn, Hans 16
Kołakowski, Leszek 181
Koselleck, Reinhart 37, 57, 165, 187n (22),
204n (44)
Koyré, Alexandre 103
Kristeva, Julia 75, 149, 166–7, 182, 208n
(17)

L
labor (concept) 32–4, 54–5, 59, 93–4, 135,
140–1, 185n (13), 193n (20, 27)
temporality of 33–4, 105, 193n (16)
Laertes (mythological character) 174–5
Lectures on Kant's Political Philosophy
(Arendt) 7, 107
Lectures on the Philosophy of History
(Hegel) 100
Levinas, Emmanuel 88–9
Lichtheim, Georg 14
Life of the Mind, The (Arendt) 4, 6, 85–6,
186n (14), 186n (16), 208n (28)
Locke, John 32
Löwith, Karl 103, 104, 180
Luban, David 35, 166
Luxemburg, Rosa 22

M
MacDonald, Dwight 14
Maier, Josef 14
Makkreel, Rudolf 122, 128, 132
Mann, Thomas 28
Mannheim, Karl 159–60
Marrus, Michael 30
Marx, Karl 2, 22, 32–3, 104, 193n (20)
marxism 15, 22, 62, 64, 89, 140, 159
Masters, Robert 62
meaning (concept) 44–5, 199n (38)

contradiction between political and historical 1–3, 43, 101, 145–54
and storytelling 142–4, 166–71, 173–6, 181
melancholy 148–9, 232n (74)
Men in Dark Times (Arendt) 79, 236n (23)
Mill, John Stuart 65
Minerva (mythological character) 150
Mink, Louis 152, 154
Montesquieu 27–8, 51
Moruzzi, Norma 1
Mussolini, Benito 25

N
narrativism (*see also*: story) 151–2, 155, 160, 176
necessity 32–4 (*see also*: history – necessity)
Nedelsky, Jennifer 125
Neumann, Franz 25
Nietzsche, Friedrich 2, 37, 47, 149, 171
Nordmann, Ingeborg 62

O
O'Boyle, Lenore 22
Odysseus (mythological character) 172–6, 183
On Revolution (Arendt) 37, 64, 171–2, 231n (58)
Origins of Totalitarianism, The (Arendt)
methodology of 53, 60, 63, 67, 156, 159–61, 179–81
reception of 13–18, 166, 185n (10), 188n (13)

P
Parker, James 15–16
Passerin D'Entrèves, Maurizio 41, 216n (30)
past (*see*: time – past)
Paul, Herman 64, 152
Penelope (mythological character) 174–6
Phaeacians (mythological character) 172, 174, 176
phenomenology 32, 43–4, 46–7
philosophy of history 3
Kant's 107, 126, 149
speculative 6, 30, 39–42, 98–101, 138–9, 195n (12)
Pihlainen, Kalle 240n (7)
Plato 113, 115, 124, 139, 202n (16), 203n (34)

Pohlmann, Julie 16–17
Popper, Karl 40, 53–4, 57–8, 67–8, 87, 202n (13)
Portmann, Adolf 78–9
process (concept) 220n (29–30)
production (*see*: work)
progress (*see*: history – progress)
Pucci, Edi 228n (152)
purposiveness 56, 65–6, 105, 107–8, 130–2, 227n (142, 144)
in itself 44
purposelessness 29, 32, 34, 66, 105, 199n (43)
without a purpose 76–7, 111–2, 125–8, 155–7

R
racism 22–3
Redhead, Mark 145
reenactment 161–3, 167–8, 170, 173
reflection (operation of) 76, 123–5, 127 (*see also*: imagination)
Reich, Richard 17
reification 75, 136, 144
Reinhold, Hans A. 14
representation
historical 135–9, 161–70
others 123–4
self 77–9, 172–7, 198n (35), 239n (83)
Ricoeur, Paul 41, 46, 102, 132, 170, 217n (35), 227n (128)
Rieff, Philip 18, 28
Riesman, David 14, 18
Ring, Jennifer 1
Rousset, David 165

S
Schelling, Friedrich Wilhelm Joseph von 140
Schumpeter, Joseph 22
science 55–8, 102–3
social 62, 65–8, 98, 164
Scotus, Duns 72, 73, 98
self 69–71, 75–9, 89, 168–9, 173–7
sensus communis 82, 120–5, 222n (31), 225n (89)
Shakespeare, William 164–5
Shklar, Judith 171
Skarga, Barbara 94
Skoller, Eleanor 163
Smith, Adam 33, 140

Socrates 81
spectator (*see*: actor and spectator)
Steinberger, Peter 182
Stern, Peter 228n (157)
story (*see also*: historiography)
    as action 166–8, 172, 176, 182
    auto/biographical 142–4, 150, 163, 170, 172–7
    fictional 37, 136–41, 144–5
    as forgiveness 182
    fragmented 156, 161–5, 181
    function of 145–8, 151–5, 169–72
    life (real) 97–8, 136–8, 150, 170, 230n (41)
    as purposive without a purpose 156–7, 180
    as reconciliation 172–3
    as representation 168–70, 175–6

T
Taminiaux, Jacques 45, 70, 86, 102
Telemachus (mythological character) 174–6
teleology (*see*: purposiveness, Kant – purposiveness)
temporality (*see*: time)
Thiele, Lesie 155
thinking 43–9, 56, 186n (16), 198n (34), 199n (37–8)
    and acting 81–3, 93–5, 214n (124), 218n (56)
    and willing 85–8
time 5–8, 41, 187n (22)
    of action and thinking 93–5
    circular 32–4, 59, 105
    discontinuity of 72–4, 141–2
    as duration 54, 102
    and fatalism 53, 58, 87–8
    future 88–90, 160–1, 165–6
    gap in 34–7, 47, 61, 93–5, 179, 183
    infinite 25, 103–4, 114
    of the mind 85–6
    past 35, 89–90, 133–4
    phenomenological 45–9
    public 79
Tocqueville, Alexis de 24–5
Topolski, Jerzy 40, 160, 195n (8), 202n (8)
Totalitarian Dictatorship and Autocracy (Friedrich, Brzezinski) 26–7
totalitarianism 25–30, 57–8, 180, 188n (13)
    explanation of 4, 24–5, 60–7, 156–7
    and ideology 51–3
    as labor 31–2, 34, 59
    and terror 27, 29–30, 66
tradition
    break in 35–7
    and revolution 171–2
Truth and Politics (Arendt) 152–3

U
utilitarianism 55, 65–6

V
Van Duzer, Charles H. 15–16
Varnhagen, Rahel 143, 145, 162–3
Villa, Dana 1, 74, 80, 82
violence 214n (108)
Virgil 141
Voegelin, Eric 17–18, 57, 62–3, 67
Vowinckel, Annette 39, 101, 146, 152, 164

W
Weber, Max 55, 80
What Is Freedom? (Arendt) 72
White, Hayden 40, 147, 152, 159–60, 231n (59), 233n (89)
Whitfield, Stephen 18, 22, 28
willing 45, 85–9, 99, 103, 151, 208n (28), 209n (33), 215n (11)
    and freedom 71–4
    melancholy of 149
Wolin, Richard 75
Wolin, Sheldon 218n (54)
work (concept of fabrication) 54–6, 202n (18), 211n (76)
    and making history 57–8, 89, 139–40
    temporality of 33, 102, 104–5
    and writing history 135–8, 146–7, 153–4, 204n (44, 46)
Wrzosek, Wojciech 40, 194n (37), 195n (8), 229n (25)

Y
Yarbrough, Jean 228n (157)
Young-Bruehl, Elisabeth 45, 90

Z
Zerilli, Linda 124
zoon politikon (*see*: action)